KASHMIR

KASHMIR

The Vajpayee Years

A.S. Dulat

with Aditya Sinha

HarperCollins *Publishers* India

First published in hardback in India in 2015 by
HarperCollins *Publishers* India

Copyright © A.S. Dulat 2015

P-ISBN: 978-93-5177-066-4
E-ISBN: 978-93-5177-067-1

2 4 6 8 10 9 7 5 3

A.S. Dulat asserts the moral right to be identified
as the author of this work.

The views and opinions expressed in this book are the author's own and
the facts are as reported by him, and the publishers are not
in any way liable for the same.

HarperCollins *Publishers*
A-75, Sector 57, Noida, Uttar Pradesh 201301, India
1 London Bridge Street, London SE1 9GF, United Kingdom
Hazelton Lanes, 55 Avenue Road, Suite 2900, Toronto, Ontario M5R 3L2
and 1995 Markham Road, Scarborough, Ontario M1B 5M8, Canada
25 Ryde Road, Pymble, Sydney, NSW 2073, Australia
195 Broadway, New York, NY 10007, USA

Typeset in 11/14 Sabon Roman at
SÜRYA

Printed and bound at
Gopsons Papers Ltd

For
My mother Raj, and my father Shamsher,
an avid reader who would have enjoyed
my Kashmir story

This above all: to thine own self be true,
And it must follow, as night the day,
Thou can'st not then be false to any man.

—Shakespeare (*Hamlet*)

CONTENTS

ACKNOWLEDGEMENTS

Since this book is about Kashmir, Kashmir and Kashmiris must remain centre stage. Kashmir has been a huge education. I have learnt more in the last ten years since I left the government than when I was in the government and thought I knew everything. I am indebted for this education, which transformed itself into a story, to innumerable friends with whom I spent endless hours talking, discussing and learning about Kashmir. It is not possible to name them all, and many may prefer to remain anonymous. But to those who have been more indulgent I owe a huge debt: my friend, philosopher and guide who helped keep the flock intact during most trying times, Prof. Abdul Ghani Bhat; manager Ghulam Hassan Mir, who was a storehouse of knowledge but also simplified my understanding of Kashmir; the kind, gentle and underestimated Firdous Syed; the more mercurial Sajad, not only TV anchor Barkha Dutt's favourite but mine also; the macho Hashim ever ready to take on both adversaries in Kashmir and even those across; Altaf, a businessman to his political fingers; Zafar, who everyone always thought was on the wrong side; Nadir, my ready reckoner; Prof. Riyaz Punjabi, who gave me my first lesson on Kashmir.

Agha Sahib—Ashraf Ali—was the most remarkable human being I have ever come across. My education of Kashmir would have remained incomplete without his words of wisdom. That he was always indulgent towards me was my great fortune and I can never thank him enough.

How can one forget Dillu (Dilshad Shaikh), not only the most beautiful woman, but warm, hospitable and with the best table in Srinagar. As Aarooji once said, 'You haven't seen the true beauty of Kashmir unless you have been to Gulmarg and met Dilshad Shaikh.' Thanks, Dillu, for your affection and great food.

My family has been a pillar of strength. As with everything in my life, this would not have happened but for the inspiration of my wife, Paran. She, most of all, made me believe that I had a story that needed to be told. During the last year and more, she has been my confidante, private secretary and typist, apart from helping with the computer and internet, about using which I am still clueless. But above all she has been by my side at times of doubt when I have thought of chucking it all up in exchange for the mess I made of the house with papers strewn in every room. She also helped me gather photographs and recollect important events as we went down memory lane.

The Intelligence Bureau (IB) and the great institution of the Friday Meeting made men out of boys. Not just the dozen chiefs I had the privilege to serve under, but so many seniors from whom one learnt so much. In particular, M.K. Narayanan not only sent me to Kashmir but also tolerated me as a roommate during my first two years in the Bureau, which gave me an opportunity to see the master at work from close quarters and get my first whiff of intelligence. I am equally grateful to my colleagues in the K-group, each one a thorough professional, which made for an excellent team that made an impact in Kashmir.

A special thanks to my colleagues C.D. Sahay and K.M. Singh, with whom I had the good fortune of working closely. C.D. and K.M. not only helped put events and personalities in Kashmir in proper perspective but helped with the editing as well. My thanks to the Research and Analysis Wing for continuing its support to me during my term in the PMO.

Finally I must thank Krishan Chopra of HarperCollins for believing that I had a story to tell. Krishan could qualify as one of Smiley's People for the way he led me up and down the alleys and staircases of Khan Market for our meetings. Thanks also to Rajinder Ganju, who provided valuable backup in taking the book through to press in a short time, and also took an interest in and appreciated the story in these pages.

Last but not the least, I must say a big thank you to 'boss', without whom there would have been no book. Aditya has been an old friend since the 1990s but when we began together (some would say he was the ghost writer but that somehow sounds spooky) as collaborators (not Ikhwanis in the Mirza Waheed sense!) he made it well known who the boss was and that's the only way it would have worked. Thanks, friend.

INTRODUCTION

Aadaab. Baat Niklegi Toh Phir Door Talak Jayegi
—Kafeel Azzer

One day during my tenure in the Prime Minister's Office (PMO)—where I unexpectedly landed after my time heading the Research & Analysis Wing (R&AW) was up—I was as usual discussing Kashmir with Brajesh Mishra, the principal secretary to Prime Minister Atal Bihari Vajpayee (who also served as India's first national security advisor). 'Do you know, Dulat, the only thing straight in Kashmir are the poplars?' he said.

Kashmir has been a part of my life since I first visited in 1987, in preparation for my posting there as deputy director in the Intelligence Bureau. The Kashmir Valley is beautiful all year round and it's difficult to say which season is most beautiful. Spring, however, is special, with fruit blossoms, tulips, daffodils and narcissi. So even after retirement, come the 'Darbar' move, Paran, my wife, and I still make our annual constitutional visit to Srinagar to savour the crispness of the air and a round or two of golf but most of all to catch up with old friends.

Paran thinks I'm nuts, interacting with Kashmiris on an almost daily basis even ten years after I left the government. She herself is acquainted with many Kashmiri voices, literally: when

I was deeply involved with Kashmir in the 1990s, our day in New Delhi normally began with a telephone call, which Paran would receive with an 'Aadaab'. This was before mobile phones. In due course she recognised regular callers to whom she assigned nicknames: 'Tweedledee and Tweedledum', 'Beehive', 'Sidekick', 'Gingersnaps', 'Drone', 'Sleepyhead', 'Aap ka Bhai', etc. God knows how she came up with these names but we would laugh our guts out; it was the lighter side of what was a stressful period. Paran's favourite was 'Gingersnaps', who was politeness personified.

In 2012 I was in Srinagar with Paran and six of her friends, and a regular visitor to our hut at the Centaur Hotel was Firdous Syed, a former militant commander-in-chief who went by the name of Babar Badr. The ladies were excited at meeting a militant and one of them, Sonia Pandhi, sacrificed a trip to Gulmarg to spend the morning listening to Firdous's story. 'How could such a decent person ever have been a terrorist?' she asked me afterwards. I explained that Firdous was not a terrorist in the way she imagined one to be, but one of many disillusioned Kashmiris who took to the gun. More significantly, Firdous understood the futility of violence as early as 1994 when he wrote of his 'shattered dream', quoting Faiz Ahmed Faiz: 'Shishon ka koi messiah nahin, kyon aas lagaye baithe ho.'

Reports of boys like Firdous coming and going to Pakistan began to trickle in as soon as I was posted to Srinagar in May 1988. There was no hint of this when I had come for my familiarisation visit six months earlier; at that time it all seemed like a holiday with a grand farewell party at Chief Minister Farooq Abdullah's residence for my predecessor K.P. Singh, who was on his way to the National Defence College, and we had vodka and kebabs by the fireside at Highland Park with Praveen Mahendru, a colleague, while it snowed outside during my first visit to Gulmarg. It all seemed like a picnic. Kashmir was at its glorious best. Soon I would also see it at its worst.

The first report of serious concern I got came a month into my tenure from an unlikely source. Praneet Sahni was a young, suave, good-looking Punjabi businessman whose father Raj owned a flour mill and used to be called Sheikh Abdullah's 'fourth son'. Praneet had a lot of Kashmiri friends, a lot of contacts, and his family was known to us. 'Please find out, whatever is happening there is not good,' he said.

'What are you implying?' I asked.

'Boys from downtown Srinagar are turning to Pakistan,' he said. 'You need to be on your guard.'

There was a lot of going-to-and-coming-from Pakistan, and for someone new in the Valley like me, who was tasked basically to keep Farooq Abdullah in good humour, it was bewildering.

I was grateful to Praneet, who sadly met a tragic end when militancy took centre stage in Kashmir in 1990. As mentioned, his father Raj was part of Srinagar's Punjabi business community; he was a post-Partition Dilliwala who went to Srinagar and started a business. In time Raj Sahni built the most beautiful house in town, standing on Gupkar Road in the same line as Farooq's place and Farooq's sister's house; his house had central heating and we would head there often in the winter because it was warm and he laid a good table. Raj, incidentally, was raided by the income tax authorities in the late 1970s, which became a political controversy at the time.

Raj Sahni had three children, two daughters and a son, Praneet, who was very smart and was taking control of the family business. Praneet got married in January of 1990 and there was a reception for him in Jammu on 1 March 1990, which I attended. I asked him how his mum and dad were.

'Dad is in Srinagar, so I'm going to Srinagar,' Praneet said.

'You have just got married. Why do you want to go to Srinagar, in this mess?' I said. It was true; there were a lot of targeted killings and it was near-anarchy in Srinagar.

'No, Dad is all alone,' he said. 'He needs me there.'

Praneet told his 19-year-old bride Upma that he would be

back in two days, after which they would have the concluding day of the month-long marriage ceremony and then embark on their honeymoon. But when he reached Srinagar, he was shot dead on his mill premises. Raj and his wife left Srinagar. Praneet was cremated in Delhi, at the Lodhi Road crematorium, and I didn't have the nerve to ask them what happened. They never went back; they wanted nothing to do with Kashmir again. Even later, I never asked what happened to their property. They were just not interested.

There was a story, though, that Praneet was involved with a Muslim girl from a prominent family. And that this was not so much a militancy killing as a revenge killing or honour killing. That Praneet had transgressed into the one area that a non-Kashmiri dare not enter. It was, in any case, a huge tragedy, and one of the stories of the exodus of Kashmiri Pandits and Punjabis from Kashmir: that someone as big as Raj Sahni had to leave in this kind of a circumstance.

Yet there were also people who refused to leave. One was a remarkable lady, Aarooji, whose husband Prakash Soni ran a photo studio in Srinagar. In better times—or maybe it was the lull before the storm—I remember Aarooji regaling the elite of Srinagar with her enchanting voice at a song recital one beautiful late-September evening in 1989. The occasion was a celebration at senior bureaucrat O.P. Bhutani's residence of his son's wedding. So seductive was her rendering of 'Aaj jaane ki zid na karo' that the guests, including Chief Minister Farooq Abdullah and Chief Justice A.S. Anand, who were in high spirits, stayed till the wee hours of the morning.

Aarooji and her husband refused to budge and stuck it out in the worst days of terrorism. When things got really bad they sometimes did not venture out of their home in Rajbagh for days on end, except to buy groceries. But they stayed on. Even after her husband passed away a few years ago, Aaroo refused to leave. I once asked her if she was not afraid of living alone and she said: 'This is my home and no militant dare touch me.'

Anyone who has been to Kashmir frequently enough realises what Aarooji meant. It is a different experience from any other part of the country. Indeed, Kashmir is unique. Over time it becomes a passion, and then an obsession.

So I was fortunate that once I was transferred out of Srinagar back to the IB HQ (the time was so hellish that I was relieved to be out of Kashmir and back to doing counter-intelligence) in March 1990, I was eventually put in the IB's Kashmir Group. Whenever someone mentions dialogue with the Kashmiri leadership, people mostly remember the talks between the separatist All Parties Hurriyat Conference and the then deputy prime minister, L.K. Advani, in 2004. But we in the government had been talking to Kashmiris since 1990. It was not easy to begin with. People like Shabir Shah and Yasin Malik were dismissive. So we talked about talking. And that opened the floodgates.

I have talked and talked and talked, to Kashmiris in Srinagar and in Delhi, and also to Kashmiris abroad. In 2013 I met a Kashmiri named Shabir Choudhury in London and the first question that he asked me was whether there was a Kashmiri leader that I had not yet met. 'Syed Ali Shah Geelani,' I said. But what he really wanted to know was whom I had met or was meeting in London. Kashmiris are happiest talking to you one on one, without anyone else knowing about it. Kashmiris generally don't trust one another.

After leaving the government, our residence in south Delhi has remained open to Kashmiris, and at times, to their deep embarrassment, separatist leaders have bumped into one another there. It has been discussed even in Hurriyat meetings. After the 2002 Jammu and Kashmir (J&K) assembly election, Farooq Abdullah met Ghulam Hassan Mir, a senior leader of the rival People's Democratic Party (PDP), at our residence. In the next election, in 2008, while campaigning against Mir in the latter's constituency of Tangmarg, Farooq publicly declared that he had met Mir at the R&AW chief's residence, thereby hoping to discredit him as no one trusts the intelligence agencies.

The Kashmiri is a most complex character, and not easy to fathom or engage with. He is the nicest, gentlest, kindest, most sensitive of human beings. Yet he can also be devious and prone to exaggeration. Ask any militant his life story and he will inevitably begin with the grievances of Kashmir and Kashmiris, sighing every now and then to express his predicament and curse his luck.

The Kashmiri rarely speaks the truth to you because he feels that you are lying to him. Brajesh Mishra was right when he bluntly said the only thing straight in Kashmir was the poplar tree. But it is we who have made him that way. The problem with Delhi has been that it sees everything in black and white, whereas Kashmir's favourite colour is grey.

Perhaps to find a way around this, the Kashmiri often resorts to symbolism, more so when he is under pressure. What he cannot say he will find some way of demonstrating. Sheikh Saheb was said to have spoken in different voices in Srinagar, Jammu and Delhi. After his arrest in 1953, the founder members of his National Conference (NC) formed the Plebiscite Front and resorted to doublespeak, the most famous example being Sheikh's closest lieutenant Mirza Afzal Beg, who went around holding Pakistani 'noon' (rock salt) to demonstrate Kashmir's affinity with Pakistan. Party flags in Kashmir all contain green, except the National Conference (red) and the People's Conference (blue), to symbolise Islam. When the Muslim United Front (MUF) was formed in 1987 it chose green as its flag's colour. PDP president Mehbooba Mufti's favourite colour is green, which she uses while campaigning. All militant organisations make free use of green.

While Pakistan has been our main concern, it does not give two hoots about Kashmir, and is often filled with contempt for Kashmiris. In the 1980s, Pakistani dictator Zia-ul-Haq, who had devised his 'thousand cuts' strategy against India, was trying to rope in the Kashmiris but was unsuccessful; he called them 'Brahmin ke aulaad' (Kashmiris are originally Nagas descended from Saraswat Brahmins). The term 'haatho' (coolie) originates from Pakistani Punjab, and in Kashmir became a familiar form of address, somewhat like 'oye'. And then there is the joke starring the famous wrestler from Gujranwala, Gama Pahalwan: a Kashmiri had Gama pinned down, but was weeping. When he was asked why he was weeping, he replied: 'When I get off him, he will thrash me.' This is what Pakistanis think of Kashmiris.

The late Balraj Puri, a noted Kashmiri scholar, once told me: 'A Punjabi Hindu can never understand Kashmir; he carries too much baggage of Partition.' As someone used to calling a spade a spade, I found it even more difficult. You need more than a lifetime to understand Kashmir and Kashmiris: there are layers within layers and you still may not get to the truth.

Kashmir has been a trouble spot since Partition because Pakistan has never accepted the finality of its accession to India; it still remains in some perverse minds its unfinished agenda, despite three wars.

Pakistan continues to fish in the troubled waters of Kashmir, raising the bogey of persecution of Muslims when all else fails. Little wonder Kashmir remains an issue and is even talked about as a possible nuclear flashpoint. And the poor Kashmiri finds himself squeezed between Pakistan's 'jugular vein' and our 'atoot ang' with his best bet being not the 'azaadi' he sometimes dreams of but normal, cordial relations between India and Pakistan. As Sheikh Mohammed Abdullah says in his autobiography, *Aatish-e-Chinar*, 'Unless India and Pakistan come close the Kashmir problem will remain. It is imperative that these neighbourly countries learn to trust one another. That is the only way to safeguard their interests as well as the interests of Kashmir.'

Kashmir acceded to India like all the other princely states except in extraordinary circumstances because of the invasion by Pakistan in October 1947, as a result of which (and the fact that it is the only Muslim-majority state in the Union) it enjoys a special status. That the accession was endorsed by the people of Kashmir owes a great deal to the common vision and special relationship between Pandit Jawaharlal Nehru, India's first prime minister, and Sheikh Abdullah, the tallest and most undisputed leader of Kashmir. As Sheikh said in a letter to Nehru in July 1951: 'I have stated again and over again that we have acceded to India because of the two luminous stars of our hope there—Gandhiji and yourself. That is why, despite several affinities between us and Pakistan, we did not join it, because we thought our programmes were not in conformity with their thoughts.' Their inexplicable falling apart (which lies buried in the Nehru–Sheikh correspondence) is one of the many tragedies of Kashmir. By taking Kashmir to the United Nations we only confounded an already complex matter by the intervention of international players with their wheels within wheels. The West sided with Pakistan till 9/11 shook the United States like no other event since the attack on Pearl Harbour. Russia has generally sided with us, and China has so far remained neutral, but for how long, with our recent tilt towards the US, it is difficult to say.

A Kashmiri friend who has repeatedly stressed that we should never underestimate Pakistan told me of an intriguing dream he claims he had recently that Pakistan was flourishing, stable and secure but when he focussed more intently he found the soldiers guarding the frontiers were Chinese!

Pandit Nehru apart, the only other prime minister who modelled himself on Nehru and had the vision, time and inclination to devote himself to Kashmir was Atal Bihari Vajpayee. As far back as early 1995, when he was leader of the opposition, Vajpayee told the separatist leader, Shabir Ahmed Shah, who met him in Delhi, that we (Indians and Kashmiris) needed to sit together to resolve the Kashmir issue. It made a big impact on the Nelson Mandela of Kashmir on his first visit to Delhi. As prime minister, Vajpayee was of the firm belief that we needed to end our permanent confrontation with Pakistan and move forward in Kashmir. That is why Atalji is still revered in the Valley long after Nehru has been forgotten.

As an IB/R&AW officer I knew I could never be totally trusted by Kashmiris. Once, though, at a wedding in Srinagar, Sajad Lone and I came out together and he said that being invited to a wedding was the epitome of social acceptability in Kashmir. I passed that test on more than one occasion.

I still continue to receive calls from Kashmir. In the winter of 2013, when our son suffered a stroke, many Kashmiri friends called to enquire about his welfare. One of the more touching was a call from Rashid Baba, who was Farooq Abdullah's man Friday for many years—he was a security officer who carried a diary rather than a gun and thus graduated to companion, caretaker, household manager, private secretary and conscience keeper to the chief minister. He was the first to inform Farooq of a revolt brewing in his party when Delhi planned his dismissal in 1984.

There comes a time in one's life when one feels it should all be put down before memory fades, without embarrassing anyone. There are endless memories and I have carried a story with me for a long time. If something had been written soon after I left the government in 2004 it would have aroused greater interest, but there were events, some of which involved me, which were too contemporary to be made public. Just as well, for I think I have learnt more of Kashmir in the ten years that I have been retired than when I was in service. So I have tried to give a witness's account of events since terrorism began in the Kashmir Valley in 1988, and Prime Minister Vajpayee's way of dealing with them.

When I first seriously thought about writing this book in 2012, I began by researching Kashmir through reading as much as I could. This was tiresome. Books at best provide information, not answers. Those come from conversations. Kashmir is far too complex to be understood from books. So I made it a mission to talk to Kashmiris of every hue whenever and wherever

I could, enquiring about events and rechecking facts which, thanks to Kashmiri friends, has yielded a wealth of information. I have relied not just on spoken words but also on shrugs, glances and whispers, which are a significant part of the Kashmiri psyche.

As veteran Kashmiri journalist Zafar Mehraj once said to me, whether facts are true or not, rumours are generally true in Kashmir. Or as Prof. Abdul Ghani Bhat put it, Kashmir is quite often a narrative of chance encounters and remarks. My one regret is that I could not get to the storehouse of knowledge that is Farooq Abdullah. Though he was one of the first to encourage me to write, he was in indifferent health when I began. So much for taking the great man for granted.

This book was written in good faith, with diligence to the truth, and as a matter of public service. Some of what I write may be contested. But the whole purpose of the book is to arouse interest in Kashmir and learn from past mistakes. In any case, mine can't be the last word on Kashmir, but I hope it will be the nearest to the truth.

At a dinner some years back I was telling the host how M.K. Narayanan, former director of the Intelligence Bureau and subsequently national security advisor in the first term of the United Progressive Alliance (UPA) government, had got me stuck in Kashmir when he passed by. He turned and said: 'Are you complaining? Do you realise that you became whatever you did only because of Kashmir?' True.

But also because of Vajpayee and Brajesh Mishra, who figured that if they needed someone on Kashmir in the PMO, it might as well be someone who had spent the previous ten years talking to Kashmiris and who had a relationship with the Abdullah family. Frankly I was surprised being drafted into the PMO as soon as I was finished with the R&AW. But Brajesh Mishra more than anyone else understood the importance of engaging with Kashmiris, and Vajpayee was clear that we needed to move forward and end our permanent confrontation with Pakistan.

Who would have imagined that a young assistant superintendent of police, overawed at entering North Block to join the IB in March 1969, would end up in the PMO? Who could think that a former R&AW chief would visit Pakistan four times in the past five years? It has all been much more than I could ever have dreamt.

December 2014

1

CUTTING THE GORDIAN KNOT

On 29 November 2014, former chief minister of Jammu and Kashmir and supremo of the PDP Mufti Mohammad Sayeed told the *Indian Express*'s Muzamil Jaleel that there was only one way for Prime Minister Narendra Modi to move forward on Kashmir and to end hostilities with Pakistan: 'the Vajpayee way'. According to Mufti, this meant only one thing—dialogue. 'The rest is a waste of time,' he said.

The occasion for this observation was the election campaign for the J&K assembly election. It had been just over six months of Modi's tenure, enough for disappointment with the prime minister to set in among Kashmiris who, unlike Indian Muslims in other parts of India, had not been apprehensive of Modi taking control of the central government. After all, Modi was the Gujarat chief minister when widespread riots in 2002 claimed over a thousand lives; he was unapologetic about it. But for the Muslims of Kashmir, Modi was the candidate of the Bharatiya Janata Party (BJP), and this gave hope that he could be like the only BJP prime minister India had so far seen: Atal Bihari Vajpayee.

No wonder then that separatist leaders like the chief priest of Kashmir, Mirwaiz Umar Farooq, who also headed the moderate faction of the All Parties Hurriyat (freedom) Conference, told journalists in April, just as the general elections were getting under way, that he felt that Modi was the 'best bet' to sort out the Kashmir dispute. 'There was forward movement on Kashmir during Vajpayee's tenure as PM,' the Mirwaiz said.

The Mirwaiz was hopeful because the ten years that the UPA was in power (2004–14) had turned out to be the Kashmiris' 'lost decade'. He not only called these ten years 'most depressing and discouraging' in press interviews, he went so far as to accuse the UPA of undoing the work of the National Democratic Alliance (NDA). Certainly Congress President Sonia Gandhi and Prime Minister Manmohan Singh couldn't clinch anything they had started on either the Pakistan front or vis-à-vis Kashmir during that time.

And despite a promising start with the swearing-in of Modi, to which Pakistan's prime minister, Nawaz Sharif, was invited, things went into deep freeze. The Mirwaiz and others tried hard to get things back on track: 'Prime Minister Modi must pick up the threads of former PM Vajpayee's peace process where he spoke of insaniyat,' the Mirwaiz told the *Hindu* in July. But not only did voices in the government speak about ending Kashmir's special status—by abrogating the Constitution's Article 370, a long-standing right-wing demand—but Modi called off the talks between India's and Pakistan's foreign secretaries when the Pakistani high commissioner met Kashmiri separatists in August—a practice that had not perturbed Indian governments for almost two decades.

Modi during his first six months belied the hope of the Mirwaiz and other Kashmiris. Modi's campaign promise to continue Vajpayee's good work turned out to be just that: a campaign promise, forgotten once the campaign was over. Modi was no Vajpayee, they felt.

What was Vajpayee trying to do that had so enamoured the

Kashmiris? As he once put it to those of us in his national security team, 'Iss gutthi ko suljhana hai': he was determined to cut the Gordian knot that was the country's lingering problem since Independence, namely India–Pakistan–Kashmir. I had joined his national security team as the head of India's external intelligence agency, the R&AW. I continued on Vajpayee's team after my tenure at R&AW ended, when he inducted me into the PMO to work with his principal secretary, Brajesh Mishra, who also functioned as India's first national security advisor. It was from this vantage point that I watched Prime Minister Vajpayee, one of India's most experienced and respected politicians, evolve a grand plan with an enlightened strategy on cutting that Gordian knot.

The strategy was simple: dialogue. But even a simple thing like dialogue requires a lot of preparation. My role in the team was to do the preparation, and that groundwork was a time-consuming process of talking. I had spent the ten years before I joined the Vajpayee team talking to Kashmiris: to separatists, mainstream politicians, intellectuals, businessmen, students, and, of course, terrorists. From December 1989, when I negotiated the release of Dr Rubaiya Sayeed, the daughter of the country's newly appointed home minister, Mufti Mohammad Sayeed, till July 1999, when I took over as the head of R&AW, I talked and talked and talked. I wasn't a negotiator: in popular perception, that's the guy who bargains urgently with terrorists or kidnappers. I was, behind the scenes, building relationships with people who had lost faith in India; and it was a long, slow process that required a lot of patience. Even at the worst of times, you just have to keep talking.

You had to talk if you wanted the separatists in the Hurriyat to enter formal talks with the government. And if you wanted peace in Kashmir, if you wanted peace with Pakistan, you had to have some kind of accord with the Hurriyat. Vajpayee grasped this, which is why I call his strategy enlightened. It's a strategy that remained relevant even ten years after he stepped down from the prime ministership.

How I ended up in Vajpayee's team was itself something that not even my wife would have predicted. First, because not long after I joined the Indian Police Service (IPS) in 1965, as a Rajasthan cadre officer, I was deputed to the Intelligence Bureau (IB), reputed to be the world's oldest intelligence agency, where I spent thirty years; and second, I was supposed to retire in 1998 at the age of fifty-eight as the second-in-command at the IB, but to my good fortune the government that very year decided to raise the age of retirement to sixty, and so I got another two years in service.

The IB, which was set up by the British Raj in 1887, gathers intelligence inside the country and along the borders, and is also responsible for counter-intelligence and counter-terrorism. Before Independence it kept a tab on Indian revolutionaries (among other things); after Independence it has been at the forefront of tackling insurgencies, along with other matters. I joined the IB in March 1969, just six months after then prime minister Indira Gandhi created a new agency by hiving off the external intelligence division from the IB, reportedly following the failures of the 1962 India-China war and the 1965 India-Pakistan war. It was named the Research and Analysis Wing of the Cabinet Secretariat; as a wing of the secretariat, it legally lay outside the purview of parliamentary oversight and audit.

I went to the IB because of a selection process put in place by the legendary B.N. Mullik, who was the director of the IB (DIB) from 1950 till the end of the tenure of India's first prime minister, Jawaharlal Nehru, in 1964. Mullik thought the best way to get officers was to select five or six fairly green IPS officers from the top ten of each new batch in the hope that they make a career in the IB. Mullik figured these officers would do six years in the IB, return to their parent cadre, do a district, and then come back to the IB. This didn't happen. Those who joined stuck on for the rest of their careers; some of those who returned to their cadre never came back to the IB. Rarely did anyone come and go and come back again. You joined the Bureau, it became a career, you stuck on.

When I joined, I was pretty excited; I was promoted from assistant superintendent of police to joint assistant director, and I shared a room with the seniormost assistant director, a man named M.K. Narayanan, already a hotshot in the IB who everyone believed would one day be DIB—the director, that is. We also received a special pay of Rs 200 to 300 in addition to our salary, which in those days was a big deal. The other bit of excitement when I joined was the fact that some of the staff were carrying desks and chairs out, and heading over to the recently created R&AW.

My career in the IB can be divided into two parts: pre-1988 and the period till I joined R&AW. During almost the first twenty years, like any other officer, I did a mix of counter-intelligence and state postings. Counter-intelligence, as the name suggests, is an activity against foreign espionage, sabotage, subversion and assassination. The state postings meant an officer was deployed in each state capital to serve as a link between the central government and the state government; the IB administratively came under the home ministry though the DIB reported directly to the prime minister. My state postings during this time included Chandigarh, where I met the chief minister and future president, Giani Zail Singh, and Bhopal, where the chief minister was the wily Arjun Singh, who would go on in 1985 to serve as governor of Punjab at a crucial time. Though his tenure as governor was only of eight months, it was during this time that Prime Minister Rajiv Gandhi signed an accord with the Akali Dal chief, Harcharan Singh Longowal, in an attempt to end the Khalistan movement. Both Gianiji and Arjun Singh were veteran practitioners of the art of politics, and I learned sufficiently from them.

My first meeting with Gianiji, in late 1975, was by chance because the boss of the Chandigarh station was out of town and the chief minister did not want to wait to meet somebody from the IB, so I had to go. I went at lunch time to the Chandigarh guest house, where I waited until the chief minister arrived with his tiffin-carrier lunch. We had some rather nice chicken curry and he asked me to tell him about Punjab politics. At the time there was dissidence brewing in the Punjab Congress. I made a remark that apparently stuck in Gianiji's head, about a Congress MP who was supposed to be close to Gianiji but was going to Delhi and bitching about him. When I told Gianiji he didn't like it.

So in 1980 when he became home minister (and I had returned from a stint in Kathmandu) he brought his secretary, Inderjeet Bindra, to Delhi to be his joint secretary. Bindra and I were friends from my Chandigarh days, when he was deputy commissioner in Patiala, and I went to say hello to him. 'Gianiji has a strange impression about you,' Bindra said. 'He told me one day, "Yeh Akali hai."' I thought if I ever bumped into Gianiji, I'd clarify.

In mid-July 1982 I was posted to Lucknow and I was to take over immediately, hence on 31 July I signed out of counter-intelligence thinking the next day I would sign in at Lucknow. But then I got a message that my father was not well. I headed home and found that he had passed away. I needed to sort things out at home and was unavailable for a couple of weeks. In the meantime someone else was sent off to Lucknow. When I returned to work I was without a job, and had to wait for a posting.

Gianiji had become President of India and in September he had to travel to Houston, USA, for an open heart surgery to be conducted by world-famous cardiologist Denton Cooley. When either the president or prime minister travel abroad they are accompanied by an IB official who is called the security officer. The DIB, T.V. Rajeswar, was looking for a Punjabi to go with the president and since I was at a loose end, he picked me. When I heard, I was sitting with my friend and colleague Ratan Sehgal, and we were with a senior officer, Dr K.V.H. Padmanabhan, who was known for his puns. He said: 'He was supposed to go to Lucknow, and look at his luck now.'

It was a small group of us who went to Houston: besides me, the military secretary, his secretary, his joint secretary Bindra, the two ADCs, and members of Gianiji's family. My job was to look after security and liaise with the local authorities for that. We spent three weeks, which were good fun, and on the way back stopped for a night in New York, where Gianiji got to know me a little better. He would tell the others to be careful of what they said in front of me: 'Arre bhai, yeh IB-wale hain, inke saamne dhyan se baat karna.'

When we returned, Gianiji's official visits began. In normal course, the job of security officer is rotated among officials posted at the IB headquarters in Delhi and very rarely among those posted in state capitals. Somehow Gianiji took a liking to me and he always insisted that the IB depute me. 'Your department was trying to send somebody else but I made it be known to them that I want you,' the president told me. I thanked him. 'No, no, security officers can't be changed like that, you must remain with me,' he said.

Obviously Gianiji felt comfortable with me. It was embarrassing at first, and especially when I was posted to Bhopal in May 1984. But thanks to him I saw the world from 1982 to '87, during his five years as president.

On and off we would chat. He pretended to be simpler than he was; actually he was very canny. Vajpayee may have been a statesman but Gianiji was a smart politician who had made quite a journey from his humble beginnings to become President of India. Like Pandit Jawaharlal Nehru he insisted on wearing a rose in his achkan. I came to appreciate his earthy common sense. I would like to think that later in my career when I talked to separatists, militants and politicians, I had imbibed many lessons from Gianiji.

He had a standard line wherever we went abroad: we have come to your beautiful country, we want to extend our hand of friendship, and my delegation has come to win you over even if you don't like us. Though he only spoke in Punjabi he was a good speaker. He required an interpreter and if no one in the delegation knew the local language then somebody from the local community would do the honours.

Once, in Athens, there was a girl at the university who knew Greek and she was roped in and given a copy of her speech, which she translated. She stood in front of him and was reading it out. Gianiji noticed she had a prepared text, and he would always deviate from whatever he was given. After a couple of sentences he got annoyed and snatched the paper from her, telling her, 'Miss, yeh aise nahin chalega.'

On a visit to Warsaw, Poland (then a communist nation), we were walking the cobbled streets in the central market area. A tall youngster from the Ministry of External Affairs was with us; he walked on one side of the president and I on the other. Gianiji saw a church in the distance, and people coming out of it. There was a Pole with us, so Gianiji said to him: 'Why in your country do they say they don't believe in God when I see a church and people coming out?'

The MEA fellow was nervy and he blurted out: 'President sir, zara dekh ke.'

'Shut up!' Gianiji snapped at him. 'I know what I'm talking.'

He continued: 'How can you not believe in God? There is God. Everybody knows there is God. Everybody believes in God. Yet you say there is no God. And there's a church here.'

The poor Pole did not know what to say. 'We have believers and non-believers,' he muttered.

Gianiji could be like that.

Once on a return from Los Angeles we made a stopover at Hong Kong, where we spent the night. Since it was Hong Kong, everyone, including the accompanying minister, N.K.P. Salve, veteran Congressman and father of Harish Salve, who would go on to become India's solicitor general, went shopping. I was told the president would like to go for a drive around Hong Kong, so I went to his room. He was all by himself. 'I was thinking what the city is like,' he said.

'It's a pretty place,' I said. 'Would you like to drive around?'

'What are you doing here? Everyone has gone shopping,' Gianiji said. 'Even my family has left me all alone and gone shopping.'

'Sir, I thought I'll go for a drive with you,' I said, and we set out. I believe he appreciated my taking him out on that occasion.

When Operation Bluestar happened in June 1984, in which the army stormed the Golden Temple to flush out Punjab militants, Gianiji was very cut up because he felt that he had not been suitably informed. He visited Sikhism's holiest site four days later, and came under heavy pressure from other important Sikhs to resign his post in protest. He was in a sulk and his relationship with the family went downhill from there, which was quite a change from when he became president and said something to the effect that he would sweep the floor if the prime minister asked him to.

Mrs Gandhi was assassinated four months later and when her son and successor Rajiv took over, his coterie put two of Mrs Gandhi's loyalists under the cloud of suspicion: her personal secretary R.K. Dhawan, who was sacked, and Gianiji. Things never improved and there was a crisis in the government in 1987 when Gianiji vetoed the Indian Post Office (amendment) Bill, which sought to empower the central and state governments to intercept or detain postal articles on certain grounds, widely seen as a form of indirect press censorship. Delhi was hit by a cyclone of rumours. Ultimately Gianiji left office after completing his term.

After Gianiji retired I met him occasionally. He had a good equation with P.V. Narasimha Rao, who became prime minister in 1991 and who would consult Gianiji on Punjab. 'I'm told you're well up with things,' I said to him one day.

'It's okay,' he said. 'But this prime minister is very crafty.'

My first year in Bhopal was eventful: a gas leak at the Union Carbide plant on the night of 2-3 December 1984 led to 3,787 deaths and 558,125 injuries. (These are state government figures.) A month before that, however, a different tragedy occurred: the November riots in Delhi that followed Indira Gandhi's assassination by her bodyguards. From 31 October to 3 November, around 8,000 Sikhs were killed around India, 3,000 in Delhi alone. Being a Sikh it was not only distressful but also scary because I had a very close call, saved by the fact that I don't wear a turban. My father, the late Justice Shamsher Singh Dulat of the Indian Civil Service, went to King's College, Cambridge, as all pre-independence civil servants were supposed to, and rather than keep washing his hair in the cold English weather he decided to cut it; the rest of us in his family have continued to do so—and that may have been what saved me.

When Mrs Gandhi was assassinated, Gianiji and I were in Sanaa, Yemen. On 31 October we returned to India, and the next day, the IB headquarters asked me to stay back in Delhi since a whole lot of VIPs would be arriving for Mrs Gandhi's funeral. Within a few hours, however, the killing of Sikhs began. Some killings were reported from Madhya Pradesh—the attitude, I'm sad to say, was that if Delhi was allowing such a thing then it was all right if a few Sikhs were murdered there; there might even be brownie points in it—so my bosses told me that I had better leave for Bhopal.

I don't know what struck me but instead of taking a 5 p.m. flight I hopped on to the Tamil Nadu Express, which left Delhi at two in the afternoon and went via Bhopal. It would get me there in time for dinner by 8:30–9:00 p.m. On the train I found myself all alone in the first class AC compartment.

The moment the train left the station it was pelted by stones. This happened each time we passed a station, where hoodlums and youngsters gathered. At Dholpur the train was held up, and on the platform there was a crowd of 100 to 150 with lathis. They barged into the train and started wreaking havoc. For three hours they went from bogie to bogie, asking, 'Sardar hain? Saale Sikhon ko dhundo.' I quietly got off the train and stood on the platform, thinking better to be a spectator than wait on the train.

It was harrowing. I did not witness this but the ticket collector later came and told me that they found three Sikhs at the back somewhere; they poured kerosene on them and burnt them alive. 'Aap toh theek hain na?' the ticket collector asked. 'Yes,' I replied, 'I am okay, but will the train move.' 'It will,' he replied.

What next, I wondered, since it was a distance from Dholpur to Bhopal.

When the train did finally leave, it was held up again in three other places and we reached Bhopal at two in the morning. I was petrified. I had seen madness from close quarters.

What saved me was that the weather at that time of year was such that you could wear a bush shirt or a full-sleeve one. Fortunately my sleeves were full, and covered my kara. Perhaps with a half-sleeve my kara would have been conspicuous, and something might have happened.

When I went to Delhi the next time, after the riots were over, I found that Sikhs were subdued all over though they were very angry inside. People I knew had gone into hiding for a week, ten days. No one in the government was willing to speak up and say that what had happened was not acceptable. So I went to the DIB, H.A. Barari, who had taken over after the assassination from R.K. Kapoor, and told him that there was extreme anger among the Sikhs. In 1987, when Narayanan took over as DIB I told him as well: I'm a Sikh and I can tell you there's huge anger.

I had overstayed my tenure in Bhopal and was expecting a posting back to the headquarters, but shortly after Giani Zail Singh retired as president, things moved forward. I got a call from my friend and former colleague M.K. Rathindran, who was at the IB HQ. Out of the blue he asked: 'How would you react to a posting in Srinagar?' It sounded great. It would be a challenging assignment and perhaps another three years away from HQ. While most colleagues preferred being in Delhi, I enjoyed whatever little autonomy an outstation offered. Being in the field was far more enjoyable than being a cog in the vast machine that was IB HQ.

I went for a familiarisation visit to the Kashmir Valley in November 1987, and one day I was with K.P. Singh, my predecessor and the then Kashmir expert and a future DIB. We sat on the balcony of his residence on Gupkar Road, having a couple of pink gins, when he told me that only 'handpicked' officers were posted to Srinagar. I had no illusions about myself, but if this was so, then I guess my five years of close association with the outgoing President of India had been a great education. It is funny how such accidents of circumstance led to a posting that would define my career and prepare me for the challenges we faced in Vajpayee's national security team several years later.

I formally took over in Kashmir's summer capital Srinagar only in May 1988, and two months later, separatist militant violence began in Kashmir. I had a hectic two years, which grew particularly rough after the Rubaiya Sayeed kidnapping. In March 1990 I was sent back to Delhi at the request of Governor Jagmohan.

In the normal course of things that would have been the end of my Kashmir experience, but in 1990, the Valley seemed like it was in anarchy. I was back in counter-intelligence for a few months, but seeing the need to reach out to Kashmiris and rebuild networks, I was reassigned and put in charge of the IB's Kashmir group, known internally as the K-group. From then on, I talked to Kashmiris, as I mentioned earlier. The K-group became the most active group in the IB, drawing in the best talent, advising prime ministers throughout the 1990s on initiatives in J&K, and getting India through one of its most difficult periods in the border state.

My career would have ended as number two in the IB and I was quite happy with that end to my career since my batchmate and friend Shyamal Datta, who was one position above me in the IPS, had become DIB in early 1998. In fact, when Shyamal became DIB, the home secretary, Balmiki Prasad Singh, called me in and told me that my batchmate was becoming the boss, and did I have a problem with that. He offered me a paramilitary organisation to head, but I had spent thirty years in the IB and was happy here. Why would I want to leave?

One day in October 1998 Shyamal caught me and asked me if I'd like to go to R&AW. I laughed.

'You want to get rid of me?' I asked.

'No, no, I'm asking seriously.'

'R&AW? What position?'

'As the boss, naturally.'

'To be boss, why wouldn't I like to go?' I said. 'To go from one agency to the other, I'd certainly like that.'

Shyamal said he would see, and then neither of us brought it up till 1 January 1999, when I went to his room to greet him for the New Year. On that day every year not much work is done in government offices, at least during the first half of the day. When I reached the DIB's room, Shyamal said he wanted to take me to the PMO, where he was going to meet the principal secretary. 'It's time I introduced you,' he said.

Twelve days after I met Brajesh Mishra for the first time, I got my orders to join R&AW. I was to be an understudy for three months to the secretary (R), Arvind Dave, and then take over from him. Of course, considering the resentment in R&AW at an outsider joining as chief-designate, it did not go smoothly, and I had to sit around for nearly six months before I took over as the chief. But there would have been a reason for the government to appoint an outsider to head the organisation; things had not been going well at R&AW and there was a void at the top. And having been an intelligence professional for thirty years, I knew a trick or two, even though my only foreign experience had been an IB posting from 1976 to 1980 in the Indian embassy at Kathmandu, Nepal, where, incidentally, I met Vajpayee for the first time.

It was the time of the Janata government (1977–80); Morarji

Desai was the prime minister and Vajpayee the minister for external affairs. Desai visited Kathmandu from 9 to 11 December 1977, and Vajpayee, naturally, accompanied him. They were put up at the palace's guest house and as the local embassy's security officer, I used to hang around. When they had an engagement, the two would come out of their respective rooms for the lift to take them down to the ground floor. Morarji would always arrive two minutes before he was scheduled to arrive at the lift (prime ministerial schedules abroad are planned down to the minute), and Vajpayee would, without fail, arrive two minutes later than he was scheduled to. At one point, Morarji could not restrain himself.

'Atalji, aap toh hamesha late aatein hain,' Morarji said.

'Pradhan mantriji, aap time se pehle aatein hain,' Vajpayee replied. They both broke into laughter.

The point of this story is that Vajpayee was an utterly confident politician and had the gumption to crack a joke with his prime minister. And it was Vajpayee's confidence which, during his foreign ministry stint in the Janata government, led him to re-establish relations with China in 1979 for the first time since India's humiliating defeat in the 1962 war; and it led him to break the ice with a visit in 1979 to Pakistan, with which relations were frozen since the 1971 war. These came as a surprise at the time, considering that the Jan Sangh, a precursor to the Bharatiya Janata Party, which was participating in the Janata government and of which Vajpayee was a member, was considered hardline in matters of security, defence and foreign affairs. Perhaps that was what gave Vajpayee the confidence to take these initiatives at the time—there was nobody to his political right to taunt him.

Thus it was no surprise when twenty years later, as prime minister, he undertook another peace initiative and on 20 February 1999 got on the first bus between Delhi and Lahore. Again, it was a visit that broke a lengthy dry spell, for it was the first visit to Pakistan by a prime minister since Rajiv Gandhi went in 1989. Hopping on a bus to Pakistan was more imaginative than any prime minister could ever dare to be, and it kindled a lot of hope—at least for a few months.

The idea of the Delhi–Lahore bus, according to the memoir by then foreign minister Jaswant Singh, came up when the prime ministers of India and Pakistan, Vajpayee and Nawaz Sharif (whom we referred to as Mian Saheb), met for lunch on the sidelines of the United Nations General Assembly in New York on 23 September 1998. This was a few months after both countries tested nuclear weapons in defiance of world opinion; the tests had given Vajpayee, at least, elbow room for an initiative vis-à-vis Pakistan. As his home minister, and later deputy prime minister, Lal Krishan Advani, put it in his memoir: 'After demonstrating that he was a worshipper of Shakti (power), he set out to prove that he was, equally, a votary of Shanti (peace).'

The idea of a bus had been discussed in various back channels and track two fora for some time. India and Pakistan have had uneasy relations from the beginning, which the Pakistanis say is because they ought to have gotten Kashmir when the British partitioned the country and left; India counters that by pointing to the legitimate Instrument of Accession to India signed by the ruler of the pre-independence princely state, Maharaja Hari Singh. The last viceroy and first Governor-General of India, Louis Mountbatten, made the accession conditional on a plebiscite, but that was not possible due to the outbreak of war in October 1947, when Pakistani irregulars joined a rebellion in Poonch and marched on to Srinagar. A ceasefire in effect partitioned J&K, and the passage of time made a plebiscite increasingly impractical in India's eyes.

India and Pakistan had fought three wars: 1947–48, in 1965 and in 1971; and in the 1990s there had been a proxy war via Kashmiri militants who were trained, armed and infiltrated across by the Pakistan army's Inter-Services Intelligence Directorate (ISI). There was a lot of mistrust, and a constant stumbling block to peace was the fact that the military controlled the country even when there was an elected government in place.

It worried the rest of the world, particularly the West, which encouraged people-to-people contact and unofficial discussions, known under the euphemism of track two meetings, and since these are unofficial, people are encouraged to speak their minds even if it isn't the official position of their respective governments; keeping it off the record does help candour. Many ideas have emerged in such meetings, including the bus, and when Mian Saheb at that lunch with Vajpayee mentioned how he had driven in his own car to Delhi in 1982 to watch the Asian Games, the bus idea came up, and it was decided to start a Delhi–Lahore service.

Obviously Mian Saheb was tickled by the idea because on 4 February 1998, in an interview to Shekhar Gupta of the *Indian Express*, he invited Vajpayee to ride the first bus into Lahore. Vajpayee accepted that very afternoon. And on 20 February, accompanied by twenty-two other Indians including Punjab chief minister Parkash Singh Badal, ageing filmstar Dev Anand and cricketer Kapil Dev, Vajpayee (who had joined the bus in Amritsar, not at its origin in Delhi) rode over the Wagah border and to Lahore and an emotional reception by Mian Saheb.

Shaukat Javed was Lahore's police chief during Vajpayee's visit. Originally an army man who had been in India as a prisoner of war during the 1971 war, he would retire as Punjab's inspector general of police, the state's top cop (and Pakistan's equivalent to our director general of police). Vajpayee was in Lahore for 26 hours, and for most of that time, Javed was part of the visiting prime minister's group. Years later I met Javed at a track two conference in Istanbul, and he told me about the excitement in his city about Vajpayee's visit.

Javed said that Prime Minister Nawaz Sharif himself took a lot of interest in the arrangements. For instance, for the evening banquet held at the Lahore Fort's Diwan-e-Khas, one of the most beautiful architectural structures in Pakistan, Mian Saheb entrusted the task to Salima Hashmi and her husband Shoaib: she was Faiz Ahmed Faiz's elder daughter and the principal of the National College of Arts. Mian Saheb supervised the minutest details and was keen that everything be done in Lahori style.

As Vajpayee's cavalcade approached the fort for the banquet it encountered a demonstration by the Jamaat-e-Islami, whose members pelted stones and damaged some of the diplomats' cars. The next morning Vajpayee asked to see Javed at the Governor's House. 'Your PM called me and everything went well,' Vajpayee told the police chief. 'These demonstrations happen in our country all the time, please don't worry about it.'

Vajpayee then visited the Minar-e-Pakistan, which was a monument to the Muslim League resolution of 23 March 1940 calling for the creation of a country for Muslims in the Indian subcontinent. Javed said his government was, in fact, not keen that Vajpayee go; it worried that he might say something about Pakistan's creation or existence that would strike a sour note. But Vajpayee was determined to go. It went off so well that though a Lahore Declaration was signed during the trip, Vajpayee's visit to the Minar was undoubtedly the highlight. Vajpayee signed the visitor's book at the monument, and wrote: 'A stable, secure and prosperous Pakistan is in India's interest. Let no one in Pakistan be in doubt. India sincerely wishes Pakistan well.'

That his statement did much to allay existential fears in sections of Pakistan was evident at a civic reception for him at the Governor's House that afternoon, hosted by Lahore mayor Khwaja Ahmad Hassan. Vajpayee told the gathering that his original plan for the trip was to merely cross the border, greet Mian Saheb, and then return home. Mian Saheb had convinced him to visit Lahore by saying, 'Dar tak aaye ho, ghar nahin aaoge?' (You've come to the door, won't you come inside?)

Vajpayee had been to Lahore twice before—as a student and as foreign minister. 'A visit to Lahore is incomplete unless you go to Anarkali Bazaar,' he said. 'But Mian Saheb has created Anarkali here, itni kaliyan chatak rahi hain.'

There were people who did not approve of his coming to Lahore—and it was the same in India; when he returned, some were sure to ask why he went to the Minar. '"Kya aap Pakistan par mohar lagane gaye the?" they will ask,' he said. 'But Pakistan does not need anyone's endorsement.' For this, he received a full five-minute standing ovation, even from those in the back who had not risen from their seats when he and Mian Saheb entered the venue together.

Vajpayee later mentioned that he and Mian Saheb had decided that they would not let war happen (though in a few months, things would turn out differently). 'Pakistan was unfortunate but the wound has healed and only the scar remains,' he said. 'One can choose one's friends, but neighbours are permanent.' His hosts were overwhelmed.

Vajpayee returned and there was great excitement, not just in the capitals of India and Pakistan, but also in Kashmir. Though I was still an understudy at R&AW with little work to do besides get myself acquainted with the organisation and my new colleagues, I continued what I had been doing the past ten years: I kept talking to Kashmiris. And one Kashmiri who met me came all the way from America where he had a furniture business that was a household name there; this Kashmiri was Farooq Kathwari, who headed Ethan Allen Interiors.

Kathwari had headed Ethan Allen in 1985 before buying it out a few years later, and it turned him into a multi-millionaire. He became an influential person in the US, selling furniture to even the White House, and setting up the Kashmir Study Group (KSG), which comprised legislators and academics. According to the KSG website, current members include Teresita Schaffer and her husband Howard, both old South Asia hands; Robert Wirsig; Representative Gary Ackerman; and Dr Ainslie Embree. Kathwari had long taken the pro-independence line on Kashmir. Along the way he had also been sobered by the fact that two of his sons died as jihadis in Afghanistan.

On 1 December 1998, just a few months before Vajpayee boarded the Lahore bus, the KSG presented a paper which generated curiosity in Kashmir and in policy circles in New Delhi, Islamabad and Washington, DC. In it, it spoke of a formula for resolving the dispute over Kashmir. KSG's proposal was 'that a portion of the former princely state of Jammu and Kashmir be reconstituted as a sovereign entity—but without an international personality—enjoying access to and from both India and Pakistan'. It went on to speak of autonomy for each of the five regions of J&K: Jammu, Kashmir, Ladakh, the Pakistan-controlled regions of Jammu and of Kashmir, and the Northern Areas (Gilgit and Baltistan). A council would decide things for the regions together; and India and Pakistan would run the regions on their respective sides of the border.

This KSG proposal would find important echoes in the years to come, as we shall see later in the narrative.

Kathwari was obviously feeling optimistic, particularly with Vajpayee's peace initiative and bus ride to Pakistan. And in Kashmir, whenever there is a glimmer of hope, there also is tremendous excitement. In that hopeful time, Kathwari came to India, and on someone's suggestion—I'm not sure whose, but continuous talking to Kashmiris both inside and outside India had got me a whole lot of well-wishers—in early May 1999, he called me up.

As I mentioned, at R&AW I was waiting for my turn to come so I didn't mind continuing my meetings with Kashmiris, particularly one whose novel proposal had come just a few months earlier.

'I'm going to Srinagar and I want your assessment of Kashmir,' Kathwari said. 'I'm told you're an expert.'

'There's no dearth of experts,' I said. 'But now that you've come, we can talk.'

I met him for about an hour, and he listened to me; and then he went to the Valley. It would turn out to be the first of three meetings I ever had with him. The second was when he returned.

'Your assessment was more or less correct,' he said.

'Then, Kathwari Saheb, you owe it to the Kashmiris to say what you're telling me,' I said. 'Telling me is of no use. Why don't you write about it? Why don't you say it?

'What are you implying?' Kathwari asked.

'We talked about autonomy,' I said.

'But autonomy is a bad word now.'

'So give it another name.'

And Kathwari began using the term 'self-rule'.

It was the first time I heard of self-rule, but it would not be the last. It did give me a new impetus for talking to Kashmiris, a lot of which would happen as the various peace initiatives by Vajpayee gained momentum. That momentum would in fact bring India as close as possible to settling the Kashmir issue with Pakistan; with a formula for self-rule, as proposed by Pakistan president Pervez Musharraf.

But that was in the future.

For right after I met Kathwari, India would learn a sobering lesson when Gen. Pervez Musharraf launched an operation in Kargil that turned into a fourth war, albeit a limited one, between India and Pakistan.

2

KARGIL AND THE COUP

George Tenet, the American spymaster and director of the Central Intelligence Agency (CIA) from 1996 to 2004, paid a secret visit to Pakistan in June 2000; from there he visited India. It had been two years since the CIA's big embarrassment, the failure to detect the May 1998 nuclear tests that India conducted. That intelligence failure would be overshadowed and forgotten fifteen months after his June 2000 visit, when al-Qaeda terrorists hijacked and crashed four commercial airliners into targets of high symbolic value on 11 September 2001. Ironically, one of the reasons for Tenet's visit was to ask the Pakistanis to check funds being diverted through certain Islamic charities to al-Qaeda, which was wanted by America for its attacks on two embassies in East Africa. He ostensibly also visited to get a first-hand look at Pakistan's army chief, who had seized power eight months earlier, in October 1999, by deposing Nawaz Sharif in a military coup. (Tenet also would have met with the head of the ISI.)

As Tenet's counterpart I invited the DCI, as he's known in his government, to a meeting at the R&AW headquarters in New Delhi. Among other matters, I asked him for his assessment of Gen. Pervez Musharraf, who had suspended Pakistan's constitution and declared himself the nation's chief executive. Tenet said that as far as the Americans were concerned, Musharraf was there to stay. He further added that the Americans felt they could do business with the General. Implicit in that remark was the suggestion that others could also do business with Musharraf.

I tried to probe Tenet some more on Musharraf, but he declined to add anything substantial. Instead, he said: 'You guys should check him out yourselves.'

This advice is one which has stuck in my mind since. As we will see, some of India's missteps can be attributed to the fact that we didn't 'check things out', be it in Kargil when there were rumours of infiltration by foreigners, or in the case of handling Shabir Shah, who was once the daddy of Kashmiri separatists and with whom we missed an opportunity of doing business.

In Musharraf's case, we did not take Tenet's advice till it was too late; as the years passed, the General responded to Vajpayee's repeated peace overtures by calling for 'out-of-the-box' solutions to the main problem in the India–Pakistan relationship, which is Kashmir. As Manmohan Singh said in his last press conference in January 2014 (and as former Pakistani foreign minister Khurshid Mahmud Kasuri revealed in 2011), the two countries came close to clinching a solution during the period from October 2006 to March 2007 but could not close the deal; and by the following year, Musharraf not only lost authority but also lost power.

The truth is also that Musharraf had made things difficult for himself with India; it was his idea to launch a military operation in Kargil in early 1999, which led to a response by India that May, and a military conflict that ended in July. Though Musharraf while later responding to peace overtures would ask India to look past Kargil, the fact was that we were taken aback by the gumption of the Pakistan army and its chief to plan such an operation even while the two countries were basking in the warmth of Vajpayee's bus trip to Lahore. And by the time we got over this betrayal, we missed an opportunity to seal peace with Pakistan.

Between the Lahore bus trip and the Kargil war, I wasn't doing much even though I was supposed to be an understudy to the incumbent R&AW chief, Arvind Dave. There wasn't much understudying going on, though; the atmosphere at R&AW was frosty as everyone there was suspicious of an 'outsider' taking over. Dave himself was surprised that with regard to the raise in retirement age, he was on the wrong side of the cut-off date, and he wondered why he should only be in service till he was 58, while others would be there till they were 60.

Dave, who was to retire on 30 April, attended a government function at Hyderabad House and for once my presence was also required, so I accompanied him. It was just before the Kargil intrusion was discovered. There we met Brajesh Mishra, who told Dave, 'Tumhare order ho jayenge,' and Dave was given a three-month extension. So I asked Brajesh, 'Sir, what about my orders?' and he said mine would be done too. My taking charge was thus pushed back to August and I had another three months of 'understudying'.

Dave was supposed to brief me extensively, particularly since I was from outside the organisation, but his briefings weren't useful as he was rather harsh in his judgment of his own colleagues. Plus he thought I was there to ease him out. So I had to learn on my own, looking around and meeting people. It took them time to accept me. Ultimately I learnt on the job as well. It took me a while to get to know the ropes, but fortunately thirty years in the IB is a long education and you learn a trick or three. It did not go to waste in R&AW. Getting to know the content of work was not a problem since the tradition in both the IB and R&AW is of a weekly meeting with the desk officers, which we call the weekly namaaz.

Eventually Dave was appointed governor of Arunachal

Pradesh after he retired and left R&AW. As it turned out, it was during his tenure as R&AW chief that the Kargil intrusion and subsequent war took place.

The Kargil Review Committee—which was set up in July 1999, after the war was over, to review the events leading up to the Pakistani intrusion and recommend measures to prevent it in future—in its report said that the Kargil operation was likely formulated by the Pakistan army as revenge for our taking control of the Siachen glacier in 1984. Siachen is the world's second longest non-polar glacier, and it is just north of where the Line of Control (LoC) between India and Pakistan ends in J&K. The committee's report said that the Kargil operation had long been brewing in Pakistani GHQ and had been twice presented to Prime Minister Benazir Bhutto, who rejected the proposal.

Kargil comprises a bunch of ridges spanning about 170 km and overlooking the Srinagar–Leh highway from heights ranging from 16,000 feet to 18,000 feet. It is located to the west of the Siachen glacier and it stands facing the Gilgit–Baltistan region of the old J&K, now occupied and administered by Pakistan as the Northern Areas, on the other side of the LoC.

The review committee sifted through Pakistani writing on the subject and deduced that the political and strategic motives of the Kargil operation were:

- To internationalise Kashmir as a nuclear flashpoint requiring urgent third-party intervention;
- To alter the LoC and disrupt its sanctity by capturing unheld areas in Kargil;
- To achieve a better bargaining position for a possible trade-off against positions held by India in Siachen.

Musharraf is said to have committed himself to the proposal when he became chief of army staff in October 1998; he even visited the Force Commander Northern Area (FCNA) in late October in pursuance of the plan.

The captured diary of Pakistani captain Hussain Ahmad of the 12 Northern Light Infantry (NLI), quoted in the review committee's report, gives an indication of the period when the intrusion began: 'Elements of the 12 NLI crossed the LoC in February 1999, losing 11 men and then another sepoy in two avalanches that struck these camps on February 25 and March 25.' In total, the report estimated that 1,500 to 2,400 troops, both regular and irregular, were deployed by Pakistan for intrusion into Kargil.

The Pakistan army had apparently gambled on a couple of factors:

'They calculated on a normal winter; a weak and vacillating Indian reaction; a strong element of surprise that would enable them to consolidate their gains along the "heights of Kargil"; their own capacity to obfuscate and a willingness on the part of traditional patrons to play along; early internationalisation of the situation, compelling foreign intervention from fear of a possible nuclear escalation.'

The intrusions were detected by 'shepherds' (as in 1965, when Pakistan tried to whip up war in Kashmir but found no support from the local population) on 3 May 1999, in the Batalik sector of Kargil; they informed the army, which sent a patrol and confirmed the intrusion on 7 May. The army then checked and detected, on 12 May, intrusion in the Dras sector (southwest of Kargil town), and on 14 May, in the Mashkoh sector (northeast of Kargil). Battalions were mobilised, several of which had just been de-inducted from Siachen, to push the intruders out.

The Pakistan army figured it would hang on to Kargil till October 1999, when the next winter set in, and when it would dig in for hard political bargaining. In any case the 1998–99 winter was mild, so the passes opened earlier and allowed a proper Indian military response. This included the use of the Indian Air Force to patrol the LoC and bomb intruders on our side; while this was a signal of how strongly India intended to reply should things escalate (far from weak and vacillating), it was also risky since the flight corridor was narrow and pilots could easily stray into Pakistani airspace. (One of our MiG-21s was downed by the other side and the pilot, Sqn Ldr Ajay Ahuja, was captured, tortured and killed.)

The military response was a fine moment for India as the army heroically and methodically began recapturing the peaks that the intruders had taken, starting with Tololing in mid-June, and then others right until the famous Tiger Hill battle in early July, just before Nawaz Sharif flew to Washington on a summons from US president Bill Clinton. It was also India's first televised war, so many of the peaks recaptured and heroes martyred became household names.

During the conflict, the two countries' foreign ministers met. Just before their meeting, our foreign minister, Jaswant Singh, held a press conference on 11 June 1999, in which he played conversations held on May 26 and May 29 between Musharraf, who was visiting Beijing, and his chief of the general staff, Lt. Gen. Mohammad Aziz Khan. These conversations were intercepted and taped by R&AW, and a decision was taken by the Cabinet Committee on Security (CCS) to publicly release these tapes.

As mentioned earlier, though, in R&AW I was still in no man's land and did not accompany Dave to the CCS meetings. When he came back from the meeting where the decision to release the tapes was taken, he let me know. As an intelligence person, the first question that struck me was why should this be made public? It would be counterproductive, for once you let the world know of a certain technical capability that you might have, the enemy knows, and your capability is likely to be neutralised.

'Sir, didn't you protest against releasing this?' I asked Dave.

'Nahin bhai, we have to do it,' he said. 'It's been decided.'

'You'll never hear Musharraf again,' I pointed out.

We left it at that.

Jaswant Singh released the tapes—he was the minister who was time and again called upon by Vajpayee to announce things to the world—and India derived huge mileage out of it. Musharraf's questions to Aziz Khan, such as 'Yeh politician log toh zyada ghabaraye toh nahin?', and the military updates he got, coupled with the restraint India showed by not crossing the LoC during the fighting, ensured that world opinion fell solidly behind India. And it severely weakened Mian Saheb's case when he went to Washington, DC.

As predicted, however, we lost a particular source of information. The fact of the matter is, if a secret conversation is overheard on a particular channel by technical means, no one is ever going to use that channel again. Why is it that these days, it's become so much more difficult to track Kashmiri militants? The same thing had happened in Punjab when militants using telephone lines were getting exposed. Once they started suffering losses and started getting caught, then they were that much more careful and that source of information dried up. It hasn't completely dried up because human beings being human still make mistakes and pick up the phone and say, 'Lagao yaar, baat karte hain.'

Because of our successes, however, a lot of disinformation was also plied into these channels. For example, whenever a VIP visit to Kashmir was planned, like that of the prime minister, a hundred messages would fly around saying, 'Usko ura dena, uski baja dena, safed ghar khatam ho jana chahiye.' The first time it alarmed me a little bit, but then I realised this was all being done deliberately: they knew we were listening and they wanted to scare us. And if you go so strictly by this information and get scared, then no VIP will ever visit Kashmir.

In any case, almost at the same time as the release of the tapes, the Indian army had recaptured Tololing, a position overlooking the Srinagar–Leh highway, and the tide had turned. We were on our way to victory. And in early July, I made a trip to Kargil.

I was in Srinagar, but I wasn't there for Kargil; what took me to Srinagar was the wedding of Chief Minister Farooq Abdullah's eldest daughter Safia. Farooq and I had a close relationship since my posting in the IB in Srinagar in 1988—as we shall see in the next chapter on the hijacking of flight IC-814 and in subsequent chapters—to the extent that when Jagmohan took over as governor of J&K in January1990 (the time that militancy exploded into a popular movement), he had me transferred out of Srinagar because he believed me to be 'Farooq's man'. For whatever that was worth, Farooq invited my wife and I for Safia's wedding and we went. We had no better place to stay than the residence of Chief Secretary Ashok 'Tony' Jaitley, another friend, one who was not only a bureaucrat but knew Kashmir better than most. He felt and behaved like a Kashmiri too, whom I had gotten to know since my tenure in Srinagar, so we stayed with him for a few days.

While I was there I told Farooq that I might as well go to Kargil. Safia's wedding was in the evening, so the chief minister gave me a helicopter in the morning in order that I could return some time in the afternoon. I flew up to visit Lt. Gen. Mohinder Puri, the man who led the 8 Mountain Division across the Zojila Pass and recaptured Tololing, which was the turning point in the war. He would rightly be much decorated after the war was over. I went to General Puri's bunker, and he gave me lunch, along with a briefing. I asked him how long it would take to wrap up the war.

'Yeah, we're getting them off our back,' General Puri said. 'They're still occupying some of our areas but we're making progress. But it will take me time. Maybe a month.'

Ironically, my visit was on 4 July 1999, the American independence day—the day that Nawaz Sharif was summoned to the White House by President Clinton. It was the day that Sharif announced that the intruders would vacate Kargil; India retook Tiger Hill the next day; and the war officially ended a week later. Of course, when I met General Puri, neither of us knew that Bill Clinton had read Mian Saheb the riot act, and when we later heard what had happened in Washington, DC we were both amused that we had expected the fighting to continue for another month.

After the war was over, the chairman of the four-member Kargil Review Committee, K. Subrahmanyam, came and met me, for by that time I had taken over as secretary at R&AW.

'Why do you think Kargil happened?' he asked, with particular reference to the build-up over the preceding winter. 'There was no intelligence.'

'First, let me clarify that I was not in R&AW in the period you're talking about,' I said. 'I was in IB and there were some bits of intelligence that I thought were quite significant. These were passed on.'

Maybe by itself the intelligence didn't amount to much, but we had information that there was unusual activity taking place on the other side of the LoC. We were keeping a watch in the aftermath of the May 1998 nuclear tests in Pakistan, and what we saw had to do with troop movement, building of bunkers, movement of weaponry. And in fact it came to my desk—I was the number two man in the IB—and I took it to the DIB.

'There's something unusual about this,' I told Shyamal.

'Why don't you send a note to the government?'

'I'll draw up a note, but I think this should go under your signature,' I said, 'because it's not just an ordinary thing.'

So in June 1998 the IB sent a note to the government. The Kargil Review Committee report, in its chapter on 'Findings', under the section 'Intelligence', said:

'The Intelligence Bureau (IB) is meant to collect intelligence within the country and is the premier agency for counter-intelligence. This agency got certain inputs on activities in the FCNA region which were considered important enough by the Director, IB, to be communicated over his signature on June 2, 1998, to the Prime Minister, Home Minister, Cabinet Secretary,

Home Secretary and Director General Military Operations. This communication was not addressed to the three officials most concerned with this information, namely, Secretary (R&AW), who is responsible for external intelligence and has the resources to follow up the leads in the IB report; Chairman JIC, who would have taken such information into account in JIC assessments; and Director General Military Intelligence. Director, IB stated that he expected the information to filter down to these officials through the official hierarchy. This did not happen in respect of Secretary (R&AW) who at that time was holding additional charge as Chairman JIC. The Committee feels that a communication of this nature should have been directly addressed to all the officials concerned.'

Obviously, neither the home ministry nor the army took much notice of the IB report, but there was something funny happening in that area. We report whatever unusual activity that we find, and this information had come to us from Leh a year before.

Whatever the Kargil committee may have said, the fact is that various governments from time to time have ignored intelligence inputs, in this case provided almost a year before the intrusions in Kargil were discovered by shepherds.

The other reality is that with our focus on counter-terrorism we are so wrapped up in actionable intelligence that we overlook tell-tale signs. This controversy was to haunt us again when 26/11 happened. It is so easy to make intelligence agencies the scapegoat, 'intelligence failure' is the general response.

And what was the army doing? It is supposed to send out regular patrols, which it had obviously stopped doing because it had become so routine. It's as simple as that.

In Kashmir, all we've done since 1989 is talk of infiltration, and it's the army which is the first to talk of it. But infiltration continues. Every summer as the snow begins to melt, you get a plethora of intelligence reports saying that Pakistan is sending in new batches of militants. Yet for all these dire warnings, people come and people go. The army has not been able to stop it.

Yet the army won the Kargil war in July, and in August I took over as chief of R&AW. Just before I took over, Dave one day said to me: 'These R&AW guys run a trade union here. I don't allow them into my room.'

The atmosphere at R&AW was less collegial than it was in the IB and that was because while the IB was homogenous in its composition of officers from the Indian Police Service, R&AW comprised several services—including its own service, the R&AW Administrative Service (RAS). The founder of R&AW, Ram Nath Kao—a man so mysterious that there was apparently no photograph of him—had envisioned R&AW would have its own service. Initially the recruitment was from the open market, much in the way the CIA or the MI6 does; Kao took from various streams, such as the postal service, the revenue service, the army, etc. His idea was that people would leave their parent services and join the RAS.

However, Kao and his deputy, K. Sankaran Nair, did not lay down clear rules of seniority for people joining from different services and this has plagued the service from day one. As a result, many people did not opt for the RAS, fearing they would lose out on the seniority their parent service offered them and defeating the very purpose the RAS was set up for. This has resulted in groupism in the RAS, unnecessary because in my experience the R&AW had officers who were as top-notch, man for man, as those in the IB despite the heterogeneity of backgrounds: for example, my successor, Vikram Sood, who had a very good tenure as chief, was originally from the postal service. Similarly, one of our bright officers who was posted in Pakistan, Vipin Handa, and who later died tragically early in a malfunctioning lift at R&AW headquarters, was from the revenue service.

One consequence of the groupism was trade unionism, as Dave put it, and I was mindful of that. As it was, the buzz going around R&AW was that Dulat was taking over and bringing in his own gang from the IB; furthermore, the rumour was that my staff officer would be someone from IB. I made it a point not to bring officers over from the IB, and I asked someone, 'Who's the most difficult fellow here? Who's the ringleader of the RAS?' 'Jayadeva Ranade,' I was told. I appointed him as my staff officer. He was very good at his work, and we're still good friends.

In fact, the irony of the matter was that as a fallout of this running rivalry between the RAS and non-RAS personnel, Ranade did not get his promotion or was made additional secretary till a few days before he retired; something that would have affected his pension had it not come through. The same government that had second thoughts about making him an additional secretary then made him a member of the National Security Advisory Board, where he was the China expert. This is the craziness of government functioning.

Appointing Ranade wasn't the only surprise my colleagues got. At the R&AW headquarters there are eleven floors, and the chief's office is on the eleventh; to access it he has a private lift at the back of the building. The building has been structured in such a way that the chief can enter the grounds, drive around and come up the private lift which goes straight to the eleventh floor, without anyone knowing. It's called 'the chief's lift'. Everyone else comes in through the main entrance, which has a whole row of lifts on the far end of the spacious lobby.

When I heard of this, I thought I can't come in sneaking around the back. In any case, I'm a guy who comes to office late, and if I come late then everybody should be able to see that I come a bit late. I wanted to make a point so I began using the main entrance. I said I would use the private lift only when I was going out during the day, or for my guests, or when I was going home at night. A colleague pointed out to me how much of a departure this was. According to him, I was the first to do so, the others used to come by the private lift and leave by it. 'Saab, aapse pehle iss taraf se koi nahin aayaa. Peechhe se aatein hain, peechhe se hi chale gaye.' It was another example of the way things were at R&AW.

Days after I joined, I decided to pay a visit to R.N. Kao, who was nearing ninety and living in Vasant Vihar, a posh colony for retired senior bureaucrats. I called him up and asked if I could visit. 'This is a good decision you have made, to call me up,' he said rather modestly, and invited me over.

He was a tall, thin man with a hawk-like nose, and we chatted about the organisation that he built. Apparently, when Indira Gandhi gave him the go-ahead to set up an external intelligence agency he went to London and met the second-in-command at the MI6, Sir Maurice Oldfield, who later took over as 'C' (and who was rumoured to be one of the models for 'C' in John le Carré's spy novels), for advice on setting up R&AW. The one thing that stood out from our conversation was his advice to me that now that I was in charge, I need not worry about anyone else; I should run it as I thought best, without looking over my shoulder. 'You've got the best job in the government,' Kao said. 'Now don't worry about anyone else, and just do your job.'

That was good advice because there weren't too many dull moments in the months after I took over. For one thing, on 12 October 1999, General Musharraf took over in Pakistan in a military coup d'état. I had been in the job for two months or so, and everyone in R&AW was caught unawares. I can claim credit for a lot of things (actually I can't, due to the Official Secrets Act) but the fact was that as far as the coup was concerned we were caught unawares.

In a nutshell, Musharraf had gone to Sri Lanka for the weekend to attend their army's 50th anniversary celebrations. On the way back, he was sacked by Nawaz Sharif, who appointed the ISI chief, Khwaja Ziauddin, in his place. The army quickly surrounded the prime minister's residence and arrested him, but not before Mian Saheb sent a message to Karachi International Airport not to let Musharraf's flight land, and instead re-direct it to India. ('Over my dead body we're going to India,' Musharraf reportedly shouted at the pilots while waving his pistol in the cockpit.) The flight was allowed to land once the army surrounded the airport, and Mian Saheb was thrown in jail; he would later be exiled to Saudi Arabia. Musharraf went to President Rafiq Tarar and declared himself chief executive.

Who would have thought that this guy would get off a flight and lock up his prime minister? Come to think of it, who would have anticipated that the prime minister would have sacked him? It all happened so fast.

We knew that this fellow was uncompromising. During Vajpayee's bus trip to Lahore, for instance, the story was that Musharraf conveniently came to meet our prime minister— without his cap. In the military, you salute with your cap, and if you're not wearing your cap, you don't salute. Musharraf obviously had refused to salute Vajpayee. And then of course was Musharraf's conversation with his number two during the Kargil war that R&AW had intercepted and that the government had played for the world.

It was a turn of events that saddened Vajpayee, for he had gotten along with Mian Saheb. Now not only was the peace process in tatters, but he was genuinely concerned for what would happen to Nawaz Sharif. I saw that there was a real shock to Vajpayee and Brajesh Mishra, but to their credit they would eventually get over it and try to do business with Musharraf. It helped that the CIA chief came and shared his opinion with us that Musharraf was someone people could do business with.

But that was still in the future, for just two months after Musharraf took over, India faced another crisis that was inspired in Pakistan and blessed by Musharraf: the hijacking of its Indian Airlines flight IC-814.

3

TWO HOSTAGE CRISES

If you were to ask me, Gen. Pervez Musharraf had to have had a hand in the hijacking of Indian Airlines flight IC-814 on 24 December 1999. The reason one can say so is that such an operation could not have been undertaken without ISI support; a hijacking was no cakewalk, even in those pre-9/11 days. And Musharraf, being the army chief and that too in a country where the military had taken direct control, was all powerful. In fact, the story we heard was that when the hijackers took the plane to Lahore they were given a bag of weapons. Thus with three events in quick succession—the Kargil intrusion, the coup d'état, and the hijacking of IC-814—there was every reason to be wary of Musharraf, who one suspected had a hand in all three incidents. The hijacking itself made for a harrowing final week of the final year of the century, what with the pressure upon the government from the families of the 176 passengers held hostage, and the international isolation in which India found herself, while the West celebrated Christmas.

IC-814 was en route from Kathmandu, Nepal, to New Delhi on Christmas Eve when five armed men, threatening to detonate a bomb onboard, hijacked the plane at around 5 p.m. They told

Capt. Devi Sharan to take the aircraft further west than its intended destination, towards Lahore, but fuel ran low and the plane had to be landed in Amritsar, where it remained for 45 to 50 minutes. That was the only moment when India could have taken control of the hijacking incident. Once it left Amritsar then the only way it could have ended was with India giving into the terrorists' demands, which is what happened.

When the hijacking became known the government convened a Crisis Management Group (CMG) headed by the cabinet secretary, Prabhat Kumar, to monitor the situation and deal with it. While the plane was on the ground in Amritsar, Punjab Police was in charge of the situation. The Punjab Police chief was Sarabjit Singh, a batchmate, who was based in Chandigarh and had taken charge a few weeks earlier. Sarabjit and I had known each other throughout our careers, and he later told me his version of what happened while IC-814 was in Amritsar.

Sarabjit had just come out of a dentist's appointment when he got news of the hijacking. As in the past, Amritsar airport would be the most vulnerable in Punjab, so he immediately spoke to J.P. Virdi, the inspector general (border), posted in Amritsar. The state police had commandos in Amritsar and Virdi had two companies sent immediately to the airport. The deputy inspector general (border), Jasminder Singh, had the presence of mind to reach the air traffic control (ATC) tower even before IC-814 landed. Jasminder kept reporting to Sarabjit on the developments as they unfolded.

Sarabjit decided to monitor the situation from Chandigarh and await instructions from the CMG in Delhi, because he felt he was not in a position to act on his own. This was not a position that former Punjab Police chief Kanwar Pal Singh Gill would have taken.

K.P.S. was the man credited with leading the police from the front in the fight against terrorism in Punjab. In 1993, he had dealt with a similar situation when an Indian Airlines flight from Delhi to Srinagar was hijacked and forced to land in

Amritsar. The hijackers wanted the plane taken to either Lahore or Kabul, but a quick operation by the paramilitary National Security Guard (NSG) ended the episode—in a span of 12 seconds, all four terrorists were immobilised and the main hijacker, Mohammed Yousuf Shah, killed. You needed a man like Gill in 1999 to make a quick assessment and disable the aircraft without wasting time waiting for clear instructions from Delhi.

Sarabjit did consider that he had at his disposal in Punjab commandos who were trained in anti-terrorism, and that they could storm the aircraft, but there would be casualties. He told Delhi, which responded that the government's top priority was that there be no casualties. Sarabjit was also in touch with his chief minister, Parkash Singh Badal, who was at the time visiting his village. Badal's instruction was: be careful. The chief minister did not want a mess in Punjab and did not want to be blamed for anything. He too said that no harm should come to the passengers.

On the other hand, DIB Shyamal Datta asked Sarabjit why he did not puncture the tyres of the aircraft and immobilise it. 'They were talking to me as if there was a bicycle there,' Sarabjit mused years later. (Since I knew Sarabjit and I knew what pressure he would be under with everyone breathing down his neck, I avoided talking to him during the crisis.)

Sarabjit said that Delhi never told him that IC-814 was not to be allowed to take off. After the event he came in for a lot of flak for allowing the aircraft to leave, and even K.P.S. joined the chorus to say that the Punjab Police should not have allowed the plane to fly away. 'I wasn't Gill,' Sarabjit said in all modesty. 'I wasn't of his stature to stake leadership because of the bad luck by which the plane landed in Amritsar.'

Sarabjit decided to sit tight and do just what Delhi instructed him. The fault, thus, would lie with the CMG, which could not come to a clear decision on what to do.

Captain Sharan also came in for criticism, but his role was

exemplary. He kept telling the ATC to help with fuel; that the hijackers had already killed a passenger, maybe two; and that even flying on reserve fuel to Lahore—which was a short distance away, on the other side of the border—was a risk. Worse, the plane was parked midway on the runway, instead of at the end from where it could begin its takeoff.

The hijackers insisted that the plane keep taxiing and told Captain Sharan to take off however he could. The body language of the hijackers showed them to be quite panic-stricken, and so the captain took off with only half a runway. At Lahore he was refused permission to land and Lahore ATC even turned off the airport lights; it was only when Captain Sharan threatened to land on a road that they permitted IC-814 to land. The hijackers had been so filled with panic that they didn't think they would get out of Amritsar and killed Rupin Katyal, ultimately throwing his body out in Dubai.

Readers may remember that IC-814 was the last hijacking that took place in India. Long before that there were lots of hijackings taking place all over the world and whenever anyone heard of a hijack they would cross their fingers and hope that the hijacked aircraft would not land in their territory. A hijacking was a no-win situation that no one wanted on their head. By the time IC-814 happened, most had gotten over the hijacking phobia, but India's most vulnerable airports remained Srinagar, Jammu and Amritsar. Soon after the hijacking of IC-814 the government decided to station NSG commandoes at these airports.

On 24 December 1999, however, the CMG debated how to deal with the hijacking, and while the CMG was debating, IC-814 flew away. It debated matters such as how to deploy the NSG commandoes to Amritsar fast enough. In all that debate the opportunity to gain the upper hand slipped away. To give credit to the home minister, L.K. Advani, he landed up at the CMG and took charge after the plane left Amritsar.

I was a part of the CMG since I headed R&AW, and several

people have asked me about what happened inside the CMG during those 50 minutes; most of the publicly available literature blames 'mismanagement' for the missed opportunity to get a handle on the hijacking. Even filmmaker Vishal Bharadwaj, who was working on a film script (and later made the excellent film *Haider*, based on Basharat Peer's script), asked me to reveal to him what happened in the CMG, but it is not my place to disclose the contents of a secret meeting.

What I can say, however, is that the CMG degenerated into a blame game, with various senior officials trying to lay the blame for allowing the aircraft to leave Indian soil on one another; the cabinet secretary, being the head of the CMG, was one target, and the NSG chief, Nikhil Kumar, became another. It was a fraught time and nerves were unfortunately constantly on edge.

In either case, the plane landed in Lahore, was refuelled and as the story went, the hijackers received a bag of weapons. Then the plane went to Dubai, where twenty-seven passengers were allowed to leave; and then the aircraft went to Kandahar, Afghanistan, at that time ruled by the Taliban. While IC-814 was in Dubai, India had contemplated a commando raid at the Dubai airport, but the local authorities refused to cooperate. We tried to prevail on the Americans to put pressure on the United Arab Emirates to allow us a raid, but as I mentioned earlier, India found itself isolated internationally. Nothing seemed to be going our way.

After the plane reached Kandahar, which incidentally was the base of the one-eyed head of the Taliban government, Mullah Mohammed Omar, we heard of the hijackers' demands: the release of thirty-five terrorists from Indian prisons, the main one being Maulana Masood Azhar, a dreaded veteran terrorist leader; and $200 million in cash. We sent a team of negotiators, the best professionals in the business, including future IB directors Ajit Doval and Nehchal Sandhu, as well as my senior colleague C.D. Sahay (who would take over as

R&AW chief after Vikram Sood); there was an external affairs ministry representative, Vivek Katju, and representatives of other departments like the Bureau of Civil Aviation Security. A truly high-powered team without much power to do anything on the soil of a country governed by people sympathetic to the hijackers.

This was evident in the fact that the Taliban surrounded the aircraft with tanks and soldiers, which they said was to dissuade the hijackers from any further violence, but which we understood was a signal to us not to try a raid by commandos to immobilise the hijackers—an option that we discussed in detail. It became clear that the airport was essentially under the ISI's control, and that the Taliban were being guided throughout the episode by the ISI. Pakistani journalist Zahid Hussain, who was in Kandahar during the hijacking, later wrote in his book, *Frontline Pakistan*: 'Afghan sources . . . revealed that the hijackers were taking instructions from Pakistani intelligence officers present at the airport.' For Hussain, 'the extent of Taliban/ISI/jihadi cooperation was revealed during the Indian hostage crisis of 1999'.

It was frustrating to be outmanoeuvred by Pakistan's spy agency. On top of that, Doval, with whom I had worked closely in the IB and who would later become PM Narendra Modi's national security advisor, was pressing me from Kandahar to get the government to find an early resolution to the hijacking. Who could blame him, for the team out there was badly stuck in a hostile environment, surrounded by Taliban. 'Take a decision quickly, sir,' he said, 'because these fellows are getting impatient and I don't know what will happen.' Eventually, after five days of negotiations the hijackers' demands were whittled down to the release of three terrorists: Masood Azhar, Ahmed Omar Saeed Sheikh, and Mushtaq Ahmed Zargar.

We had arrested Masood Azhar back in 1994, when he had come to India to settle some disputes between different factions of his outfit, the Harkat-ul-Ansar. He was of such high value that to get his release, his group floated a front group, al-Faran, which in 1995 kidnapped six foreign trekkers in south Kashmir and held them hostage in the mountains, demanding the release of Masood Azhar and twenty other terrorists. The six were Britons Keith Mangan and Paul Wells; Americans John Childs and Donald Hutchings; German Dirk Hasert; and Norwegian Hans Christian Ostro. Childs managed to escape. Ostro was beheaded (and the name 'al-Faran' was carved on his chest). The other four were never heard from again; a few months later al-Faran claimed they no longer held them, and their bodies were never found. Much later there were reports that in late 1995, the al-Faran leader, Abdul Hamid Turki, was killed in an exchange with our army, and that nine days after Turki's death, the hostages were shot dead. Masood Azhar was not released.

We spent a year trying to spot the al-Faran/Harkat-ul-Ansar kidnappers and their hostages. It proved very tough in the mountains of south Kashmir. At the time, as I've mentioned earlier, I was heading the Kashmir group in the IB, and we got a whole lot of information every day—there had been a sighting here, there had been a sighting there, another sighting somewhere completely different. The Bakerwals—a pastoral community inhabiting the hills and mountains of Kashmir—and some Gujjars would bring us these stories, and in one sense, the avalanche of information was farcical. The truth is that the kidnappers had taken the Westerners deep into the forests, and no technical intelligence, satellite imagery, or Gujjar ears and eyes on the ground could nail them.

In fact, one day the minister of state for home affairs, Rajesh Pilot, who used to take a keen interest in Kashmir affairs and who was encouraged in doing so by his prime minister, P.V. Narasimha Rao, summoned both the vice-chief of the army staff, Lt. Gen. Surinder Nath, and me to his room in North Block. General Nath had earlier been commander of the Srinagar-based XV corps so he had a working knowledge of the Valley. Pilot shot off a bunch of questions.

'What the hell is going on?' the minister said. 'Why can't the army get to know where the hostages are? And when we give the army information, why aren't they able to do anything?'

Pilot was himself from the Gujjar community and was well aware of the intelligence that was coming in from them. He spread out on the table a large map of the Kashmir Valley.

'General,' he said. 'Tell me, suppose I tell you that these guys are here,' he pointed to a mountainous spot in south Kashmir, 'how long will it take for your people to get there?'

And in typical army parlance, General Nath began his long-winded answer: 'It will have to be a brigade-level operation.'

So Pilot folded the map he had spread out before him and the general left. We were back to square one.

We were keen to get the hostages back; by that time, we were sick of kidnappings. It was a phenomenon that began in December 1989 with the kidnapping of the home minister's daughter, Rubaiya Sayeed; the success of that hostage trade-off made kidnapping an everyday occurrence in Kashmir. It became a lucrative business. A militant would pick someone up and extort good money. It became so that a target could be kidnapped in the morning and released in the evening; people had no choice but to pay up and smile.

In fact, just before the al-Faran incident there was a high-profile kidnapping of *Financial Times* correspondent David Housego's son Kim; the journalist made use of his network of contacts to get his boy released. The picking up of the six Western trekkers marked the peak of the kidnappings; and in the way IC-814 was the last hijacking, the al-Faran abductions became the last kidnapping. After this, it faded and stopped, because it had become counterproductive for everyone.

Some people allege that India strung out the al-Faran kidnapping, or that India half-heartedly searched for the kidnapped trekkers, because it was proving to be a public relations disaster for Pakistan and that it was one of the factors that helped India get over the international hostility it faced over Kashmir and thereby subsequently manage the political problem. This is nonsense.

What was an unexpected consequence of the kidnapping was that the Western governments used it to their great advantage in building up their networks in Kashmir. The Americans, for instance, made a lot of trips to Srinagar on the pretext of monitoring the kidnapping, for one of their nationals was still involved. They sent their diplomats and they sent their intelligence professionals; we knew each and every visitor to the Valley. In a sense, then, the al-Faran kidnapping was the first opening up of Kashmir, for until this incident, very few foreigners used to go to Srinagar once violence broke out in 1990; perhaps there would be the occasional visit by the first secretary (political) or the political counsellor of a Western mission. The al-Faran kidnapping became a good excuse and some professionals did build up a good network. The British also showed a lot of interest—they worked closely with the Americans—and they developed a well-informed political section.

You could say that everyone got something out of the al-Faran kidnapping except the kidnappers themselves, for Masood Azhar remained jailed, and so Harkat-ul-Ansar tried again the next year when it kidnapped four Western tourists and kept them as hostages in a village in Saharanpur, Uttar Pradesh. The person who lured the tourists into a trap was a former London School of Economics student, Omar Sheikh, who Musharraf in his memoir *In the Line of Fire* alleged was recruited by the British MI6 while he was at LSE (Musharraf also claimed MI6 sent Omar Sheikh to the Balkans). Again Omar Sheikh and company demanded the release of Masood Azhar, as well as ten other terrorists, but the police were able to foil the kidnappers, release the hostages unharmed and capture the kidnappers including Omar Sheikh, who spent the next five years as a guest at Delhi's Tihar Jail.

The third terrorist whose release the IC-814 hijackers sought was Mushtaq Zargar, a particularly brutish, ruthless, low-life Kashmiri terrorist, quite unlike the militant chiefs who were committed to their separatist cause, who had intellectual curiosity and who were not ideologically dogmatic. From a neighbourhood near Srinagar's Jamia Masjid, he joined the movement and took up the gun early on, launching his own tanzeem, al-Umar Mujahideen. He is responsible for forty murders, including a string of killings of Kashmiri Pandits which contributed in no small measure to the exodus of Hindus from the Valley once violence took centre stage in 1989–90. He is somebody I have always found highly distasteful.

Once Ajit Doval and the other negotiators had whittled the IC-814 hijackers' demands to these three terrorists—Masood Azhar, Omar Sheikh and Mushtaq Zargar—the government had to take a call. There was great pressure exerted by the media, which kept showing visuals of the protesting families of the hostages gathered at the entry to Race Course Road, where the official residence of the prime minister is located. With very few cards to play, Vajpayee's team had little choice but to agree to release the three terrorists.

Suddenly it occurred to everyone that the J&K chief minister, Dr Farooq Abdullah, would have to be informed; it also dawned on everyone that he might object and pose a hurdle. The national security advisor asked me to go. Jaswant Singh made an official call to Farooq on behalf of the CCS, and advised the chief minister that the R&AW chief was being sent to him.

I was picked to do the dirty job as I was reckoned to be close to Doctor Saheb since my days as the IB head in Srinagar in the late 1980s. Since it was winter, the J&K government had shifted to Jammu, and I called Farooq and told him that I was coming to Jammu. He immediately guessed why the government was sending me. He responded by saying, 'You might as well come and stay with me.' I had not expected it to be a pleasant encounter and had taken a colleague along as moral support. He did not take the full bombardment that I was to get for three hours plus. He tactfully excused himself saying he had to go for dinner.

As my R&AW aircraft landed in Jammu, the sun was setting on 30 December. It was the month of Ramzan. I went straight to Farooq's residence, where I found him sitting at his dining table by himself. 'I know why you've come,' he said. 'Just let me go and say my prayers.'

After his prayers he came out and had his juice. And then he angrily said: 'You again? Tumne Mufti ki beti ke liye kiya tha, phir wohi kar rahe ho.'

What he was angry about and what the small irony of our situation was, was the kidnapping of Rubaiya Sayeed on 8 December 1989, an eventful episode like the hijacking of IC-814 a decade later, and one where both of us were involved. In both episodes, he was chief minister; during the earlier incident, I was the head of the IB in Srinagar. In both episodes I had asked him to release jailed terrorists, and in both episodes he had initially refused, saying presciently that doing so would have dire consequences for militancy in his state. In both episodes I persuaded him to ultimately give in, on orders from the top in Delhi.

As mentioned earlier, Rubaiya Sayeed was the daughter of the newly appointed Union home minister, Mufti Sayeed, who had taken charge following the election defeat of Rajiv Gandhi's Congress government and the installation of a National Front government led by Vishwanath Pratap Singh. She was kidnapped as she came out of the hospital where she interned, the Lal Ded Memorial Hospital, by boys of the Jammu and Kashmir Liberation Front, and kept in captivity somewhere in Sopore, as some JKLF boys later told me.

The JKLF was founded in 1977 by Pakistan-based Amanullah Khan and Maqbool Butt, who was hanged in 1984 following the kidnapping and murder of Indian diplomat Ravindra Mhatre in England, and whose execution was mourned annually by Kashmiris to defiantly show their anger with India. The tanzeem was the dominant 'nationalist' separatist group in the early days in Kashmir, espousing independence. Later it was overtaken in power and influence by other groups which wanted Kashmir's merger with Pakistan.

Most of the boys who first crossed over into Pakistan for terrorism-training under the ISI, following the fraudulent assembly elections in 1987 in which many of them were involved as poll agents for the new opposition party, the Muslim United Front (most of whose leaders would six years later form the separatist All Parties Hurriyat Conference), did so under the aegis of the JKLF. (Mushtaq Zargar was originally a member of the JKLF till he fell out with the group in 1989 and formed his own tanzeem.) The JKLF's leaders were known by the acronym HAJY, standing for Hamid Sheikh, Ashfaq Majid Wani, Javed Mir, and Yasin Malik; they committed the first acts of terror in Kashmir between 1988 and 1990, though their unwavering commitment to independence made them suspect in Pakistani eyes.

The JKLF had been hatching a kidnapping plan for some time; their first target was actually the chief minister's eldest daughter, Safia Abdullah. The boys, however, found it difficult to get to Safia because Gupkar Road, where the chief minister stayed, had enough security and protection to make a kidnapping difficult. Also, she did not go out too much in those days. After a while, the JKLF gave up on the plan to kidnap Safia and their next target was the daughter of the senior superintendent of police (SSP), Allah Baksh. Though he was a straightforward policeman, who only spoke the language of the 'danda' and followed strictly whatever orders he got, he was one of the officials blamed for the rigged 1987 elections, as his policemen allegedly picked up many MUF workers and threw them in jail for the night.

While they were planning this kidnapping, on 5 December 1989, Mufti was sworn in as the Union home minister, and one of the JKLF fellows had a brainwave: why not pick up Rubaiya.

With Mufti becoming minister, Farooq had in any case receded into the background, and in those days, he had left Kashmir feeling down and had gone to England, as he occasionally did (he had studied there and he met his wife there, so it was a natural getaway for him). And Rubaiya, Mufti's middle daughter, was a 23-year-old medical intern at the Lal Ded hospital; she went in every second day; someone said she went in at such-and-such time and left at such-and-such time; so it would be an easy pick-up.

Thus on 8 December, at about a quarter to four in the afternoon, when she was half a kilometre from home, Rubaiya was pulled out of the mini-bus she was in and put into a Maruti car and driven to Sopore. She had been kidnapped.

All hell broke loose. Where was Mufti's daughter, everyone kept asking me. The kidnappers called up the office of the *Kashmir Times* and claimed responsibility. They demanded the release of several militants including JKLF leader Hamid Sheikh, who was in custody. Since it was winter and the government was in Jammu, I took the next morning's flight to Srinagar, and immediately people who had any link or connection to Mufti got into the act.

Chief Secretary Moosa Raza, a Gujarat cadre officer from Tamil Nadu, was the main negotiator, but all the back-up was provided by IB, and I worked in close tandem with him. Moosa rarely left the IB office from where operations were conducted, but for obvious reasons the IB was kept in the background. The first two guys on the scene were journalists, Zafar Mehraj of the *Kashmir Times* and Mohammed Sayeed Malik, both of whom had deep connections with Mufti. Sayeed came to do a recce, basically to report to Mufti what was going on, and whether the men in Srinagar were showing seriousness in tracking down Rubaiya.

But Zafar Mehraj hung around and was helpful. He arranged a meeting with the father of Ashfaq Majid Wani, one of the JKLF top guns and one of those involved in the actual kidnapping. Ashfaq was already a legend in Kashmir for his bravado, and the legend grew after he died while trying to lob a grenade at some CRPF personnel in March 1990. His father, on the other hand, was a humble government clerk.

We met in a government flat and sat on the ground, and Ashfaq's father was very emotional, not least because there was some anger in the Valley that the boys had kidnapped an unmarried girl, which they considered a highly un-Islamic act. Ashfaq's father kept saying Delhi had always let down Kashmir and Kashmiris, and then he would launch into an emotional speech about how the boys were actually nice boys, that they wouldn't harm anyone, that he could vouch for them, and that Rubaiya was like a sister to them.

Ashfaq's father told us that the kidnapping was basically to get Hamid Sheikh freed. He had been injured and so was being kept in the hospital, and the JKLF wanted him released so the whole kidnapping was for that, plus whatever publicity they could get.

'Okay,' I said. 'But if he's to be released, where do you want him released? In Lal Chowk?'

Ashfaq's father was not very clear. 'Why don't you hand him over to the Iranians?' he said.

'There are no Iranians here,' I said. 'Which Iranians do you want him handed over to?'

'No, you could hand him over to the Iranian embassy.'

'How will you take him and hand him over to the Iranian embassy?' I asked. 'Suppose the Iranians refuse, then what will we do with him?'

He kept saying vague things like that, perhaps bits of conversation that he had himself heard. The JKLF had apparently seriously considered options like this.

'Why don't you leave him at the border?' Ashfaq's father suggested.

'If the government agrees we could,' I said. 'So many are going, he could also go.'

In the end, in half-disgust, half-bravado, and half-theatre, he grabbed my wrist and said: 'Let me tell you one thing. These boys are very good boys, and even if Delhi does nothing, no harm will come to Rubaiya. She is like their sister, she will be released.'

That was the conversation. And it gave us confidence that the whole episode would have a good ending, and that we need not jump the gun. We felt that Rubaiya might be released for no one, or at the least, in exchange for just Hamid Sheikh.

A lot of other fellows got into the act. There was the judge, Moti Lal Kaul, who reported faithfully back to Mufti; there was an MLA, Mir Mustafa of Lasjan, who was later killed. Moulvi Abbas Ansari, a decent man who was instrumental in setting up the MUF and later joined and headed the Hurriyat, and I met him through a colleague in the J&K police during that time. Moulvi Abbas was close to the JKLF boys, who had a lot of faith in him, and after I met him he volunteered to help by going and talking to the boys holding Rubaiya. Unfortunately, by the time he got into action, things were moving at a fast clip and nobody needed too much help.

The home minister's daughter was a hostage and there was intense pressure on us, so I was meeting a lot of Kashmiris. Indeed, this was the beginning of my career as a person talking to as many Kashmiris, of as many hues as possible, as I could, not a start in the best of circumstances. In fact, one of the first people I approached was Dr Abdul Ahad Guru, the cardiothoracic surgeon who was an ideologue of the JKLF and who basically told me to get lost.

I went and met Dr Guru at his residence-cum-clinic in Barzalla at eight in the morning on a bitterly cold December morning. I had been told that if I wanted to go and meet him, I should go there at eight o'clock. There was a long queue of waiting patients outside his house. He came out of his room and asked me, 'What can I do for you?'

'You know our problem,' I said. 'This Hamid Sheikh is in

the hospital and he has a lot of regard and respect for you. You could help us resolve this whole matter.'

'Hamid Sheikh is a patient of mine,' Dr Guru said. 'It's just a doctor–patient relationship. I'm not getting involved in any of this. Sorry. Can't help you.'

He said it straight, and his message was clear. I left, empty-handed.

(Incidentally, Dr Guru was murdered in 1993 by the pro-Pakistan Hizbul Mujahideen, which was on a mission to wipe out the pro-independence JKLF.)

On the morning of 11 December 1989, Farooq arrived in Kashmir on his return from London. As I've said once, without Farooq Abdullah there was no National Conference and in fact while he was away, the cabinet was pretty much dead except for one meeting in which no one knew what to do or what to decide. On his return Farooq immediately called for a cabinet meeting and his senior ministers complained that they had no idea what was going on.

'Everything is being handled from the office of the IB,' one of them said. 'Even the chief secretary has stopped reporting to us; he only reports to the IB and spends all his time sitting in their office. We have not been kept in the loop at all.'

As usual, this was one of those things you could say was 'almost true'.

Farooq promptly summoned Moosa, who had been projecting himself as the interlocutor, and told him: 'You're no longer the interlocutor.'

The hapless Moosa wondered why, and Farooq said: 'How the hell could you not report to the cabinet?'

'But there was no cabinet in your absence,' Moosa pointed out. 'I didn't know who to report to.'

The truth was that poor Moosa was reporting to the cabinet secretary in Delhi, a gentleman by the name of T.N. Seshan, who would go on to gain a reputation for being an assertive chief election commissioner and for clamping down on electoral malpractices. Moosa was flabbergasted by Farooq's rebuke, and he told Seshan that he might be removed as chief secretary. As a result I got a frantic call from Delhi saying that they had heard that Moosa was being removed. I told them, the chief minister's back and he's in a bit of a huff.

I went to Farooq and said, 'Sir, I'm told you're really angry with Moosa. It's not really his fault. Given the limitations in which we're working, he's doing his best.'

Farooq relented and said, 'Okay, we'll reinstate Moosa.' And then he said to me: 'What the hell is going on?'

What was going on is that the gang in Delhi who kept repeating ad nauseam that Farooq was not serious were gunning for him and now they had a good excuse: he wasn't in J&K at a crucial time like this and it had taken him three days to come back. That he was no good. Farooq was no fool and he saw that two parallel games were playing out in Delhi: one was for the release of Mufti's daughter, and the other was the chance to get rid of the incompetent, no-good, holidaying-in-London Farooq Abdullah. And one thing influenced the other.

I have to say that from the 11th to the 13th, when Rubaiya was finally freed, Farooq cooperated totally with whatever Mufti and Delhi wanted—except for the point about releasing five terrorists. M.L. Kaul was the one who went and met Farooq with Mufti's message that all five terrorists had to be released, and Farooq was furious.

'How has it gone from one to three to five?' he asked. 'Even if it were my own daughter I would not release them.'

Yet he did call up Mufti, in my presence, because there was a lot of talk going around that Farooq was just not bothered about the kidnapping because it was Mufti's daughter; the usual Delhi Darbar nonsense. Farooq called up one evening and said, 'Look, we are doing our best, I assure you we will not allow anything to go wrong. Mufti Saheb, I am doing as much for your daughter as I would have done for my own daughter.'

The end of the story is that on 13 December, two ministers

arrived: Inder Gujral and Arif Mohammad Khan. We had been talking to Delhi with regard to the negotiations till about midnight. It was still a stalemate. Seshan, who was still the cabinet secretary, read the riot act to Moosa. 'Enough is enough,' he said. 'We will tell you what has to be done. Tell your chief minister to fall in line.'

After all this, around midnight, we each left the control room to go home. Soon after I reached, however, I received a call that the two ministers were arriving. In those five days I think I slept a total of eight hours, and now I was told that these two ministers would arrive at five in the morning by special plane. No chance of sleep, I told myself, so I shaved and then lay down for a 90-minute nap. At around four I got ready and then realised that I hadn't informed Farooq yet. Farooq did not like surprises.

I drove by Farooq's gate and said, 'Doctor Saheb so rahe honge?'

'CM Saheb utth gaye honge,' the guard said. 'Namaaz ka time ho raha hai.' It was 4:30 a.m.

I told him to get Farooq on the phone. He came on the line and asked: 'Hello, what are you doing?'

I told him the two ministers were coming, so I guessed he knew. 'So what if they're arriving?' he said. 'Why do you need to go to the airport?'

'The DIB is also coming,' I said, as IB chief M.K. Narayanan was with the two ministers.

'Bring them straight here,' Farooq said.

It was dark when the plane landed and the ministers said they wanted to wash up at the guest house. I said the CM has called you straight home, he's waiting for you, so we went to Farooq's house, and he took us to the hamam downstairs. It was around 6 a.m., and just about daybreak. As soon as we all sat down, Farooq said, why don't you hear it from the IB chief here in Srinagar. So I briefed them and gave the whole spiel in a nutshell.

Frankly, I don't know if Gujral and Arif came to Srinagar to genuinely listen to Farooq, or if they were just playing good cop/bad cop. Whatever Farooq would say, they would say, 'We didn't know this!' Whatever Gujral didn't like he would pretend he had not heard and he would tap his hearing aid. Arif would say something and Gujral would say, 'Kya kaha aapne?' The whole thing was a charade.

This went on for two hours, we drank three cups of tea, and then the two ministers took Farooq outside and told him, 'This is what is to be done.'

He said, 'Okay, you want to go ahead and release them, do it. But I want to lodge my protest.'

Farooq was a sharp cookie, he sensed that once V.P. Singh and company came, his days were numbered. He was just playing along.

But he clearly told them that if the government held out, Rubaiya would be released unharmed and without having to free terrorists. If the government caved in, it would burst the dam, and there would be no looking back for terrorists in Kashmir. 'We will have to pay for it,' he told the two ministers.

He proved right.

I had gone to see the Delhi team off at the airport and on the way back found that it had become Diwali. The entire city of Srinagar was illuminated and there were lots of boys going around and collecting money on the roads, collecting funds for the movement. It was now under way in right earnest. The whole mood in Srinagar had changed. Azaadi was now around the corner.

So, on 30 December 1999, during the hijacking episode of IC-814, when I arrived in Jammu to advise Farooq, he took one look at me and said: 'You again.'

Most people would be wary of raising their voice with the R&AW chief, but the chief minister was in a fury and for three hours he shouted at me.

'You were there during Rubaiya's kidnapping,' he said. 'How could you come back again?'

'Sir, I was solidly with you that time, but this time I'm with the government of India,' I said. 'Then I was pleading along with you. This time I'm pleading with you.'

'I said then that whatever you are doing is wrong, and I'm saying it again,' Farooq shouted. 'I don't agree with it.'

He experienced waves of anger. He would calm down and then he would start all over again. Calm down and start again. Then he was at it: how weak Delhi is, how big a mistake this is, what a bunch of bloody idiots, buffoons. It just went on and on and on. Part of it was theatre; when Farooq gets into it, he likes to milk the drama for all he can.

'Sir, there is no other option, this has to be done,' I told him.

He called up Jaswant Singh and gave him an earful. 'Aap jo bhi kar rahe hain, galat kar rahe hain.' He called others up in Delhi. He kept banging the phone down.

Then at the end he said: 'Those two bloody Pakistanis or whatever they are, I don't give a damn. Let them go to hell.' He was referring to Masood Azhar and Omar Sheikh. 'But I will not let this Kashmiri fellow (Zargar) go, he's a killer. He will not be released.'

'Sir,' I said. 'It will not happen without Zargar.'

'I don't care if it happens or not.'

Finally he said: 'Okay, I'm going to the governor and giving my resignation.'

I had figured something like this might happen, so I said: 'Sir, if you're going to the governor, then at least take me along.'

He was agreeable, so at 10 p.m. we went to see Governor Girish Chandra 'Gary' Saxena. Gary Saxena was also prepared since Farooq had sent an advance message that he was coming over.

'These fellows want these terrorists released and I've told the R&AW chief I won't be a party to it,' Farooq told his governor. 'I would rather resign, and that's what I have come to do.'

Gary Saxena, incidentally, was a former R&AW chief. He dealt with the situation extremely well.

'Doctor Saheb, come-come, sit down, relax,' Gary said. 'You're a fighter, you don't give in so easily.'

Out came the bottle of Black Label. As he poured the Scotch, Gary said: 'Doctor Saheb, you can't throw in the towel so easily. Sit down, relax.'

Farooq listened to the governor. He always had regard for age and things like that.

'These bloody fellows don't know what they're doing,' Farooq ranted. 'They're making a huge mistake.'

'Maybe,' Gary said, pouring another. 'But at this point of time there is no other option. This must have been thought of and discussed in Delhi, and if they've decided that there's no other option, then we have to go along with it.'

I kept my trap shut. I had already got it for three long hours.

Farooq said his bit, the drama was over, we went back home.

The next morning I judged that before I went back to Delhi, I had better make use of the three hours of shit I got from Farooq. So at breakfast I said, 'Sir, I need a few things done from the state government.' Farooq typically was all charm the next morning, and whatever I asked he said, 'Done.' Done, done, done. Just like that. Transfers and other favours for friends in Kashmir, matters that normally have to go through the grind of the state bureaucracy.

There were no calls from Delhi, as everyone assumed I would get Farooq to come around and release the two guys in J&K. Omar Sheikh was in Tihar Jail, but Masood Azhar was in Kot Bhalwal jail on the outskirts of Jammu, and Zargar was incarcerated in Srinagar. Both were brought over to the airport, all the legal formalities were sorted out with a magistrate, and they were put aboard my R&AW aircraft, a small Gulfstream jet.

Azhar and Zargar were not allowed to see me. They were

blindfolded and put on board before I got on the aircraft. There was a curtain in the cabin, and they were made to sit in the back. I sat in the front. There was no question of my having a chat with these fellows, much as I prided myself on talking to anyone and everyone in Kashmir.

As we were taking off I was told to get down to Delhi as quickly as possible because Jaswant Singh was waiting to go to Kandahar. When we landed in Delhi, they were taken to Jaswant's aircraft, where Omar Sheikh was also waiting.

Jaswant Singh was a very lonely man. When twenty-seven passengers, mostly women and children, and the dead Rupin Katyal were released in Dubai, the tourism minister, Sharad Yadav, raised his hand and said I want to be there. He quickly flew out to Dubai and took charge of the release and he waved his hand on TV. So when the time came for Kandahar, Jaswant Singh raised his hand and said: 'I'll go.'

Nobody was helping us out. Relations with Pakistan were strained post-Kargil, and we were yet to come to terms with Musharraf. The Americans were out on their Christmas week, so no CIA to plead with; my meeting with George Tenet (CIA chief) was in the future. Jaswant kept calling the Taliban foreign minister, Abdul Muttawakil, but that fellow wouldn't take his call. When he showed up in Kandahar for the exchange, he was the one on whom everybody who had felt frustrated with the whole incident in India focused their frustration.

In any case, on 31 December 1999, it was all over. What some would have said—that it was not a good year for Indian intelligence—was now finally past. After a week of drama and intense pressure, I got home in time to bring in the New Year with my wife, sipping cognac by the fireside.

As far as government policy goes, when the UPA government took power in 2004, the matter of IC-814 was raised and people felt that we ought to review our policy with regard to terrorism and hijacking; it was felt that the government's policy should be to never compromise with terrorism. Never give in.

But I remember Jaswant Singh spoke up—bravely, I thought—and said these policies are good and fine, but at the time there was no other option; and that we might again be faced with a situation where we had no option but to negotiate.

The fact of the matter is everybody compromises. Even the Israelis compromise. You can act big and say we don't compromise with terrorists. But everyone does. I had seen it first-hand on two occasions. It may have been the end of the year, but it was not the end of the world. We would move forward in the next year, and that's what we did.

4

KASHMIR'S MANDELA OR DELHI'S AGENT: SHABIR SHAH

In the year 2000 two terrorists returned to India. One of them, Hashim Qureshi, was among the first Kashmiri terrorists along with Mohammad Maqbool Butt; in 1971 Hashim had hijacked an Indian Airlines plane to Pakistan. The other, Abdul Majid Dar, headed the most lethal home-grown terrorist group, Hizbul Mujahideen, and by virtue of that was currently the leader of Pakistan-based militants. Each of their stories are apocryphal in the lessons they hold for Kashmiris as well as New Delhi: of how close to a breakthrough we've been, and how it always manages to slip away.

That both returned, one from Amsterdam and one from Pakistan, could happen only because even though I was now the R&AW chief—someone that most militants would run a mile away from—talking to Kashmiris had helped create a conducive atmosphere. During this time, several other separatists and militants began to harbour doubts about the direction in which their movement was headed, and whether the violence they had unleashed had gotten them anywhere. There are two stories in particular that illustrate what went on: that of the man known as the Nelson Mandela of Kashmir, the eldest of the modern generation of separatists, Shabir Shah; and that of his commander-in-chief, one who had kidnapped the first foreigners in Kashmir, Babar Badr—a nom de guerre for one Firdous Syed.

How I got talking to Shabir and Firdous and many others is itself a story; because it nearly never happened. In 1990, when my tenure in Srinagar as head of the IB station came to an end, I should have moved on to other matters, as was the normal course in the Intelligence Bureau. Frankly I was glad that my tenure was over because the last few months in Srinagar, when militancy overwhelmed everything, were hellish.

Srinagar in the winter of 1989-90 was an eerie ghost town witnessing the beginnings of a war dance. Rubaiya Sayeed's kidnapping opened the floodgates of insurgency. Killings were almost a daily occurrence. Bombs and firing occurred not far from the chief minister's residence in the most secure zone down our road. Gun-toting youth in trucks were seen close to the cantonment. Military parades by terrorists were held in downtown. Kashmiris believed that they were on the verge of liberation. Many even put their watches back half an hour to Pakistan time. It was prime time for Pakistani spies; not just militants but reputed businessmen, doctors, engineers and government officials were meeting their handlers in Delhi, Kathmandu, Lahore and Rawalpindi. Everyone was suspected of being a Pakistani, no one trusted anyone else.

The state government was in Jammu; there were hardly any central government employees left in town except those from the agencies. Everyone who could was running away. There was negligible presence of the army and the CRPF in the city, no security paraphernalia or bulletproof cars either. The J&K police was under heavy attack from the militants; there were reports of sympathisers within the movement. One was left to one's own devices. Everything changed overnight.

My ultimate nightmare then was what would happen if the

large crowds which had started gathering after Jagmohan arrived in Srinagar for his second tenure in January 1990 decided to march to the Raj Bhavan. There would have been no way to protect the governor or his residence; resistance would have led to large-scale bloodshed all over.

It started with the Rubaiya kidnapping, mentioned in the previous chapter, though it wasn't the first incident of terrorism; the blasts on 31 July 1988 at the Srinagar Club and outside the Central Telegraph Office marked the first incidents in this era. Yet, at the time, there was no panic. A year later people's uncertainty and caution grew but they had still not panicked.

For instance, in September 1989 the state government's advisor, O.P. Bhutani, one of my earlier mentors in Kashmir, was busy celebrating his son's marriage with lots of singing and dancing. My wife and I were at his place one night and attended the wedding at Centaur Hotel the following night. There was to be a general reception the next day at the Shalimar Bagh, the famed Mughal Garden in Srinagar. But that night—on 28 September—the separatist Shabir Shah was arrested at Ramban in Jammu. His repeated incarcerations had helped build a myth around him and his popularity grew with young Kashmiris during the turbulent 1980s. News of his arrest led to riots in various places including his native Anantnag and in Srinagar; so Bhutani had to cancel the reception. We were cautious, but that was it.

The dam burst the night the JKLF boys were freed in exchange for Rubaiya's release. As Farooq had predicted, the government's caving in emboldened many Kashmiris into thinking that azaadi was possible. 'The price we will have to pay,' were Farooq's prophetic words.

Despite Rubaiya's kidnapping, till after Christmas I was still driving around Srinagar on my own. Most of the infrastructure that the IB has today grew during the prime ministership of Rajiv Gandhi for he took a keen interest in intelligence matters and it helped that he had a cerebral DIB like Narayanan.

During my time in Srinagar the IB had a few Ambassador cars plus that swanky—actually a small, but nifty, hatchback—new car, the Maruti 800. I loved driving the Maruti and whenever I wanted to leave the driver behind I would take it out and drive my wife into the city, buzzing from one place to another. This continued till 3 January 1990, when the first of my IB colleagues was shot dead by the JKLF boys.

The militants, who had come trained and armed from camps across the Line of Control (LoC), had been advised by the ISI to try and roll the State back in Kashmir. Those targeted included Kashmiri Pandits who worked in the government, like Neel Kanth Ganjoo, the judge who had sentenced Maqbool Butt to death, and Lassa Koul, the director of Doordarshan TV's Srinagar station; they included mainstream politicians from the National Conference, which was denounced by militants as pro-India; and the uniformed services, as part of which was the gunning down of a Central Reserve Police Force (CRPF) detail, or of four air force officers. And it included four IB officers in a span of around five weeks.

As mentioned earlier, the IB was most active, most feared and most denounced in Kashmir. The ISI, itself being an intelligence agency and emboldened at having recently defeated the mighty Soviet Union in Afghanistan, knew exactly how key the IB was to the central government's hold on Kashmir; it told the militants to target the IB. Most of our officers on the ground were Kashmiri Pandits, who lived among the ordinary Kashmiri folk, and they made for easy targets.

The first IB officer shot was a Bihari, though: R.N.P. Singh. He was killed in Anantnag, in broad daylight. In those days silencer pistols were used. Someone could just walk up to you and shoot you and no one would know. You would just drop dead. As the others were killed—Kishen Gopal in Badgam on 9 January, M.L. Bhan in Nowgam on 15 January, and T.K. Razdan in Srinagar on 12 February—we knew we were being targeted. It suddenly became scary. All of us were under threat.

The IB office on Gupkar Road has completely changed now, but in those days it had a steep staircase coming down, with a landing halfway down. I used to walk down from the top of those stairs to the bottom every day, and I began to think: if there's a guy sitting across the road with a sniper rifle then I'm a dead duck. Just the walk from the house to the front without even leaving the compound was a heart-stopping experience—on a daily basis.

Although we got bulletproof vehicles, things that winter were so bad that every time you went out, you didn't know if you were going to come back or not.

One day, we were invited to lunch by Joginder 'Tiger' Singh, then the CRPF's IG (and later director of the Central Bureau of Investigation) and we drove there via the big Rajbagh bridge. We were on the bridge when a bomb went off.

A lot of woodwork flew over the car. The driver stopped the car and I shouted at him, 'What the hell, get a move on.' We reached Tiger's, and it took a while to calm down. Finally, while I had my lunch the driver went and did a recce, checked up and returned. He said that there was a house at the edge of the bridge and the bomb had gone off in that house.

Jagmohan was appointed governor on 19 January and arrived in Jammu, where there were celebrations. To impress the new governor, Joginder Singh had about 300 youngsters rounded up in downtown Srinagar. The night of 20 January was one of the most infamous nights of Kashmir. All of Srinagar came out on the roads in protest and there was a lot of wailing and shrieking that rose and fell unnervingly.

On 21 January, I was summoned by the governor to meet him at 10.30 a.m. at Raj Bhavan. I was ushered in immediately on arrival into the governor's office overlooking the Dal Lake. Jagmohan was sitting at his desk wearing a grey suit. He was livid with Joginder Singh for rounding up the boys without his 'permission'. Joginder Singh was shaken but mostly kept quiet. I can't remember if we even exchanged a word, such was the tension in the room. I was embarrassed. Jagmohan was to get considerable flak for what happened in those early days of his second term. The events of those two nights were to cast a shadow on what followed.

In the afternoon of 21 January, there was again a protest in the city and protestors, consisting mainly of youth, had to be fired upon, leading to a number of deaths at Gow Kadal in the old city. Such was the atmosphere that Jagmohan was to later claim in his memoir, *My Frozen Turbulence in Kashmir*, that he stopped Kashmir from joining Pakistan on 26 January 1990.

The night of 20 January, I was at dinner at the residence of the resident R&AW officer, Duj Nath, and he lived in Barzalla, which is quite far from Gupkar Road. During dinner the loudspeaker of the mosque outside suddenly came on and started broadcasting wailing at high volume. A large crowd collected. Duj's house was at the rear of a large compound and at the gate was a lone sentry. There were six of us there and we watched the whole tamasha from the house. I was certain that were the crowd to break the gate and storm the house, the six of us would be lynched alive.

My assistant director back at Gupkar called and asked where I was. He told me not to return that night. 'It's not safe,' he said. 'Stay where you are.' As luck would have it, one of the dinner guests was the Kashmir Valley sub area commander, Brig. Madan Mohan Lakhera, and he called for an army column. So a long two hours later we were back home.

During that killing spree of IB officials there came a day when I was sort of gheraoed by my IB colleagues in my office. The staff came out, all twenty of them, and they told me they felt very insecure in Srinagar. What had happened was all the central government employees had run away from Kashmir that winter; they had all disappeared, leaving behind nobody. The only people left were the IB. The staff said, we're the only ones left and the place is not secure. In those days, there was no army, and minimal paramilitary presence. As far as safety went, we were left to our own devices.

'Secure or not secure, I'm not going anywhere,' I said, 'and neither are you guys.'

When Razdan was killed (the last of the winter, the next IB official would be killed in July 1990) he was shot with one of those silencer-equipped guns and we got a call from the police saying they had a body at their control room and that it might be one of our people. The police asked us to come and identify the victim, and I went. Razdan was one of our tech officers, a Kashmiri Pandit from Habba Kadal. I had one of the Pandit officers with me and I said, 'You would know his house, will you go and inform his parents of what's happened?'

The officer said he would but then I thought, no, I should do it myself.

The four of us went to Habba Kadal. It was lunch time. The door opened, and inside we saw an elderly couple about to sit down for their meal. The man had a bowl of rice in his hand, and one look at us and he understood what had happened. He bitterly said a few words in Kashmiri and flung his bowl against the wall.

I spent my time those days sending these bodies down to Delhi. They were grim days.

When our new DIB, Rajendra Prasad Joshi, visited Srinagar he saw that I was looking drawn. (Joshi had taken over from Narayanan after the formation of the new National Front government of V.P. Singh.) 'Aren't you drinking too much?' he asked one night before dinner.

'Sir, there's nothing else to do here,' I replied. I had nobody for company, nobody to talk to. My wife was in Jammu because my daughter was preparing for her class 12 boards. Nobody trusted anyone, nobody relied on anyone. Srinagar was like a ghost city.

We had a young domestic helper by the name of Farooq. We had hired him in the summer of 1989. My wife found him soft-spoken and a good worker. But when things got bad one of our chaps suggested I not let Farooq into the house. 'How do you know he's not been infiltrated here,' the colleague said. 'He's new here?'

'Yeah, if he's infiltrated, he's infiltrated,' I said. 'Now it's too late. Next you'll ask me to start looking for bombs under my bed.'

We had a gardener, Sultan Wani, and he had been kept because he turned the IB compound into one of the most beautiful gardens in Srinagar. He was so old that no one knew when he retired, but he kept working there. And someone suggested to me that he was not okay. 'What do I do with him?' I said. 'I can't afford to chuck out the old man.'

It was that kind of time, a bad time, and for me it came to an abrupt end. The day Jagmohan was appointed, Farooq Abdullah carried through with the threat that he had made to the new prime minister, V.P. Singh—if the new government sent Jagmohan to J&K, he would quit. Jagmohan was the governor in 1984 who was sent to J&K to deal with militancy that had exploded in the Valley, knowing that Farooq would also resign. V.P. Singh had no choice, however, and when Jagmohan's appointment was announced Farooq quit.

I had been warned that I was also going to be removed, and the person who warned me was Vijay Dhar, a friend and a neighbour on Gupkar Road. Vijay was the son of ambassador D.P. Dhar; the father was a confidant of Indira Gandhi, the son a confidant of Rajiv Gandhi. Vijay knew I was preoccupied during the Rubaiya kidnapping; it ended on 13 December at 5:30 p.m., and the next day he came and asked to have a cup of coffee. 'I just want to warn you that people in Delhi are gunning for you,' he said. 'You should be careful. You've been branded as a Farooq man.'

'Who are these guys?' I asked.

'Arun Nehru and company,' he said. This included the home minister, Mufti Sayeed, whose daughter's release I had worked for and who never really liked me; and Jagmohan, whose previous term had overlapped with mine and who didn't like how close I was to Farooq. I took it in my stride but that's exactly what happened. In early March I was relieved; and I only got to know that I was being turfed out to Delhi the day my successor, R.C. Mehta, was coming to Srinagar.

I got a call in the morning that R.C. was arriving and I didn't immediately get it; I said if he's coming, don't worry, I'll go and receive him at the airport. They said, no, he's going to be there for a while. That's when it hit me.

Actually I was happy to get out of there. When I reached Delhi I heard that it had taken them a while to find someone willing to go to Srinagar. In fact, Jagmohan, genius that he was, sent a message on the IB channel asking for K.P. Singh, who had been posted in Srinagar before me during Jagmohan's earlier tenure, to be posted again. Thus I knew that my time would soon be up. Trouble was that K.P. turned down the offer to return to Srinagar. He had done his bit. He told Joshi, the DIB, 'Sir, I have already been there. Will you send whoever Jagmohan asks for?'

They tried a few senior officers and finally R.C. figured, 'Chalte hain.'

While I was in Srinagar, Joshi had said something that gave a way forward. Things were going badly in the Valley: Kashmiris began to sniff azaadi, for they were taken in by the ISI's bluff that if they started something big enough, the Pakistan army would come and liberate them from India, much in the way India had helped Bangladesh's liberation from Pakistan. Insurgency in Kashmir was masterminded by Gen. Zia-ul-Haq and his henchmen as revenge for Bangladesh. Kashmiris were crossing the border in droves. The IB's sources dried up because no one would talk to us; no one wanted to be seen going to Gupkar Road. We were in a mess. The Pakistanis were enjoying watching Kashmir burn.

Thus, in 1990, we needed the army to contain militancy, but if it were not for the IB and the intelligence it provided the army wouldn't have known what to do: it would have been fighting blind. In that very difficult period the army operations were guided by the IB, and frankly I did not contribute anything because I had been pulled out: the successes in fighting militancy during that time were a tribute to the work by colleagues posted in Srinagar after me. They rose to the occasion and took out some key militants. Some militants got killed, some of them disappeared, and some went back to Pakistan, and that is what encouraged separatists like Shabir or militants like Firdous to come out of the shadows.

The way forward that Joshi inspired was that despite the killings and despite the IB being targeted, what was most important was for Delhi to reach out to the Kashmiris, and for the IB to do so too. Joshi knew that the IB never had the best reputation in the Valley since the time of Sheikh Saheb.

Perhaps Joshi's insight had to do with the fact that he wasn't like the rest of us. Joshi came to the Bureau late. He wasn't like those of us who had been earmarked right at the beginning of our service; he entered the IB at the level of deputy director, which was exceptional in our organisation because the IB likes people to grow from within. As a result, he had more experience than the rest of us of being a police officer in the field; combined with the fact that he was down to earth, simple and practical, it helped; he saw straight in many matters.

Joshi became chief quite by accident; though he was second in seniority to Narayanan (they were from the same batch), everyone assumed Narayanan would be in the saddle till he retired. But when V.P. Singh became prime minister he eased out Narayanan to the Joint Intelligence Committee (JIC) and made Joshi the chief. And in the one year that Joshi was in the saddle—V.P. Singh was prime minister for just a year—he made this point: we must understand that we have to reach out and befriend the Kashmiri so that he doesn't feel Delhi is always hostile to him.

When I returned from Srinagar in March 1990 I was asked to handle this, since it was assumed that I must know some people, though the fact was I knew nobody. I was wondering where to start when I was suddenly transferred to counter-intelligence. For most intelligence officers that would have been the end of their Kashmir experience.

What happened, however, is that V.P. Singh's government fell and Chandra Shekhar became the new prime minister with the support of the Congress party. He brought Narayanan back as the DIB. And as soon as Narayanan took over he called for me and said: 'You've had enough of a holiday, now come back and do some serious work. I want you to again take over.' And so I was put in charge of the IB's Kashmir Operations Group in December 1990, after a few months of counter-intelligence, and till the time I went across to R&AW eight years later I did nothing but Kashmir.

We began talking to Kashmiris. There were three types.

One type comprised Kashmiris who were on the periphery of the movement. They thought they were in the movement, but they weren't really because they weren't into killing people. These guys were close to the JKLF but they were not ideologues— you could say they were hangers-on. Somebody who knew Yasin Malik, somebody who knew Shabir Shah, etc. They would visit Delhi and would come with stories and we would talk to them. They were basically general Kashmiris supportive of or sympathetic to the movement.

The second category was a readymade group of the people who really mattered, the people who were all in jail. By early 1990, the former Muslim United Front leaders who would later form the All Parties Hurriyat Conference, or the JKLF guys, were in different jails. We thus had the opportunity of reaching out to whoever we wanted to by visiting them in jail. Like Shabir Shah, Yasin Malik too was contacted when in jail.

The third category were the militants. Obviously, this was a slightly more difficult group, for how do you get to some boys who are in the field, or underground? Like Firdous and others, we got to them but it took time.

Eventually, there was nobody in Kashmir whom the K-Group did not reach out to. So, with that, besides the analysis and operations and other stuff that we did, we got very involved in talking to Kashmiris. And we spent a lot of time cultivating relationships like the one with Shabir Ahmed Shah, the headmaster of the boys who took up arms in the late 1980s–early 1990s.

Shabir had been in and out of jail since 1968, when he was only fourteen years old. The only Kashmiri who had spent more time in jail than Shabir was Sheikh Abdullah. The fact that Shabir was older than the new lot of militant boys and the fact that he kept going into and coming out of jail made him the object of respect and admiration of Kashmiri youngsters. Myths grew around him such as the one that he unfurled a Pakistani flag at an international cricket match between India and the West Indies in Srinagar in 1983. He wasn't even at the match.

But he didn't mind all the publicity and all the time in jail: it saved him from ever having to lay out an agenda or a roadmap to freedom. In fact, being in Jammu jail quite often during the 1980s put him in touch with Sikh boys who were jailed for Khalistan-related terrorism, most of them with the Sikh Students Federation. Hence some networking had started, which picked up pace in the early 1990s, between extremists from both Punjab and Kashmir. For Pakistan this was good news for they could try to exploit both together. However, what I understood from the Sikh boys later was that they got disillusioned with the Kashmiris pretty quickly. They said the Kashmiris were faint-hearted and talked big but would do nothing: 'In mein dum nahin hain, kucch nahin karenge,' they said.

In any case, Shabir and like-minded Kashmiri separatists formed the People's League in 1974 in protest against the negotiations that would lead to the accord between Sheikh Saheb and Indira Gandhi the following year. In late 1986, a close associate of Shabir, Mehmood Sagar, was instrumental in patronising anti-India youth in Srinagar city while Shabir was in jail, leading to the formation of the anti-India Islamic Students League (ISL). Some of its members, like its general secretary, Yasin Malik, actively worked for MUF candidates in the 1987 state assembly election, and they were thrown in jail when they protested against the blatant electoral malpractices of those polls. The ISL would later morph into the JKLF while Shabir remained in the People's League. The ISL, however, had a close bond with Shabir, who was then the emotional voice of Kashmiri youth.

Shabir caught my attention in late 1988, when an interview of him by Zafar Mehraj appeared on the front page of the *Kashmir Times*. Shabir being underground made the interview big news. By that time he was also known as an Amnesty International 'prisoner of conscience': he was quite taken by such monikers. And then almost a year later he and his lieutenant Nayeem Khan were arrested at Ramban in Jammu while the two were making an attempt to cross the Line of Control to take charge of separatist activities in Pakistan-occupied Kashmir. The ISI guys were waiting for him and had wanted him to come across for a long time; he was a most sought-after separatist.

Years later various former comrades of his would allege that Shabir himself avoided going across because he lacked the courage to do so. Perhaps it would have put him to a real leadership test; several militants later told me that once you go across, you don't know if you're going to be used or misused. Or perhaps he didn't want to get too tangled with the ISI because once you've been to that 'randikhana', it is very difficult to get back out. A Kashmiri militant once told me, guys who've come into proper contact with the ISI are never going to be in a position to work something out with Delhi.

And incidentally, Shabir is the only separatist leader who has never been to Pakistan.

When I started talking to Kashmiris then, the obvious choice to start with was Shabir. The entire JKLF leadership at that point looked up to him (the Hizbul Mujahideen hadn't become the dominant group yet), he had his own militant tanzeem, and he seemed to have a certain amount of ego that we could massage. The fact is that anybody who is somebody or who thinks he is somebody in Kashmir has a big ego. And at that point Shabir was the headmaster to the rest of the militants.

Yet even though I had no problem in walking into the jail where Shabir was being held, there was no guarantee that he would utter a word, much less begin talking to me. It would have been good to have an intermediary and I stumbled across one through a mainstream politician, Prof. Saifuddin Soz, who was then with the National Conference. Soz was a strange character: he would never look anyone in the eye when he spoke and instead directed his gaze at a point just above one's head. He was a complicated character, voting against his own party in 1999 and bringing down the one-year-old BJP government (which was re-elected anyway), for which Farooq threw him out of the party.

In the winter of 1990, however, Soz approached me and asked me for help with a friend who was in jail. 'Please help him, he's a personal friend of mine,' Soz said. 'And he could be of use to you also.'

'Whether he's of use to me or not, if he's a personal friend of yours we'll help him,' I said.

Soz's friend was a prominent businessman. At that time in Kashmir—an unusual time—there were business people, some of whom money was extorted from and some of whom were giving money to militants. Some of these business people with links across the border were pivotal in sponsoring terrorism. The same people would help us in the government of India in our fightback against militancy. In the way that there were obvious separatists or obvious militants, there were also obvious business families involved in the same racket, in some aspect or another. Since they had public dealings, being businessmen, they were more easily approachable for the IB than a militant. Some of them were in trouble and they came to us; some of them we heard about and we approached on our own; some became friends. Obviously they will need to remain anonymous.

Soz's friend was part of a flourishing business family and he was in jail because Jagmohan, despite his short tenure the second time around—he took over in January 1990 and had to resign in May due to the firing upon a procession of mourners of the assassinated Mirwaiz Moulvi Farooq—zealously went after those he thought were funding and financing militancy. If there was an allegation against a business person, Jagmohan had that person picked up. Thus, this friend of Soz's from a prominent business family was thrown into jail and was there for five or six months before Soz finally came to me.

The businessman was eventually released and I went to meet him. He was distrustful of me and had lots of reservations about talking to the IB. Yet while he spoke little, he did mention to me that there was nobody better than Shabir at that point to target or talk to. 'He could be the answer to your problems,' this businessman suggested to me. 'If Delhi is serious about a dialogue with Kashmiris, then Shabir is the right person.'

That businessman was close to Shabir and remained so as long as Shabir was the focus of things in Kashmir.

Shabir was in jail with his lieutenant Nayeem Khan, who had left the ISL to join with Shabir in the People's League. Nayeem was a good, practical influence on Shabir, who had dreams and visions. Nayeem helped our cause as a voice of reason at Shabir's side because when we started talking to Shabir, the prisoner of conscience had typical Kashmiri reservations. 'What are we going to talk about?' he said to me.

'Let's talk about talking,' I replied.

When I say typical Kashmiri refrain, what I mean is that at the back of the Kashmiri mind are all the sacrifices they have made for their movement and all the deaths that have taken place; that all of it has only grown and multiplied; and that there has to be something shown for it. 'It has to be peace with honour,' Shabir would tell me. So from talking about talks, we began speaking about the futility of the gun, and then about peace with honour. It was a slow process.

Sometimes I met him in jail, bringing along a bottle of Rooh Afza and a box of grapes, and sometimes I met him at a Jammu nursing home. We began to talk of dialogue. I began to call him the Nelson Mandela of Kashmir, and he liked to be known that way. We spoke of a settlement with India and that he could become chief minister—or even prime minister—of Kashmir in the way that Sheikh Saheb was in the period 1947–53.

Once other separatists were released in 1993—the MUF guys who formed the All Parties Hurriyat Conference—he began to feel ready for release. We really massaged his ego, encouraging him to think that he had a monopoly on Delhi and that we wanted to see him as chief minister. 'Shah Saheb,' I said. 'Now we want to see you there. I want to come and stay with you.'

Shabir would laugh about it, but he was also concerned because he was going along with the flow and once in a while he would wonder whether he had gone too far or whether he had gone too fast, and where all this would end up. 'I will be responsible,' he said repeatedly to us, and insisted that there had to be peace with honour. 'Of course,' I said. 'If there's a dialogue, there has to be something for the Kashmiris also.'

The people around him—Nayeem, Shabir's commander-in-chief Firdous (who was caught by the army during those years), and even that businessman who put me on to him—all wanted Shabir to move a little faster. Yet since he felt he was senior and superior to all the other separatists he wanted to wait till the government of India released the big-name separatists before they released him. Indeed, the last big name released before Shabir was Yasin Malik in May 1994, and in October 1994 Shabir was released.

When Shabir was out, he decided he would march to Poonch, then back to Jammu and then climb up through Bhaderwah and Kishtwar in Doda (a part of the Jammu region) on his way to Anantnag in south Kashmir. It was a good plan. By the time he reached Srinagar he was like the Pied Piper of Hamlin: everyone was following him. His each stop was thronged by excited Kashmiris. *India Today* put him on its cover on top of a bus. I was taken aback by the massive reception and asked a Kashmiri friend, 'Is this guy really that big?'

The Kashmiri turned around and said: 'Look, there is a feeling that he has done a deal with Delhi and therefore he gives us a lot of hope. That is the reason so many people are backing him or following him.'

Shabir was the right man at the right moment. Kashmiris had gone through almost five years of unrelenting violence without any of the azaadi that the ISI had promised them. They wanted relief and they wanted peace with honour. Shabir tapped the sentiment and in Baramulla he made a speech where he said that he had come with a needle and thread, looking to sew together a peace. It seemed that in 1995 he would seize the moment and give Kashmir a new direction. He had even gotten married in 1995, something that not only ended his penchant for repeatedly going to jail but also fuelled his personal ambition. He spoke to his friends about the possibility that he could win a Nobel Prize.

And then, nothing happened. Shabir began to have second thoughts and he began backtracking.

Some of it was his own fear of stepping up to the plate, and some of it was Delhi. In March 1995, for instance, Shabir came to Delhi and he met a whole bunch of politicians, including those in the ruling Congress party, those in the Left, and even Vajpayee, who was then the leader of the opposition. While he was in Delhi he told us that he needed to go to Kathmandu, and he asked me to facilitate the trip. 'I'm going to meet Mehmood Sagar,' he said, referring to his Pakistan-based senior colleague in the People's League. Sagar used to own a shop in Maharaj Bazaar, and in 1987, boys would congregate there before they crossed the LoC. Shabir apparently wanted to consult his senior colleague, who was himself now across the LoC. 'I can only meet him in Kathmandu,' Shabir said. 'So I must go to Kathmandu.'

I judged that it was no big deal. If we were to do business with him then we should let him go, even if it was obvious that Sagar would not be the only person he would meet. It would be Mehmood Sagar-plus; the ISI would want a word or two as well. 'No big deal,' I thought.

I was overruled by my panicky bosses in Delhi. 'No, no, this is very risky,' they said. In intelligence work, you have to follow the chain of command. And so Shabir, who was in Varanasi on his way to Kathmandu, was called back.

Shabir never let me forget that. 'Aap humko trust nahin karte,' he said. To put it in the words of George Tenet, we should have taken that chance to check him out.

As Shabir began to lose steam the people around him became increasingly disillusioned. As 1995 progressed, all that Nayeem and Firdous ever saw was Shabir having a ball, travelling around India and meeting politicians and activists, going to places like Calcutta and Trivandrum and being feted as The Next Big Thing From Kashmir. The prime minister, P.V. Narasimha Rao, who was thinking of a breakthrough in Kashmir (he had already had a breakthrough in Punjab with the 1992 state assembly elections), encouraged the political class to pump up Shabir. Shabir even set up shop in Delhi: he established the Kashmir Awareness Bureau in south Delhi's Malviya Nagar, and it was inaugurated by I.K. Gujral, a later prime minister. It was part of Shabir's getting known in Delhi and becoming a part of the political firmament.

And all that Nayeem and Firdous ever heard from Shabir was how he should get the Nobel Prize. This didn't help the militants who wanted to join him overground. They were in a more precarious position because the lifespan of a militant was two to two and a half years before they would get bumped off by the army or the police or somebody else. They needed a dialogue to begin, and a peace initiative to work. We even suggested to Shabir that he depute a team to continue the dialogue on his behalf but to no avail.

Narasimha Rao was so keen to rope Shabir into play—he didn't like Farooq much and wanted to see a fresh leadership in Kashmir—that I was sent by the DIB to brief him on Kashmir before he left on a foreign tour as prime minister in November 1995. It was the only time I ever met the man, who also never looked me in the eye, but asked me: 'How necessary is Farooq for the revival of the democratic process in Kashmir?'

Narasimha Rao was obviously looking towards a state assembly election in J&K the following year and it was clear that he was placing great hope in Shabir. He had even asked me to introduce Shabir to his finance minister, Manmohan Singh, another future prime minister. And to cap it, on that trip to Africa, when the prime minister was in Burkina Faso, he announced that the government was willing to discuss any kind of political arrangement with Kashmir; any quantum of azaadi. 'The sky is the limit,' were his famous words. He was signalling to Shabir that he was ready to give Kashmiris peace with honour.

Shabir, however, did not see it that way because he did not check Narasimha Rao out. For some reason he thought Narasimha Rao's offer of the sky was for Farooq and the National Conference to draw them in and thereby legitimise elections. That was the unintended consequence of all this: Farooq and his party worried that they could get left behind in New Delhi's attempt to woo the separatists and so they jumped into the fray in the 1996 state elections. And since Shabir dithered, the National Conference won big and formed the government.

The dithering in 1995–96 did not go unnoticed by Shabir's lieutenants, who ultimately got disillusioned with him—Firdous before the elections, Nayeem after the elections. Firdous and several other militants we were speaking to in fact decided to no longer wait for Shabir to make up his mind and in early 1996 they came overground, laid down arms, and began peace talks with the government of India. This was also a setback to Shabir because he believed he had a monopoly with New Delhi. When Firdous and other militants began a dialogue then Shabir began to think that Delhi was double-dealing with him.

As mentioned earlier, perhaps Shabir felt things were going too fast and he didn't feel he knew where it would all end. It was basically a matter of he not having faith in himself.

The irony is, because of the way we pursued him and the offer that the prime minister made, things opened up in Kashmir. More and more Kashmiris began to come forward and the National Conference won power; so that by the time of the next election in 2002, Shabir had missed the bus. There were more players and he was no longer a big deal. Had Shabir jumped into the fray in 1996 he could have had it all and a chance to forge his people's destiny.

I had a long chat with Shabir during the 2002 elections, when I tried to persuade him to contest, but he said, 'What can I do single-handedly? I can at most win one seat. If I had more people I could win probably three seats. And anyway it's decided that Farooq Abdullah or his son Omar will become the chief minister.' I told him he was wrong, but he did not listen.

After the 2002 elections, Mufti Sayeed became the chief minister without having won the largest number of seats, and I told Shabir he had been wrong. I told Nayeem and him that they could have been ministers if they had become MLAs. Naeem agreed and said, 'Yes, we made a mistake.' But Shabir was bitter. 'Big deal,' he said. 'Mufti is the other side of the same coin as Farooq.'

Things were never the same for Shabir after that: his career drifted aimlessly and now he's in his sixties he has a Hurriyat Conference of his own after once joining it and splitting it. He has of late tilted more towards Pakistan, which funds him, and gets money and hangs around in Srinagar. He is cynical, like most Kashmiris, and will tell anyone who listens about how insincere Delhi is.

It reminded me of what Firdous once said to me in 1995, when his frustration was reaching a zenith. He asked me whether the IB had psychiatrists.

'No,' I said. 'Why do you ask?'

'How do you analyse personalities?' Firdous persisted.

'By talking to them,' I said.

'No,' he said. 'Shabir is not so easy to analyse.'

Shabir was a hell of a letdown. They all thought that, even Yasin. It was a disappointment for me, having spent so many years talking to him, trying to get the ISI out of his head, trying to get him to get up and stand up for his people. But in retrospect it wasn't such a big disappointment because one, the thread of dialogue with Shabir can be picked up again, at any time. And two, the experience was a step in the successes we had in bringing militants in from the cold, be they Shabir's commander-in-chief Firdous, Hashim Qureshi, or Abdul Majid Dar.

5

PROXY WARRIOR

If terrorism suspects voluntarily returned from abroad during my time as the R&AW chief, the main reason for doing so was their disappointment with Pakistan. Perhaps they had matured, grown older and wiser, and had developed familial responsibilities; perhaps it was exhaustion and a desire to come home and breathe easily; but what was undeniable in all cases was a sense of betrayal and the shattering of their dream that Pakistan would help liberate Kashmir from India.

I had seen this repeatedly after 1994 and up close in great detail with Shabir's commander-in-chief, Babar Badr, whose real name was Firdous Syed. He and his group, the Muslim Jaanbaz Force (named after the people's militia that Pakistani military dictator Zia-ul-Haq had propounded), had in April 1991 kidnapped Swedish engineers Johan Jansson and Jan Ole Loman, working on the Uri hydel project just 18 km from the LoC in north-western Kashmir. It was the first time foreigners were kidnapped in Kashmir. Even the United Nations secretary general, Javier Perez de Cuellar, appealed for the Swedes' release. The Swedish government paid off the MJF in Pakistan and in three months the engineers were allowed to walk to freedom. Not long after they were kidnapped, though, the army caught Firdous and a couple of his boys, and after the usual detention and interrogation, we at the IB got word from the army that here was a militant who was unlike the others: he was reasonable, he was good, he spoke sense, he talked peace.

Firdous was not at all the run-of-the-mill militant. He was a middle-class boy from an 'NC family', one that traditionally supported the National Conference. He was from Bhaderwah in Doda district, which lay on the Jammu bank of the Jhelum river—the metaphoric cusp of both the Kashmir and Jammu regions—so Doda's Muslims comprised Kashmiris and non-Kashmiris who strongly identified with Kashmiri culture. Firdous's father was in the timber trade, and since politics in J&K was based on patronage—timber contracts were doled out by the government in exchange for political support—theirs was a hardcore NC family. One of Firdous's childhood memories, in fact, was at the Jammu railway station with his folks to receive Sheikh Abdullah following the Sher-e-Kashmir's release, after two decades of imprisonment, and return to J&K in 1975.

Firdous was a teenager during Sheikh Saheb's twilight and the abbreviated first tenure of Farooq Abdullah. That was a time when there was much turmoil in the Muslim world, first with the Islamic revolution in Iran in 1979, and then with the Soviet Union's invasion of Afghanistan leading to a resistance manned by Islamists, funded by Saudi petro-dollars, and armed by the CIA. It still surprises me that a cultured and sensitive fellow like Firdous could have gotten involved in aggression and militancy but that was the trend in the 1980s, particularly after the 1987 assembly election that the Muslim United Front (MUF) felt was stolen from them. Though he was close to Shabir Shah—the headmaster of those boys that comprised the first wave of militancy—he did not join the Islamic Students League (ISL), which later became the Jammu and Kashmir Liberation Front (JKLF), and instead formed his own group, the MJF.

In 1988, soon after the assembly election, groups of boys crossed LoC for arms training by the ISI. Firdous was among those youngsters and he went across with Shabir's other lieutenant, Nayeem. After their return, the MJF was involved in several incidents of terrorism, and then came the 1991 kidnapping of the Swedes and Firdous's subsequent capture. After a month of futile interrogation by paramilitary forces like the CRPF and the Border Security Force (BSF) he was handed over to the army for solitary confinement.

This was a key period, for Firdous as well as for us, because during the eleven months that he was with the army's 10 Garhwal Rifles a lot changed for him. For one thing, he had time to introspect about the movement, the violence, and whether or not it was worth it. A free run of the regiment's well-stocked library contributed to this process, and though Firdous's involvement in rebel activity and militancy meant that his formal education had been curtailed, he read voraciously during that time, going through about fifty books ranging from Gen. Douglas MacArthur's memoirs to Faiz Ahmed Faiz's poetry. It probably helped that he was in solitary and not among other prisoners, who were more likely to be spending time in planning jailbreaks (as he would later in Jammu jail).

The man who allowed him a free run of the library was the commanding officer, Brig. Naseeb Singh Katoch. This professional soldier talked to Firdous; and that was the second thing about the change Firdous underwent. The two of them debated Kashmir, the movement—a separatist militant and a man totally committed to India. The man in uniform impressed Firdous with his knowledge, his patience. Brigadier Katoch generally dispelled a stereotype that Firdous and other militants (not to speak of their ISI handlers) had of Indian soldiers in particular and Indians in general. Firdous found that Indians were reasonable.

The army also realised that Firdous was nothing like the crude, uncouth, illiterate and sometimes barbaric militants they ordinarily came across. The unit sent word to us at the IB that here was a reasonable fellow whom we might want to talk to at length.

In the IB, the whole idea of talking directly to boys who had taken up the gun was two-fold: one was that we needed to detach any militant—and in this case, Firdous was an important militant—from militancy and violence and bring him overground. This would be to our tactical advantage. The second was that we could try and get him involved in talks, because that would be the best way to end militancy. The army and the paramilitary could eventually manage the violence, but we wanted to end it completely, and that would only come through the movement changing tack from violence to politics—and talking was the way to get that strategic advantage.

In Firdous's case he was close to Shabir as well, and we were trying to break the ice with Shabir. By then Nayeem had also been arrested and he had started talking to us, and so if we had both of Shabir's lieutenants talking to us then Shabir would have no choice but to move forward; otherwise he might get left behind by his own lieutenants.

So my people went and met Firdous and talked to him, in the hope that he might be of some value. I also met him once in 1993, by which time he had been shifted to Jammu jail. But I did not meet him in jail. He came to Delhi, dressed as a Sikh in a turban, and was brought here on a special aircraft to secretly meet Rajesh Pilot, the minister for internal security. Pilot was meeting several such militants. I also got to meet Firdous at this point, and I wondered what the hell is this and who is this Kashmiri pretending to be a sardar.

When Shabir got to know that the government was talking to Firdous, he threw a fit. Not because a Kashmiri militant might be compromising with the government, but because Shabir believed that as the leader he should be the only one talking to anyone in the government. Shabir believed that any political negotiation should be done by him and him alone, for he not only saw himself as the next Sheikh Abdullah, he went beyond that: he was not unhappy being known as the Nelson Mandela of Kashmir.

Shabir had a brainwave. Firdous had spent two and a half years in jail and his detention under the Public Safety Act would soon come to an end. Usually when a militant's detention ended, we had them re-arrested just outside the gate of the prison and sent them back in. Shabir suggested we let Firdous go free instead of re-arresting him. He would send his commander-in-chief on a special assignment, and since Shabir was then very important to the government's plans, particularly those of Prime Minister P.V. Narasimha Rao, we agreed.

The special assignment that he sent Firdous on was across the LoC. With both Shabir and Firdous in jail, their militant groups were running into funding problems with the ISI. Though two very senior colleagues of Shabir's were across the LoC—Mehmood Sagar and Irshad Malik—Shabir asked Firdous to go across and spend some time there sorting out things. He need not hurry back.

Shabir had sent Firdous to get him out of his hair. Unexpectedly, Firdous came to a crossroads in his life. In January 1994, Firdous crossed the LoC and after some time at the training camps near and around Muzaffarabad, he decided to tour Pakistan and see the country and its people. It was an eye-opening experience for him.

One of the people he hung around with was Irshad Malik, who at one point became the secretary general of the United Jehad Council that was established in Muzaffarabad in Pakistan-occupied Kashmir; it was a coordinating body for all the militant groups that were operating out of PoK and other places. Once Irshad helped Firdous with sorting out their various financial difficulties, Firdous in March 1994 embarked on his tour of Pakistan. This included visiting relatives and other Kashmiri migrants, such as the entrepreneur in Sialkot who made footballs for the international sporting goods company Adidas. This friend was obviously a big shot. Yet when Firdous visited him, the friend gave him advice: 'Yahan aaye ho, yahan baithna nahin.'

Firdous was puzzled and angry; he assumed the friend had taken Firdous to be a freeloader, and was thus advising him not to stay long in Pakistan. Firdous did not realise then that the friend was only giving words to his own disillusionment with Pakistan.

Firdous went to Karachi and met Mehmood Sagar's uncle, a retired admiral of the Pakistan navy. The uncle told Sagar that whatever he did, he should one day return to their homeland, Kashmir. Then he turned to Firdous and said: 'Promise me that your goal will always be independence and never accession to Pakistan.' Firdous was stunned to hear a former member of the Pakistan armed forces telling a Kashmiri freedom fighter not to join or settle in Pakistan.

Firdous visited a cousin in Muzaffarabad who was director of education in PoK. She told him not to settle in Pakistan; since he was likely to be killed if he returned to Kashmir, she suggested that like many other Kashmiris he migrate to London and settle down there. 'You're still young,' she said.

It was the same refrain everywhere that he went. Each and every Kashmiri that he met in Pakistan felt they were in an alien land.

The real shock came when Firdous visited Lahore and made the acquaintance of Majid Nizami, the chief editor of the *Nawa-e-Waqt*. Nizami also ran a relief fund for Kashmiri militants and was thus considered a big shot in separatist circles. Yet all Nizami would talk about was the two-nation theory and how Kashmir could only become a part of Pakistan. At a seminar at the Avari luxury hotel in Lahore on its foundation day, Firdous listened with disbelief as Nizami said that the third option for Kashmir, that of independence, was un-Islamic and unpatriotic, and a disgrace to Mohammed Ali Jinnah, the founder of Pakistan.

Nizami's argument was this: an independent Kashmir would reduce Pakistan's strategic depth, as the international border would only be 10 km from the arterial Grand Trunk Road that connected Lahore to Rawalpindi; and an independent Kashmir would deprive Pakistan of water, since all of the water that irrigated the breadbasket in Punjab came from the Mangla dam in Mirpur. For Nizami, this was what all the Kashmiri sacrifice—the lives and livelihood lost—was for: a secure Pakistani border, and water.

Firdous then realised that Pakistan's priorities and Kashmir's priorities were two separate things. And in the bargain, Kashmiris were losing out, quite disastrously.

Firdous's final straw was his meeting with the ISI before he was due to return to India. The man running the Kashmir operations was the ISI's deputy director-general, Lt. Gen. Syed Iftikhar Hussain Shah. Under General Iftikhar were two officers, Brigadier Faisal, who looked after the political cell, and Brigadier Fahd, who looked after the military cell. Firdous was given intensive training in bomb making, and once he became an explosives expert, Faisal and Fahd briefed him.

Brigadier Faisal told him that Pakistan wanted violence to be taken to the next level in Kashmir with the use of explosives. Firdous was to take the fight to Jammu and beyond, to the very heart of India. Faisal wanted the militants to give India 'a thousand cuts' and thus bleed her to death. Brigadier Fahd said the main aim was to prevent normalcy from returning: 'Most of all, you are to make sure that assembly elections do not take place.'

Firdous was surprised at how Pakistan, which in 1990 promised militants like himself that it would invade India and take revenge for Bangladesh once militancy got fully under way, was in 1994 asking the same militants to prevent elections. What a climbdown.

To make sure, Firdous sought and got a meeting with General Iftikhar, where he asked the ISI's number two man for surface-to-air missiles (SAM). The ISI had provided the Afghan Mujahideen with SAMs, and these had turned the tide of the resistance against the Soviet Union. Bringing down a helicopter or two would cause real panic in India.

General Iftikhar turned him down. 'Why do you want to waste your money?' the general asked. 'We have SAMs, we will decide when Kashmir needs SAMs.'

As Firdous tried to argue the point, he realised that the ISI did not want to provoke India beyond a point; it did not want the proxy war to escalate into an open one, which the use of SAMs was sure to do. The ISI was not interested in raising the violence above India's limit of tolerance. The ISI was not interested in the fact that the Kashmiris had gone all out to fight their dirty war for them.

Firdous gave brigadiers Faisal and Fahd a piece of his mind, ranting against the two-nation theory, saying that Kashmiris were being used, and that Pakistan ran the risk of disillusioning the Kashmiri militants. But the brigadiers were not interested in any debate; they were only interested in Firdous going back and using bombs against India. They told him as much.

What a contrast to Brigadier Katoch, Firdous realised. The Indian solider engaged him in intense debate, listened to him, and answered his points with his own. The Pakistani soldiers, on the other hand, looked bored; talking to them was like banging one's head on a brick wall.

On top of this, the rumour among the Kashmiris who were in training was that whenever they got their pay from the ISI, there was always ten per cent missing.

This bitter experience made Firdous's break with Pakistan final and complete. He left.

When he returned to the Valley, Shabir Shah had been released a month earlier and was travelling around Kashmir speaking of mending things with a needle and thread, and drawing large crowds. At first Firdous was excited because he now knew that with Pakistan not committed to the Kashmir movement, the violence was of no use. And if the violence was of no use, then it had to be replaced by a dialogue. Firdous saw the crowds as an endorsement by ordinary Kashmiris of a new path that the movement should take. Yasin Malik, who was released a few months earlier, in May 1994, had already announced that he would continue the movement through non-violence, which was another indication that disillusionment had set in all round, and the very people who had started the militancy were now looking to end it.

Shabir, however, was carried away by his own importance, and instead of charting out a plan for initiating a dialogue and bringing peace to the Valley, all Shabir was doing was talking about whether or not he stood a chance to win the Nobel Peace Prize. He was not taking the movement's next step seriously; he was just marking time. He did not look to be going anywhere. This Firdous found to be equally disillusioning.

Firdous began to get impatient because he was still underground, still a militant, and either he would get arrested or he would get bumped off. Or he would have to go back to Pakistan. Firdous was thus worried about his own safety. On top of that he saw Shabir wandering about India, parading around Kashmir, having a good time. Firdous became restless.

After Firdous returned, our guys in the IB found out and instead of arresting him or anything like that, I sought a meeting with him. We had lots of sessions together, and over time Firdous and I became good friends. We talked a lot, and remember that was my role on behalf of the government: to talk. We talked a lot about Shabir. Once, on a visit to Delhi, when he was staying at a hotel I went and met him and he asked me the question about whether we had psychiatrists in our department.

'How else do you assess a personality like Shabir Shah?' Firdous said. 'Because this fellow needs a psychiatrist.'

I laughed then and said that we did assess people but we did not use psychiatrists. His question, though, gave me the first doubt that these fellows were drifting apart.

The next time we met was in Jammu, and he said that he had had enough of Shabir.

'Yeh kya ho raha hain iske saath?' I asked Firdous.

'He will not do anything, I'm convinced,' Firdous said about Shabir. 'I've told him, aap ko jo marzi kariye, hum jo marzi karenge.'

Both Firdous and Nayeem had had a lot of respect for Shabir and somewhere along the way, they lost it. This is also true of Kashmiris in general; after that tumultuous reception he got all over the Valley, the people lost respect for Shabir. Firdous and Nayeem thought that Shabir was cooking a deal with the government of India, and that's what Kashmiris in general, tired of militancy and its violence, had also hoped. When Firdous and Nayeem realised it wasn't going to happen, they were disillusioned with their former leader. Nayeem parted company with Shabir over a dispute about money but is back with him again.

Firdous walked out on Shabir first. The occasion was a meeting of the All Party Hurriyat Conference, a conglomerate of thirty-odd separatist groups headed by the former leaders of the MUF that was tightly controlled by Pakistan. The Hurriyat wanted Shabir to join, but Shabir gave some conditions: that the Hurriyat merge into a single unit, that it elect a single leader, that it give representation to Jammu and Ladakh, among others. The Hurriyat did not want to do so. So Shabir held off joining until May 1995, when a crisis developed at the Chrar-e-Sharief shrine, taken over by a Pakistani militant named Mast Gul. Shabir, without warning his lieutenants, went to the Hurriyat meeting and signed up. In July 1995, Firdous walked out.

Firdous's misfortune was that Shabir flopped. Had Shabir taken charge and forged ahead, he would have been bigger than the Hurriyat. All the militants looked up to him in the beginning, and when the peace process began, he was the most sought after by Delhi. The US ambassador, Frank Wisner, first visited

Srinagar in 1996, and he had a special lunch meeting with Shabir in a houseboat. Obviously, Wisner thought Shabir was important enough to talk to one-on-one, and wanted to check Shabir out on whether he was serious about moving forward. The irony is that the Hurriyat, which had hurriedly taken Shabir Shah in just a year earlier, now sacked him after he met Wisner, on the charge of indiscipline.

After Firdous walked out on Shabir, he got in touch with a handful of friends of his in militancy, and they were like-minded in that they agreed to come out and talk peace with the government of India. They included Bilal Lodhi, the chief of al-Barq, which was Abdul Ghani Lone's militant group; Imran Rahi, a divisional commander of the Hizbul Mujahideen; and Ghulam Moinuddin, a divisional commander of the Muslim Mujahideen. In February 1996, the four held a press conference at Ahdoos Hotel in Srinagar, denouncing the Hurriyat and stating that they were ready for a peace initiative with New Delhi.

It had an explosive effect. The Union home minister, S.B. Chavan, welcomed the initiative and invited them to Delhi. The four now-former militants went to a former NC minister named Ghulam Hassan Mir, who defected from Farooq Abdullah's first government in 1984. Mir had been an important player in Kashmir, and he saw the chance to be a peacemaker; so he got involved in Firdous's peace initiative by bringing the four to Delhi. This was how he got to be called 'Manager'.

It was a major breakthrough that paved the way for the democratic process and took the wind out of militancy that year. On its own, however, it did not take off, probably because the limitation that the four ex-militants had was that there was no political leader among them; none of them was big enough to drive their initiative forward. From Delhi's point of view, it was a godsend in that they got some top militants out of the game. No one was more kicked than the DIB, D.C. Pathak, who felt that Shabir's C-in-C had more than made up for his indecisiveness. But soon after, the government changed, the home minister changed, and the biggest change of all that happened, the biggest setback to militancy, was the holding of assembly elections in J&K in 1996.

Those elections brought Farooq Abdullah back into power, and once he was in the saddle, Firdous and his friends would only have a secondary role. In fact, I took the four of them to meet Farooq and I said that now that the National Conference had come to power, the two sides had to make a deal. Farooq was willing to accommodate them. But they were not willing to join the mainstream political party. Perhaps it was too soon for them.

Firdous did get accommodated the following year, in February 1997. I was always fond of Firdous as he struck me as more sincere than the other militants, and the years after Farooq became chief minister again (before I went to R&AW) were years when I could have gotten any favour out of Farooq. So I said to the chief minister: 'This boy is an extremely good fellow, why don't you accommodate him somewhere?'

Farooq's reaction was immediate and positive. He told me to bring Firdous over to his place, and the next morning we met the chief minister on his verandah, where Firdous explained how he was from a traditional NC family. But at that time, Farooq didn't even need an explanation.

'Sure,' Farooq said. 'I'll give him an MLC's ticket.'

And just like that, Firdous was on his way to becoming a member of the legislative council.

'You can come and meet me any time you like,' Farooq told Firdous. 'Don't hesitate.'

When it started, it was a great honeymoon, for Firdous was also taken up by Farooq; this was only natural because Farooq's personality is also fairly larger than life. And to begin with, Firdous was allowed direct access to the chief minister a couple of times. But then Farooq must have thought, why does this guy need to see me? So he put him in touch with party general secretary Sheikh Nazir Ahmed. That's when Firdous's NC experience began to sour.

Though Sheikh Nazir is Farooq Abdullah's brother, the two are totally different. You could say Sheikh Nazir was the old school of the old school, the old guard of the old guard in the NC—the kind that never forgave Delhi for anything, least of all the way Sheikh Abdullah was arrested in 1953 and thrown into jail for a series of incarcerations that lasted nearly twenty-two years. This man reacted quite differently to Firdous; he never allowed Firdous to feel comfortable.

'Mere ko bulate hain, phir kucch nahin kehte hain,' Firdous would complain to me. 'Main bolta hoon kya karoon, woh bolte hain kucch nahin.'

Sheikh Nazir just would not trust Firdous, and simply because Firdous had come to the NC through me, a senior IB official. In Sheikh Nazir's eyes, once an IB agent, always an IB agent; why should he be in our party? Which was quite unfair to Firdous since he was always his own man, even after we became friends. But he was never let into the inner workings of the party.

Firdous went back to Farooq but I don't think he got much joy out of that. And four years later, when the end of his term was in sight, Firdous was himself 50-50 about continuing; he knew that he might not get another term but he was keen on it. He came to me to ask me to speak with Farooq. 'Meri toh koi sunwai nahin hai NC mein, aap Doctor Saheb se baat karenge?'

'Kyon nahin karenge?' I said. 'I have no reservations.'

It was the winter of 2001 and I was by that time in the Prime Minister's Office. I went to Jammu to deliver a lecture, and met Farooq. He bluntly turned down my request with a straight no.

'Sorry, but he'll have to wait,' Farooq said. 'He's done a term, we'll accommodate him somewhere else, but I have to see about other people.'

'He's a good chap, sir,' I said.

'Yeah-yeah,' Farooq said. 'Isko kahin aur accommodate kar lenge.'

Firdous left the NC. He was extremely demoralised. You might say he lost heart quickly, but then he was a militant who had been across the LoC twice and had taken up arms against India. He was no longer with the anti-India folks and now a pro-India party had left him feeling rejected.

When the 2002 assembly elections came, I told him that if he was interested in politics, he ought to contest the elections.

'As what?' he said. 'As who?'

'As Firdous Syed,' I said. 'Go home, back to Bhaderwah.'

'Wahan nahin hoga, I'm mostly in Srinagar,' Firdous said. 'If the Hurriyat backed me, I would contest from downtown Srinagar.'

'So go meet the Mirwaiz,' I said.

He met Mirwaiz Umar Farooq, the chairman of the Hurriyat Conference, but the Mirwaiz did not show much interest. Firdous threw his hands up. 'Mere se nahin hoga,' he said. 'I can't win an election, I'm not fit for politics.'

He didn't have the gumption to face the voters.

His political career fizzled out, and he has been a bit of a recluse ever since. He started a think tank and did some writing in newspapers, but even his think tank wound up when the UPA government took charge in 2004 and stopped giving it grants. It came to the extent that in 2014 he didn't even have a passport; simply because the government did not trust him and did not want to give him such a document. Firdous is a man who wanted peace, but it seemed as if no one wanted him.

Firdous's story is typical of most Kashmiris who became disillusioned with Pakistan, even old hijackers like Hashim Qureshi. Yet it was not easy getting such men back to India. It was finally managed on my watch as R&AW chief, in 2000, making for some interesting stories.

6

TINKER, TAILOR, HIJACKER, SPY

I first met Hashim Qureshi in Paris, in the early summer of 2000. He had driven down from his home in Amsterdam, Holland, in his red Passat, and when we came face to face he extended his hand and said: 'I'm Hashim Qureshi.'

'Mujhe Dulat kehte hain.'

Hashim smiled. 'Aap apna sahi naam batayenge?' he asked. 'I have met many people, nobody tells me his real name.'

'What can I say, this is my name.'

'You're the only one who's ever given me his real name,' Hashim said. And so began our relationship.

Hashim had obviously met a lot of spooks: from Pakistan, from India, and as he told me, from the Netherlands and the United States. Hence, from the very beginning, he was always suspect. It was always difficult to figure out who he was working for. Perhaps it depended on that very moment.

I had first heard of Hashim in September 1989, when an article of his was published in a Kashmiri newspaper and in a national newspaper. Of course, I had heard of the hijacking he had done in 1971; at that time, two years into my career at the IB, I was posted at the headquarters doing counter-intelligence and the hijacking was no small matter. It grew curiouser when the hijacker claimed that he worked for the BSF, and even curiouser when the Pakistanis claimed that the hijacking had been stage-managed so that Indian airspace could be closed to Pakistani aircraft during Bangladesh's liberation war that would come later that year. These were all stories that made the affair head-scratchingly mysterious.

But when I read his article in 1989, I frankly did not connect it with the man who had committed the hijacking eighteen years earlier. The article itself was anti-militancy and anti-Pakistan, and I said to myself, here's a brave Kashmiri to be writing against militancy: for by this time in 1989, targeted killings had begun and fifteen people had been assassinated; the JKLF had called for a quit Kashmir movement in the beginning of the summer; and when Shabir Shah was arrested that same September there were riots resulting in three days of civil curfew and four persons dead. The storm had been brewing (and it broke only three months later, in December, following the Rubaiya Sayeed kidnapping episode), and all Kashmiris looked sullen. On the other hand, here was a guy who sounded like Farooq, the chief minister, in his anti-militancy article. No Kashmiri could have thought well of Hashim after what he had written. I then heard that he was living in Holland and so I shrugged, thinking Kashmiris living in Holland have the liberty to say whatever they like. I put him out of my mind.

Four eventful years later, in September 1993, I was in London to attend an intelligence-liaison conference that the British hosted. I had three nights, so I thought I should call up Farooq who was in England those days; ever since he quit in January 1990 and till he was re-elected in October 1996, Jammu and Kashmir was under governor's rule. Mainstream politicians had gone underground while the government was grappling with the security situation and while we were laying the ground for getting the political process up and running again. Farooq was mostly in England, in and out of Delhi and Srinagar, because he was number one on the terrorists' hit list: we had heard that the ISI's largest bounty was offered for Farooq's head.

One day I found myself free and so I called Farooq and said, 'Sir, I'm in London.'

Dr Abdullah was not living in London but in Southend by Sea, Essex, an hour and a half's drive east from London. 'Will you be coming into London?' I asked.

'I'll come to London whenever you want,' Farooq said. 'But first you must visit us at home.'

Farooq and his wife lived in a modest corner house near the beach, but that is the kind of man he is, adjusting from the good life in India quite easily. Also, there seemed to be no security, considering how we Indians are obsessed with it. 'Do you have no security at all?' I asked.

'Sure,' he said. 'The police know I'm living here. They've given me a number that I can call in any emergency, they'll come immediately. They have their own way of doing this thing, so I'm not worried.'

Farooq and his wife Mollie and I went to a club for lunch. When we returned home I sat in the drawing room while he went into an adjoining room and came back with a whole stack of literature. He handed me something by Hashim Qureshi. 'This may interest you,' he said.

'Okay,' I said, thumbing through Hashim's writings.

'He may be useful to you,' Farooq continued. 'Why don't I get him to speak to you?'

Then Farooq called up Hashim and we exchanged greetings. It was as simple as that.

Hashim later told me that he had first met Farooq just a few months before we spoke on that first phone call from Essex to Amsterdam, during the summer of 1993. In his telling, Farooq called him on the phone.

It wasn't that extraordinary a thing because Kashmir is in many ways a small place, and a part of Hashim's extended family were traditional National Conference supporters. 'Like most Kashmiris, I worshipped Sheikh Saheb,' Hashim told me about the Sher-e-Kashmir, Sheikh Abdullah. Hashim said that Sheikh Saheb used to visit Hashim's parents' place in Nowhatta, and later, whenever Farooq travelled to Bandipora, he would stop by and pay his respects to Hashim's mother. There were photos of Farooq with Hashim's father and at Hashim's brother's wedding.

According to Hashim, when he hijacked a plane in 1971, the forces came and took his father, Mohammed Khaleel Qureshi, away. Hashim's maternal uncle, Mohammed Sikander, was close to Sheikh Saheb, who was still under arrest at the time, so Hashim's mother went to Begum Sahiba and successfully pleaded for her husband's release. Sheikh Saheb later scolded Hashim's brother: 'Did your father have to produce this kind of son?'

Farooq and Hashim met in 1993 in Hyde Park, of all places. 'Let's eat,' Farooq told him. 'There's a Bengali restaurant with superb food.'

They met several times after that around Europe: in Switzerland, in Belgium, at conferences. And Hashim claimed that Farooq had told him: 'Because you ask for azaadi, we Kashmiris get some respect.'

A few months into my tenure as R&AW chief, Hashim made contact, and I responded. He was a Dutch national, wanted for the almost-three-decade-old hijacking, so we had to meet in Europe. But he didn't want to meet in Holland. Perhaps it had to do with the fact that he earned an occasional salary being a consultant to their intelligence service. So we decided on a third country whose capital I was passing through on other official work.

When we met, he said he wanted to come back.

'When did you first contact the government about coming back?' I asked.

It turned out that Hashim had written to the then prime minister, Rajiv Gandhi, possibly in 1985. In the letter, he claimed, he had warned the PM of what was likely to happen in due course, that is, the militancy in Kashmir. Rajiv Gandhi passed on the letter to R&AW, but there was too much suspicion of the hijacker who had spent nine years in Pakistani jails. Do we trust him, went the internal debate, which continued for several years.

In due course, R&AW made contact with Hashim in Amsterdam. Interestingly, when I met Hashim, our man in Holland was Rabindra Singh, the same R&AW officer who defected to the USA in 2004 after it was discovered that he was a CIA mole in India's spy agency. Hashim, however, claimed that Singh was a dud: he was a womaniser, used to drink heavily, and talked loosely. Perhaps what he said of Singh was true, but it didn't mitigate the fact that Singh betrayed India. By the time Singh returned to headquarters, I had left R&AW.

Hashim talked to me at that meeting of coming back, and I asked: 'What will you do?'

'Now that the political process has begun, I will also find a role in it,' Hashim said.

'Where will you fit in?' I persisted.

He had heard that we in the government had been talking to Shabir Shah. He claimed Shabir was his friend. 'Shabir mera dost hai, uske saath hum tie-up kar sakte hain,' he said, optimistically.

I was trying to discourage him because I felt that whatever little he might be in Holland, back in Kashmir he wouldn't fit in. Also, it was my responsibility as a human being to warn him that he might return to a bad mess. Hashim, however, was keen to return home and do something for his people, as he told me. And he sounded more Punjabi than Kashmiri: he was proud, talked openly and with a lot of confidence. That was the sort of thing that got Kashmiris bumped off by the ISI. In Delhi, even the IB was impressed with Hashim. My friend Ajit Doval spoke to him at length and told me, 'Yeh to kaam ka banda hai.'

'Yeh Shabir tumhara dost hoga,' I said sceptically, but Hashim did not let me complete.

'I will set him right if he misbehaves,' Hashim said.

I laughed and so Hashim immediately called up Shabir and put it on the speaker. 'I'm thinking of coming back to Kashmir,' he said.

'Welcome, welcome,' Shabir said.

I shook my head in resignation. You don't have to be R&AW chief to recognise the smelly stuff being nonchalantly thrown around.

Hashim told me that the 1971 hijacking of the Indian Airlines plane 'Ganga' was Maqbool Butt's idea.

Kashmiris regard Maqbool Butt as one of the first martyrs of their movement. According to Hashim, Maqbool was the chairman of the armed wing of the Plebiscite Front—the front started by Sheikh Saheb's right-hand man Mirza Mohammed Aslam Beg in 1955, two years after Sheikh Saheb was arrested, that called for a popular plebiscite to determine the finality of Kashmir's accession to India, as promised by the first governor-general, Lord Mountbatten. It was known as the Jammu & Kashmir National Liberation Front (JKNLF).

Maqbool was hanged in Delhi's Tihar jail on 11 February 1984. He had been sentenced to death for the 1966 murder of a policeman as well as the murder of the manager of a Kupwara bank; he escaped from Srinagar jail in 1968 by digging a tunnel out and then went to Pakistan. He returned to India in 1976 and was arrested; his hanging eight years later was ostensibly as payback for the kidnapping and murder of Indian diplomat Ravindra Mhatre in Birmingham, England, on 3 February 1984. The anniversary of Maqbool Butt's execution is observed annually in Kashmir as a day of anti-India shutdown and protests, but in recent years this anniversary has been losing steam. Instead, it now seems likely that the anniversary of the 9 February 2013 hanging of Mohammed Afzal Guru, for his complicity in the December 2001 attack on Parliament—a charge that many Kashmiris found dubious and vindictive—will be observed as the major anti-India day instead.

Hashim said he met Maqbool Butt for the first time as a fifteen- or sixteen-year-old, when he went to Pakistan with his family in early 1969. Khaleel Qureshi, Hashim's father, was a member of the Political Conference, the party founded by Mohiuddin Karra in 1953 as the first party openly for accession to Pakistan. Hashim stayed in Peshawar and was enthused to meet the renegade Maqbool Butt, who was admired by many youngsters. During Hashim's five months in Pakistan he was influenced by Maqbool's argument against accession to Pakistan but for azaadi. According to Maqbool, the international community would not support Kashmir's accession to Pakistan, but it would support azaadi—on both sides. The insight, that the world would not take sides between India and Pakistan, unless it sided against both, impressed Hashim. He joined Maqbool Butt and the JKNLF.

Maqbool told Hashim that the organisation and its cause needed to get some publicity, and he sent Hashim back to Kashmir to try and enlarge the JKNLF. Hashim did just that, forming cells around urban Srinagar and clandestinely putting up posters that called for an armed struggle. Naturally, the cells he had set up now asked for arms.

At this stage Hashim one day walked into the Royal Haircutting Saloon at Regal Chowk and made the acquaintance of a fellow customer, who happened to be a BSF inspector. They became friends.

Hashim told the BSF inspector he was thinking of crossing the border into Pakistan, and the inspector promised to help him, provided Hashim got information for him on an organisation called al-Mujahid. Hashim agreed, because al-Mujahid was nothing more than an organisation on paper, set up by the self-styled first mujahid of Kashmir, Sardar Mohammad Abdul Qayoom Khan, who was occasionally either the president or the prime minister of PoK. 'It was rubbish,' said Hashim, who agreed to the inspector's terms. The inspector took Hashim to meet his superintendent of police, Ashok Patel. In early April 1970, Hashim went across the border.

Hashim went to Rawalpindi, where JKNLF (and future JKLF co-founder) Dr Farooq Haider lived and had a clinic where he treated Kashmiri migrants for free. Dr Haider would have a prominent role in militancy for he was very close to the ISI. He was originally from Jammu and went over to Pakistan back in 1947 because of the communal rioting, in which his elder brother, Malik Ajaz Ahmed, was killed. This embittered Dr Haider. It was at Dr Haider's house that Hashim caught up with Maqbool Butt; and now the ISI was watching over them. Hashim told Maqbool how he had come across with the help of the BSF, and they all had a good laugh. He then told him that the boys were asking for arms for training and they all sobered up.

One of them recalled the Karachi airport incident from 18 June 1969, when an Ethiopian Airlines plane was attacked by three armed rebels of the Eritrean Liberation Front. Part of the Boeing 707 burned, but fortunately there were no casualties, and the three Eritreans were caught, convicted and sentenced to a year of hard labour. It had been quite sensational. In the JKNLF discussion the idea to do something similar came up, a terror attack, something that would internationalise Kashmir and also their JKNLF. That's how the idea of the hijacking first came up.

Dr Haider's brother-in-law, Javed Minto, was an ex-pilot of the Pakistan Air Force, and he acquainted Hashim with aircraft training. He took Hashim to the Chaklala airbase in Rawalpindi (now known as the PAF's Nur Khan base located at the international airport) where there was a Fokker F-27 Friendship. The ISI, told about the JKNLF's intention, was happy to grant them permission to learn the basics of aviation. Javed and the ISI showed Hashim how the wireless worked, how the compass worked, how to take charge of an airplane, and what to do if he needed to take control of it. Hashim passed with 'flying colours', so to speak.

Hashim returned to India in August 1970, via the Sialkot-

Shakargarh sector south of Jammu. He carried with him a pistol and a grenade, and a plan to hijack a plane from Jammu. But he was caught by the Border Security Force (BSF).

This was a possibility that Maqbool Butt had prepared him for. Maqbool had told him that if he got caught, he should immediately own up and avoid getting bashed, which was pointless. He was to tell his captors that he was being trained— and that there were two others being trained, by the names of Javed Sagar and Naseem Rana. This would make the BSF want to look for the other guys, rather than just lock Hashim up and throw away the key.

The BSF confiscated his pistol and grenade, and Hashim asked for his friend, the BSF inspector from the Royal Haircutting Saloon. Hashim gave him his story of how three of them were being trained by the ISI for terrorism. Ashok Patel landed up in Jammu for the interrogation; even the director general of police got involved, and the IB sent people from Delhi for the interrogation.

Ultimately the BSF gave him the benefit of the doubt and released him to look for the other two. Not only that, they told him he could function as a BSF sub-inspector and play that cover to keep a watch at the Srinagar airport for the two other fellows. However, to Hashim's enduring chagrin, they did not give him an identity card, just a plain piece of paper which said he was a sub-inspector. It was a farce, Hashim felt, and he was now determined to hijack a plane.

Luckily for Hashim, the BSF posted him at Srinagar airport and this made his job easier. Hashim began watching the arrival and departure of planes, and he reconnoitred the airport and its aircraft. He also began training his cousin, Ashraf Qureshi. In the absence of any weapon they made a wooden grenade and obtained a fake .22 pistol. The .22 pistol looked so realistic that it not only fooled the aircraft captain but also the security forces in Lahore.

The flight they hijacked was the Srinagar–Jammu–Delhi

flight of 30 January 1971. The aircraft was a Fokker F-27, one of the oldest planes Indian Airlines had, that had been decommissioned and then weeks later, in a typical bureaucratic flip-flop, re-inducted. It took off from Srinagar at 11:30 a.m.

As the flight began its descent into Jammu, Hashim and Ashraf ran up the aisle towards the cockpit. Hashim, holding the fake gun, ran inside, while Ashraf held the fake grenade and stood outside the door to the cockpit, facing the passengers. Ashraf asked the passengers to raise their hands in the air and warned them: 'Zyada hoshiari dikhane ki zaroorat nahin.'

Inside Hashim stuck his gun's muzzle to the back of the pilot's head and took control of the plane. He told them to take the plane to Lahore. Captains Kachroo and Oberoi protested and argued, but Hashim was menacing enough for them to fall in line. At around 1:30 p.m., the plane landed in Lahore, in an airfield dotted with aircraft of Pakistan International Airlines (PIA). Security forces surrounded the Fokker. The plane door was opened, a couple of aluminum boxes were thrown down to use as steps, and Hashim stepped off the airplane.

The rest of the people deboarded and were greeted with tea and Lahori bread. Then, to everyone's surprise, the Pakistani external affairs minister, Zulfikar Ali Bhutto, arrived at the airport. He greeted Hashim and Ashraf, exchanged a few words, and invited the passengers to lunch with him. Following the lunch, Bhutto held a press conference.

The hijackers demanded political asylum in Pakistan and the release in India of about two dozen jailed JKNLF colleagues. India and Pakistan spent a couple of days negotiating all this, which ended with the passengers being sent overland to Hussainwalla border, from where they returned to India. This was because on 2 February, at 8:00 p.m., Hashim and Ashraf set the Fokker on fire—at the behest of the ISI.

K.H. Khurshid, a Kashmiri originally from Srinagar who became personal secretary to Pakistan's founder, Mohammed Ali Jinnah, was a witness in the hijack case, which went to trial later, and he told the court that he had arrived at Lahore airport at 7:00 p.m. on 2 February, and was told the situation was tense. PIA had stopped serving food to Hashim and Ashraf, kept in custody at the airport. Khurshid and Maqbool Butt, who also arrived at the airport, were taken to a room where they met Hashim and Ashraf. The hijackers told them that the ISI was pressuring them to burn down the aircraft.

Maqbool apparently thought this would be unwise, and till now Hashim had followed all his instructions implicitly. But after he and Khurshid left, the ISI insisted the hijackers burn the plane as the only way of finishing the episode. So they did.

Incidentally, while the Ganga's hijacking focused world attention on Kashmir, it also led to India banning all Pakistani flights from its airspace. This ban was serendipitously timed, because East Pakistan was erupting with protest and when the war took place later in the year, Pakistan said it could not transport enough troops to quell the rebellion due to the ban— as if that would have stopped the inevitable secession of Bangladesh. Yet it provided enough grist for conspiracy theories for years to come, as to whether Hashim's hijacking was merely a ruse to provide a justification for the ban.

Hashim and Ashraf remained heroes in Pakistan till 14 April, when Hashim was arrested in Murree. Pakistan had appointed a commission to look into the hijacking and what it now felt was an Indian conspiracy. After prolonged interrogation other JKNLF leaders were arrested, including Maqbool Butt and Dr Haider; these men were in jail for two years until the Lahore High Court challenged their detention, exonerated them and released them, calling them 'patriots fighting for the liberation of their motherland'. Even Ashraf was released (he went on to become a renowned academic in Pakistan). Only Hashim remained in jail.

Though he was found guilty under a mountain of charges and sentenced to nineteen years in prison, Hashim spent nine years in various jails: in Attock, Sahiwal, Faisalabad, in camp jail Lahore, and in Multan. The Supreme Court reduced his sentence. 'Only I know how I was ill-treated, how I was tortured,' Hashim said of his Pakistani prison experience.

His fellow Kashmiris visited Hashim in jail and kept him abreast of what was going on. He learnt that Maqbool, who was released in 1973, met Bhutto on a number of occasions starting in 1974. Bhutto, now the prime minister of Pakistan, told Maqbool that something had to be done in Kashmir.

'Nothing less than independence,' Maqbool responded.

'Pakistan or independence, India must be out of Kashmir,' Bhutto said.

Hence Bhutto was the only Pakistani who agreed with Maqbool that it was all right even if you talked of Kashmiri independence. He struck the Kashmiris as a practical leader. Whereas before 1971 Pakistan pursued Kashmir as the unfinished agenda of Partition, after 1971 it became revenge for Bangladesh. Bhutto wanted revenge. (In Kashmir people were quite upset when General Zia executed Bhutto in 1979. But typical of Kashmiris, they protested against Bhutto's execution and later against the death of his executioner.)

Maqbool, in 1974, not only met Bhutto for the first time, but also Farooq Abdullah. Farooq was working in London and was sent to Pakistan by Sheikh Saheb to gauge reactions while the negotiations for the eventual Sheikh–Indira Accord of 1975 were on. In PoK, the Plebiscite Front hosted Farooq. During his visit to Mirpur, which is in the Jammu part of PoK, Farooq is said to have made a public speech where he said, in reference to the ongoing negotiations (or the Beg–Parthasarathy consultations, as they were called) that nothing short of independence would be acceptable in Kashmir.

When Farooq met Bhutto, however, the prime minister advised him to tell Sheikh Saheb that as Pakistan, having lost in 1971, could do nothing for him at this juncture, Kashmiris should take whatever they could get from Delhi. This was the signal from Pakistan for Sheikh Saheb to go ahead with the accord, which he did, and following which he became chief minister of J&K till he died in 1982.

Maqbool returned to the Valley in 1976 with the intention of organising the JKNLF, and was soon arrested. Eight years later he was put to death.

Hashim was released from jail in 1980, after which he kept agitating for an independent Kashmir in PoK. This did not go down well with the ISI, and he was picked up repeatedly and released, thanks to Dr Haider, who was his link to the ISI.

In 1983, Hashim again thought of hijacking an airplane, to seek the release of Maqbool Butt. Hijacking seemed the only way of getting things done in those days, but no one was willing to help him. The ISI gave Hashim a passport on which he travelled to London and met with Amanullah Khan, the man who would found the JKLF in London (it was formed in phases: in 1977, the London unit of the PF turned into the JKLF, and then set up a unit in PoK in 1982, and a unit in Kashmir in 1987). Hashim claimed that it was Amanullah who gave the go-ahead for the killing of Mhatre, thereby virtually signing Maqbool's death warrant.

This sort of game went on in the early 1980s. After Bhutto it was General Zia-ul-Haq, for whom the 1979 invasion of Afghanistan by the Soviet Union provided Pakistan with the perfect opportunity to divert men and material to Kashmir. Pakistan was the West's key ally and also the base for the Afghan war, so it was in a position to virtually blackmail the West. Incidentally, this was also the time a young US State Department diplomat and former CIA analyst, Robin Raphel, began referring to Kashmir as disputed.

The key role in Kashmir was that of the ISI chief, Gen. Akhtar Abdur Rehman Khan, who gained fame for running the Afghan war against the Soviets and in the bargain significantly expanding the capabilities of the ISI, turning it into the powerful 'state within a state' that it was known as thereafter. Following Farooq's dismissal by Governor Jagmohan in 1984, there was a serious effort to destabilise Kashmir, and Dr Haider arranged a meeting with the ISI of selected JKLF leaders in a safe house in Islamabad, and four or five meetings after that. Hashim came face to face with General Rehman during one of these meetings. That's when Rehman told them to get boys from the Valley for training, and wait for a signal: 'We would like to replicate Bangladesh in Kashmir by creating something like Mukti Bahini, and by cutting off the Valley,' the ISI chief said. 'Pakistan would attack at the appropriate time.'

This did not work out due to the reluctance of the JKLF boys. Indeed, it was only after Amanullah Khan was thrown out of England in 1988 for terrorism and he came to Pakistan that the boys started coming across (Amanullah's arrival happily coincided with the boys' fury over the 1987 rigged assembly elections in J&K).

The ISI told Hashim to start militancy, but he refused. As it was, the ISI was getting irritated with Hashim's agitation against accession and for independence. So its officers told him to return the passport and identity card and other papers the ISI had given him; it had been a big mistake, they told him. Hashim, instead, filed a writ petition in Rawalpindi in the court of Justice Yusuf Saraf. The judge took Hashim aside and told him that he had been approached by the ISI with regard to his case. 'Flee,' Justice Saraf told Hashim. 'It is better you leave the country.'

What took me by surprise while listening to Hashim's story was the following part: that the CIA advised him to shift to the Netherlands. It is an interesting anecdote, but Hashim did not elaborate.

Despite being on the ISI's blacklist, Hashim bribed his way through the airport—no doubt the CIA might have given a slight nudge to his efforts—and in August 1986 left for Amsterdam, where he sought political asylum. India's first reaction was that Hashim was probably setting up a base for the JKLF in the Netherlands at the behest of the ISI. Hashim told me that the Dutch gave him more than asylum; they gave him work helping with analysis by their intelligence service; and in 1992, they gave him citizenship. Hashim's background attracted intelligence services. In the Netherlands he was their 'South Asia' expert.

Hashim did return to Pakistan once, in 1993, on a visa, which he admitted he got with the help of the Americans. The ISI chief at the time was Lt. Gen. Javed Nasir, an extremely pro-Islam, anti-India chief, and he wanted to meet Hashim. But Hashim refused to meet him. Hashim went to Rawalpindi and stayed with Dr Haider and met with leaders of the Jamaat-e-Islami, who were by now at the forefront of Kashmir militancy through their armed group, the Hizbul Mujahideen. Hashim also went to Muzaffarabad, the capital of PoK, and dropped into the office of engineer Tariq Shura, who introduced him to a major in the ISI. Hashim rebuffed the major as well. He went to Pakistan, he claimed, to check out the fate of Kashmir and Kashmiris.

Hashim was repeatedly approached by the ISI, but he wanted nothing to do with them. He had enough experience of Pakistan—not just its jails, but also its insistence that Kashmir should join Pakistan, not fight for independence—that he was disillusioned with the country. In fact, in 2010, his old friend Shabir Shah approached him and asked him to meet the ISI. 'They're very keen to meet you,' Shabir told Hashim.

'Pakistanis are zero per cent for Kashmir,' Hashim replied. 'Even if India is only 30 per cent for Kashmir, we can still deal with India. It is impossible dealing with Pakistanis. I have enough knowledge of Pakistanis, thank you very much. I would rather not have anything more to do with Pakistan.'

Hashim then asked his old separatist friend how it was that Shabir had never visited Pakistan. Every single separatist, be it a militant or a politician, had been to Pakistan—except Shabir. 'It's because you're scared of Pakistan,' Hashim said. 'Yet you are recruiting on behalf of the ISI.'

In the course of time, Hashim met me and said: please bring me home.

It was six months before he could make it back, during my final days at R&AW. It took him that long because first, he wanted to make sure he had our approval and that he wouldn't land in a legal soup after reaching India; and second, because he had to make arrangements for his family. He had married his cousin Zaib-un-Nisa Baig, a Pakistani citizen, in 1982, a couple of years after he was freed from prison; and they had four children.

Finally, on 29 December 2000, he flew into Delhi and was arrested at the airport as soon as he landed because of a 'lookout warrant' issued against him by the J&K government. He spent a fortnight in Delhi's Tihar jail, where among his visitors was Muzaffar Baig, who would later join Mufti Sayeed's PDP and become deputy chief minister of J&K. In the new year, Hashim was transferred to Srinagar, where he spent almost a year in the joint interrogation centre. He was released on bail for Eid in November 2001.

Yet the two things that he wanted did not materialise. First, the hijacking-related case against him still hangs, despite his plea of double jeopardy. The case, as of this writing, has been carrying on for thirteen years, since 2001, but the wheels in justice move slowly and also lower-tier judges are wary of ruling against the State. The case is so absurd that the State's witnesses don't recognise Hashim any more. And that's not because he is a threat, or a menacing fellow. 'This case is total rubbish,' Hashim said, pointing out that Satnam Singh, one of the five men who hijacked an Indian plane on its way to Srinagar to Pakistan in September 1981, was let off. Satnam was thrown in jail in Lahore where he spent thirteen years, and then he migrated to Canada. In February 2000 he also returned to India; he was arrested and produced before a magistrate to whom he showed his papers and said, 'I've already been punished for the hijacking.' The magistrate said, double jeopardy: no one can serve twice for the same crime. She had him released.

Hashim got in touch with the chief minister, Farooq Abdullah, and said: 'Mine is also a case of double jeopardy. How can you charge me?'

'Yes, I know,' Farooq said. 'But you have to get through this somehow.'

Of course, what Hashim did not know was that Farooq had his plate full at the time, in 2001, to which we will come a couple of chapters from now.

'These IB, R&AW guys don't realise that if I get a sentence here then the Indian judiciary will face questions in front of the whole world,' Hashim said. 'I'm a Dutch citizen. When I was arrested, they raised it in their parliament, and it will get raised again. And then they will ask, what is India doing in Kashmir?'

This brings us to his other grouse: that even fourteen years after he returned, he's still a Dutch national. I had promised him Indian nationality, but it turned out to be too difficult, particularly since my tenure as R&AW chief ended two days after he arrived. Left to me, I would have made him a citizen, because then he could have been used politically in Kashmir. Yet there are people in the government who don't trust him because nobody is certain whether he's an Indian agent or a Pakistani agent or a Dutch agent or an American agent. Even Farooq, who, if you recall, introduced me to Hashim, pretended as if he did not know him at all and did not want to deal with him. And the home ministry seems gloriously uninterested.

He came out on bail and spent his years fighting his cases, setting up a non-governmental organisation to help widows, and even set up an office right opposite the Hurriyat party's office. Nothing came of it. Many years later, I reminded him: 'Hashim Saheb, what did I tell you, what will you do here?'

Hashim replied to that with an Urdu couplet, which roughly translated says: I live in a city of such jealousy where even during namaaz people think ill of others. 'The Kashmiri has a huge problem,' Hashim said. 'He doesn't want to speak the truth, he doesn't want to hear the truth.'

'I speak the truth, so they call me an Indian agent,' said Hashim. 'My group has an office in front of the Hurriyat office. I say that the Hurriyat people should give up the accession to Pakistan, as should our people. Sixty-five years have passed, another 500 years will pass, Kashmir will never become Pakistan. You can write it down. All these groups, Mirwaiz (Umar Farooq), (Syed Ali Shah) Geelani, even Shabir who once roamed around with the needle and thread and now roams around with scissors, all three of these are for Pakistan; why don't they become one party? And people, don't sacrifice your children, you're not going to get anything from their struggle. If you're sincere, then say both India and Pakistan should get out of our land.'

Hashim said he made a great mistake in 2000. 'My son said, everyone thinks you're a Delhi man, and Delhi doesn't think you're their man,' he said. 'You should have come to Delhi and said, fellow Kashmiris, Pakistan is the best. India would have raised you on a pedestal, made you Wazir-e-Alam, you would have got Arab money. He was right.'

Instead, Hashim has had a stressful time. He has two daughters and two sons. One boy was studying in Amsterdam and stayed back; by now he has a job in a bank. The other son was a small boy when they returned, and as of the writing of this book, had grown up and gone off to Holland to study. Of the two daughters, one got married in 2007 and lives in Dubai. I attended her wedding, as also that of his son, Junaid, though I asked Hashim if he was sure I should attend because I was a former R&AW chief; it would mark him out in Kashmir. He laughed and said, let them say I'm your agent. As it turned out, at Junaid's wedding, many of the separatists who attended came over for a chat—because I knew them all.

Hashim's other daughter ran away from home. It has depressed him. She ran first to her sister in Dubai and then went to London, where she now lives and plans to marry (incidentally, her love interest is a Kashmiri boy; yet Hashim is still disapproving). Hashim's wife also left. An attractive Pakistani woman, coming from Holland to Kashmir was quite a letdown for her, and she chastised him for the 'third-class' world he had brought her to. There was a lot of disruption in Hashim's family.

When his daughter ran away, he rang me up for help in locating her. His wife was not there, he was all alone, lonely and stressed out. 'Please, aap logon ke har jagah contacts hote hain,' he begged me. 'Please isse dhoondhwaye.' Finally she was traced in Dubai.

All of this took its toll: in 2013, Hashim had to have a heart bypass. Fortunately, his wife is now back with him.

You wonder why, after all this, Hashim stays in India. 'There's no country freer than India and people don't realise it,' Hashim said. 'You can pee anywhere you like and nothing will happen to you. America is a great democracy but has not even spared our ministers from physical searches. I know one minister from Tamil Nadu who went there; he had long hair coming out of his ears, and they searched that even. What's so great about the US?'

'India has let down a lot of people, no one more than me,' Hashim said. 'They have no morality. But at least they are humane.'

As I mentioned at the beginning, it helped that militants who were once anti-India were rapidly disappointed with Pakistan. Our success with Hashim at the beginning of the summer helped the next man come over, a far more dreaded militant named Abdul Majid Dar, who came over in what was a storybook operation.

7

THE DEFECTOR WHO SHOOK PAKISTAN

The story of Abdul Majid Dar is a love story. He was the most important Kashmiri terrorist in Pakistan, and he returned to India in what was an operation that turned on a matter of the heart. The ISI, which got burned, had Majid Dar assassinated. And then they went and shot his wife.

As with many stories, the episode began while I was in the IB. A Kashmiri boy had been caught and was interrogated. An officer of the force interrogating the boy came to me and said the boy was an interesting fellow. 'You should talk to him,' he said. We did so.

As you might have guessed, some of the details of this account will have to remain sketchy due to reasons of operational secrecy. Besides the confidentiality that I'm sworn to, lives could be at risk—beyond the ones already lost.

The boy being interrogated said: 'Do you know Abdul Majid Dar?'

Who didn't? He was the operational chief of the Hizbul Mujahideen, the lethal pro-Pakistan Kashmiri militant group. It was considered the armed wing of the Jamaat-e-Islami, but it was pretty much a power unto itself. The Hizb was led by Syed Salahuddin, whose real name was Mohammed Yusuf Shah, a Jamaat-e-Islami preacher who contested the 1987 J&K assembly election on an MUF ticket, from the Amirakadal constituency. He lost. The winner was the National Conference's Ghulam Mohiuddin Shah, the focal point of allegations of rigging in those flawed elections. Yusuf Shah was thrown in jail, and though his Jamaat was reluctant to join the armed militancy that was brewing (prescient Jamaatis argued that terrorism would only lead to Kashmiris killing Kashmiris), when violence finally took centre stage in 1990, the Jamaat-e-Islami gave the go-ahead to the formation of the Hizb in April 1990. The first chief was a killer named Ahsan Dar, who convinced Yusuf Shah to join; the latter adopted his nom de guerre after Saladdin the crusader.

Salahuddin took over as chief in November 1991, but he was just the chief for name's sake. The brainstrust was the operational chief, Abdul Majid Dar: a man of guts.

Majid Dar was not an original Hizb recruit, though he had a strong Jamaati influence as he grew up in Sopore, in Baramulla district, one of the Kashmiri towns that have historically been hostile to India. Born in 1954, he was enrolled in the degree college at Sopore but had to leave before he could finish his bachelor's. He married in 1978, and for a while it is said that he ran a dry-cleaning shop in Sopore. In the early 1980s he joined Shabir Shah's People's League and began visiting Pakistan. When People's League members began joining militant groups in the late 1980s—recall that Shabir Shah's lieutenants such as Firdous Syed formed his own group, and Nayeem Khan joined the Islamic Students League—then Majid Dar followed a fellow named Sheikh Aziz and formed the Tehreek-e-Jehad-e-Islami (TJI).

In the early 1990s, Majid Dar's group dominated north Kashmir, from Sopore to Kupwara. It was also a time when groups were splitting into smaller and smaller factions, and hence there was a move by group leaders to unify their followers/ soldiers so as to be more effective against the government. By the end of the year, Majid Dar's TJI merged into the Hizbul Mujahideen, and Ahsan Dar made him deputy chief.

As I said, however, he was the one who really ran things. He was a guy with brains, and had a much better understanding of the militancy and the situation in Kashmir. As a result, he had better contacts and links with the ISI. Also, he grasped quickly when things were going bad; he grasped how Pakistan was waging its own war and had made Kashmir its battlefield; he grasped that the ISI was shifting its focus away from the Hizb after 1995, and towards trans-national jihadi groups, particularly the Lashkar-e-Toiba; and he grasped that his people were tired. 'Compared to Majid Dar, Salahuddin was a pygmy,' his wife later said.

Hence the boy being interrogated said that Majid Dar might be interested in coming back to Kashmir, because his wife was very keen to return. And Majid Dar was very much in love with his wife, Dr Shamima Badroo.

It was the second marriage for both of them. Shamima was also from Sopore, an attractive divorcee with a forceful personality; it is said that Majid Dar had fallen in love with her and forced her to get a divorce. Majid Dar, who had married early, as happens in traditional families, particularly those in semi-urban or rural areas, left his first wife behind in Sopore. And then he went across to Pakistan in 1991.

Shamima followed him there, so they had apparently fallen in love and were already having an affair. She got a visa and went to do a postgraduate degree; she stayed with a friend, met up with Majid Dar, and they got married. Because she was working at the cantonment hospital in Muzaffarabad, Majid Dar was spending a lot of time in the PoK office of the Hizb, rather than in Islamabad where Salahuddin wanted him. That Majid Dar was besotted with his wife earned him much scorn from the Hizb cadres, particularly those closer to Salahuddin.

That's why, the boy under interrogation said, 'You can target Majid Dar.'

Our ears perked up. 'How can you say that?'

'He's very much in love,' the militant said. 'His wife is very keen to come back.'

Our files told us that Majid Dar had left his wife back in Sopore, so it took some explaining before we realised he had married again. Once we realised that this was his second wife he was in love with, it struck me that she must feel uncomfortable living over in PoK, which by all accounts was a drab and backward place. She must have judged that this was no life, that it was better to go back.

At the time, however, there wasn't much I could do because I was in the IB, and Majid Dar was based in Pakistan. This was out of the IB's domain. All Pakistan matters were handled by R&AW, and though our agencies cooperate, they are also competitive. The IB and R&AW are no different from other intelligence agencies in the world, each of which is naturally possessive about its turf.

When I became the R&AW chief, Majid Dar's possible vulnerability was one of the matters I remembered, and I told myself that now was the time to get something going. We got a group of colleagues to engage with him. Obviously there was a limit to how much we could check him out, given that he was inside Pakistan, our arch enemy and a place where even normal Indian diplomats were subject to relentless surveillance and suspicion. Hence, in this business, some of these matters are based on trust, and you have to take a leap of faith.

We could take that leap with him because he was a good guy, a confident fellow who was completely for ending the militancy. Our assessment in R&AW was that this was an intelligent guy, perceptive and sensitive, attested to by his love affair. When we dug into his past, we found that he had never actually killed anyone, and some of our guys doubted that he had ever fired a gun at all. We knew that at that point of time, there was great disillusionment with Pakistan, in Pakistan, among Kashmiris. Majid Dar was likely among those who realised that the only people suffering in the militancy were the Kashmiris themselves.

Plus, it was obvious he wanted to get his family back here. He had a young boy whom he was extremely fond of. We worked out a plan. We crossed our fingers, and we began to pray that he would find a way and come over.

Majid Dar found a way, and it was pretty straightforward: he went to the ISI and told them he wanted to go back to Kashmir—as their agent. He needed the approval, if not just the support, of the ISI to return. He convinced his ISI handler, a fellow named Brigadier Riaz, that he would go as their man, and seeing that Delhi was prepared to talk to militants, he would go and engage India in dialogue, while secretly carrying out the ISI agenda. Brigadier Riaz checked with Salahuddin, who was okay with it despite his growing differences with Majid Dar. He came armed with a resolution from the Hizb Supreme Council authorising him to engage in dialogue. Brigadier Riaz then went to the ISI chief, Lt. Gen. Mahmud Ahmed, who approved Majid Dar's return to Kashmir.

(General Mahmud was the same ISI chief sitting in Washington, DC when the 9/11 attacks took place. He was removed just before the US attacked the Taliban regime in Afghanistan a month later.)

Majid Dar slipped into Kashmir, and later it was rumoured that he came to India via Dubai (which is pretty much ISI turf). He remained underground for a while, so no one knew he was here.

And then one fine day, on 24 July 2000, Majid Dar surfaced in Srinagar and announced a unilateral ceasefire. He said it was to facilitate talks for a settlement. Of course, this caused great excitement because no group had done this before; while individual militants like Firdous Syed had given up the gun and entered talks with the government in 1996, never before had a group, and that too one that had dominated militancy in the way the Hizb had throughout the 1990s before the pan-Islamists began taking over. Ordinary Kashmiris who had long tired of the violence but had been let down before, notably by Shabir Shah, were intrigued.

In Pakistan, Salahuddin acknowledged his support to the ceasefire. The government of India reciprocated with a three-month ceasefire of its own.

The Union home secretary, Kamal Pandey, responded and on 3 August he and other home ministry officials flew in from Delhi and met four of Majid Dar's commanders, including his nominated interlocutor, Fazl Haq Qureshi, at the Nehru Guest House in Srinagar. It was a start. It looked as if a major breakthrough had taken place. Majid Dar himself became rather enthusiastic about the dialogue, and immediately began planning to broad-base it with the participation of other Kashmiri separatists and militants.

Then on 8 August, just five days later, Salahuddin, in an announcement from Pakistan, withdrew the ceasefire. But for the first time, as a Kashmiri friend put it, Kashmiris realised that there could be life in Kashmir without violence.

The ISI had chickened out. In its view, Majid Dar had been turned by Indian intelligence; the ISI had lost control of him and he had been won over and become an Indian agent. Shamima later said that it was a big shock for the ISI because while Majid Dar was in Pakistan, he was the last word in the Hizbul Mujahideen as far as the ISI was concerned. The ISI respected him a lot. His turnaround after his arrival in Kashmir was thus a shock to the ISI—particularly since he had come with Pakistani permission, Pakistani approval, on a Pakistani mission. It broke the back of indigenous militancy and was to have far-reaching consequences, not least of which was the success of the 2002 elections. The Hizb remains decapitated to this day with the Dar loyalists in Pakistan refusing to accept Salahuddin's leadership.

The ISI began planning Majid Dar's assassination.

Despite Salahuddin's withdrawal of ceasefire, Majid Dar was spending his time productively; he had his agenda for dialogue and so he went around meeting people. He met the Jamaat-e-Islami supremo and senior Hurriyat leader, Syed Ali Shah Geelani, a few times. He met Mirwaiz Umar Farooq. He met Yasin Malik. He must have met Shabir Shah as well. Initially he was checking them out but then he began to suggest to them that they should begin talking. He was trying to build a lobby and form a consensus in favour of dialogue.

Majid Dar came across as a confident, positive person, enthusiastic above all else for peace. He got the separatists to think without and beyond Pakistan. Had he been around when the government began talking to the separatist All Party Hurriyat Conference—the then deputy prime minister, L.K. Advani, did so in January 2004—he would have very much been a part of it (in fact, his interlocutor, Fazl Haq Qureshi, did join the Hurriyat talks).

It was clear that in his mind, the Pakistan story was over. He told everyone that what got him started thinking about a dialogue was the Kargil war.

Pakistan's misadventure in Kargil was an eye-opener for Kashmiris operating out of Pakistan, Majid Dar said. It was a big disappointment particularly because US president Bill Clinton had called up Nawaz Sharif and told him to pull his troops back. That's when Kashmiris realised that Pakistan could do nothing for them even if it wanted to; and that veneer had already come off with the indication, over the past few years, that Pakistan's anti-India agenda did not necessarily translate into a pro-Kashmir agenda.

Majid Dar was disillusioned with Pakistan and categorically said that Pakistan's tap of terror could be turned off immediately, at any time, by the Americans. 'Pakistan has no interest in freeing Kashmir,' he said. 'Pakistan just wants to bleed Kashmir.'

And so, the Kargil war had got him and many others thinking about dialogue with India.

The other thing that bothered Majid Dar was the corruption of the movement. For much of the 1990s, the tanzeem that had sustained the movement was the Hizb. And he made the point to other Kashmiris that though the Hizb was different from the JKLF, it was actually pro-liberation. But then in 2000 it began to look as if the Hizb would not survive for long; it had been diminished operationally and others had been given more importance, particularly the mercenaries. Control was being taken over by the Lashkar-e-Toiba. Now his Hizb was playing second fiddle to the Lashkar.

This resonated with other Kashmiris such as Abdul Ghani Lone, an important Hurriyat leader who often argued with Geelani that the Lashkar and the Taliban and other jihadis were not welcome in Kashmir. 'Yeh hamare mehmaan nahin hain,' Lone said. 'These guests are coming here and killing Kashmiris.'

The ISI did not like any of this at all and it even tried reaching out to Majid Dar. But in 2001 Majid Dar stopped taking calls from the ISI chief, General Mahmud. That undoubtedly firmed the ISI's resolve to finish Majid Dar.

Salahuddin's rift with Majid Dar also widened. Majid Dar had always been loyal to the Hizb supreme leader, despite Salahuddin's close proximity to the ISI, but he began to find Salahuddin's duplicity intolerable. Their estrangement now was reflected in the increasing internecine battles in the Hizbul Mujahideen in Pakistan: many fights erupted between Majid Dar's boys—many of whom had their roots like their leader in the TJI—and Salahuddin's boys. The Salahuddin people began bumping off Majid Dar's people, starting with those who participated in the 3 August talks with the government of India, Hamid Tantray and Farooq Mircha. And, of course, it included the murder of Majid Dar himself. Fazl Haq Qureshi was also later targeted and shot and critically wounded while coming out of a mosque in Srinagar on 4 December 2009. He was lucky to survive and continue in the moderate Hurriyat, still very much a votary of dialogue, even though he was one of the first Kashmiri separatists to indulge in violence in Srinagar, being part of the infamous al-Fatah.

Majid Dar, in the meantime, was beginning to realise that the job of getting people together, persuading them that talking was a positive and beneficial step for them, for Kashmiris, was a little more difficult than it might have looked from across the border. The Hurriyat in particular was so much under the control of Pakistan that he could not progress. Then he must have understood that what he needed to do was go back to Pakistan and talk to the ISI to loosen its reins on the separatists.

When word filtered down, we saw no logic in going back to Pakistan because he was no doubt a persona non grata there. One reason was that Majid Dar's ceasefire had started a chain of events, including Prime Minister Vajpayee's announcement of a unilateral ceasefire during Ramzan, which was during September 2000.

How that happened is that Yousuf Tarigami, the lone flag-bearer for the Communist Party of India (Marxist) in Kashmir and assemblyman from Kulgam, came and met me at my official residence one morning. 'Eid is coming,' he said. 'Kucch karwa dijiye.'

'Ceasefire toh hua tha,' I told him. 'Hizb has backed out. What should we do?'

'Why don't you have a unilateral ceasefire declared,' Tarigami suggested.

I took it to Vajpayee, and the idea appealed to him. A Ramzan ceasefire was announced, and this really caught the fancy of Kashmiris. It was one of a series of pronouncements that endeared Vajpayee to Kashmiris long after he left office. Above all, it was a critical factor that improved the atmosphere for the 2002 assembly election in J&K, which was a success.

In the ISI's panicked eyes, it was further damnation of Majid Dar, if more was needed. In December 2001, Salahuddin threw him out of the Hizbul Mujahideen. And when he let it be known, after the 2002 assembly election, that he would go back to Pakistan—he was supremely confident that he could go and deal with the ISI any time he wanted to—they had him killed.

In fact, the idea of his going to Pakistan was a dangerous one, and one worried that he would be killed there, in Pakistan; but he was killed right here. Of course, it was delayed a bit, till March 2003, due to the ISI's assassination of Abdul Ghani Lone in May 2002 (which we will come to in the next chapter), and the ISI's need to wait for things to cool down after Lone was murdered, but in the end Majid Dar was killed here so that the blame would not fall directly on the ISI. And also, to send everyone in Kashmir a message: never to cross the ISI.

When we began receiving his decision to go back to Pakistan, to us in R&AW it was incomprehensible.

A common friend told Dar, 'Don't go back. As far as Pakistan is concerned, you're finished. You will get into trouble there. You might never be able to come back out, or worse, they might just kill you.'

That probably steeled his resolve to return.

There was precious little anybody could do to save him, because Majid Dar was on his own, underground, and we in the government only occasionally heard that he had been in such-and-such place, or that he had met so-and-so. Though we had successfully managed his return, once he was back he was a free person. Plus he was underground.

His wife Shamima Badroo later said that it was Brigadier Riaz, the ISI officer who had helped make the case within the ISI to let Majid Dar cross over, who whipped up an atmosphere against Majid Dar in Pakistan. Shamima said, and there's no way of verifying this, that the ISI plan B, if his assassins could not get to him, was to kidnap her and the son that he doted on.

The threat to him grew so serious that one of Majid Dar's men warned him, during the last few days, against visiting Sopore. On Friday, 21 March, one of his friends in Srinagar told him so: 'Aap Sopore mat jaye.'

On 22 March, he spent the day with his Hizb colleagues.

One 23 March, he went to Sopore, despite all the warnings, because he said he had to go and say goodbye to his mother whom he loved immensely. It is said that while he was in hiding his mother would send him his favourite Wullar fish personally cooked. A mother's love and his own over-confidence contributed to his tragic end. And around 11 a.m., he was shot dead.

We assumed the Hizb killed him, the boys with allegiance to Salahuddin, on orders from the ISI. When the ISI felt the time was right, Majid Dar was put down. It was unfortunate, to say the least, because if he had been around when talks with the Hurriyat came out into the open in 2004, Majid Dar would have been a huge asset to everyone; he had leadership qualities.

Worse, though, was what happened to his wife. For on 28 November 2006, she was shot at her house in Chhanpora, Srinagar, and though she survived, she was left paralysed. Again, I suspected the Hizb, and what I was told was that many militants were still settling scores with her for Majid Dar's return to Kashmir. I heard that Majid Dar's own divisional commander was involved in the shooting; yet why should his own men kill Majid Dar's wife?

The Hizb boys knew that she was the reason he came back, and they were convinced by the ISI that Shamima was an Indian intelligence agent who, during the seven or eight years of their married life in Pakistan, worked on him to return, thereby cleaving into two what used to be the premier militant group, Hizbul Mujahideen.

The shooting left her wheelchair-bound for life and in a bad state, both emotionally and financially, yet still this gutsy woman went to Pakistan in January 2014 and confronted the ISI. She said that she tried to meet the ISI chief, but he didn't meet her; instead, she met Brigadier Riaz, who apologised and said that Majid Dar's death was a great loss. A former lieutenant of Majid Dar's, Zafar Bhat, later revealed that Majid Dar had some land in Pakistan and that she probably went back to dispose of it. Perhaps this was the unfinished business that Majid Dar sometimes spoke of. Basically he wanted to go back to apprise the ISI of the ground situation in Kashmir: to tell them there was no other way but dialogue. It's doubtful that we will ever know the complete story, but such is the messy business of espionage.

There were other Kashmiris that we would have liked to have brought back home, but when my tenure ended on 31 December 2000, there were guys who were left out in the cold.

One of the guys whom I had very much in mind was Irshad Malik. If you remember, Irshad Malik was the secretary general of the United Jehad Council in Muzaffarabad and a colleague of our friend Firdous Syed, who caught up with Irshad when he visited PoK and Pakistan in 1994.

Irshad had been a practising lawyer in Baramulla, was the organiser of the district bar association, and actually worked for the government, representing the local cooperative bank. He had been sympathetic to Shabir Shah's People's League for many years and was arrested in 1982 for some minor disturbance on 14 August, which is Pakistan's independence day. In 1987 Irshad was asked by the MUF to contest the 1987 elections, though he was not confident enough. The MUF had wanted him to contest independently and split the NC vote so that the MUF candidate would win; Baramulla constituency had a 55:45 rural-urban ratio, and the countryside was where the NC was strong. The MUF was confident of taking the urban vote, but Irshad, not confident he could achieve anything, declined their offer.

One of Irshad's friends at university was a commerce student named Aijaz Dar; Dar was one of the founding members of the JKLF who would later gain notoriety as the first militant killed when he was shot dead during an attack on the residence of the deputy inspector general, A.M. Watali, in September 1988. Aijaz hung around two other students who would later become prominent militants, Shakeel Ahmed Bakshi and Hilal Beg. That was how Irshad started meeting militants and became familiar with many of them.

I met Irshad more than two decades later, in London, where he had sought asylum in 2004 after fleeing Pakistan out of disillusionment. Irshad told me that when he lived at home, in Baramulla, his best friend was a fellow named Shahid Ali Shah, who came from an important NC family and was the nephew of Khwaja Mubarak Shah, a former state minister and MP from Baramulla, and known as one of Sheikh Abdullah's trusted lieutenants. In 1989 and 1990, as mentioned earlier, militants who burst upon the scene were targeting various groups of people, one of which were members of mainstream parties. In January 1990, some militants came to Irshad's house in Baramulla, looking for his friend Shahid Ali.

The militants told Irshad to guide them to Shahid Ali's place. The ringleader was Prince Khan, who was Nayeem's brother; Irshad knew Nayeem of course as a close lieutenant of Shabir Shah, and since Nayeem was a distant relative of his. He also realised that these militants, led by Prince Khan, were going to kill Shahid Ali and had surrounded his house. Thus, to save his friend, Irshad said he would join the militants. Fortunately, as Shahid Ali was unavailable, the militants went away.

One thing led to another, and in June 1990, at the age of twenty-four and having fathered a daughter who was now fifteen months, he crossed the LoC. As soon as he did so he wept, the weight of the moment coming down on him. He realised he might never go home (he still hasn't been able to return to Kashmir); that he had lost his identity, his daughter, his roots. His companion during the crossing, another advocate named Abdul Salam Rather, told him to cheer up.

In December 1990–January 1991, the Jehad Council was formed, and about ten of the militant representatives gathered in Islamabad to discuss its formation and who would sit on the council. Irshad was selected as the secretary general, and when the time came to choose a chairman, a veteran militant named Azam Inquilabi spoke up and told the gathering that they had to decide who it would be; and then he walked out of the room. Obviously his message was that they should pick him. So they did.

The ISI, when it learnt of this, was not amused. The ISI's Kashmir group officers summoned a couple of the militant representatives and asked them what was going on. Basically, according to Irshad, the ISI wanted total control of the jehadis and anything happening without their knowledge was unthinkable. The consequence was that there was a Kashmiri Jehad Council and a Pakistani Jehad Council for some time, until the ISI realised how bad two councils looked and got them to unify. The whole episode was telling of Pakistan's true intentions; after all, this was a Kashmiri movement. It was the beginning of Irshad's disillusionment with Pakistan.

When I was in R&AW, Firdous reminded me of his friend Irshad. 'Irshad Malik se baat kariye,' Firdous said. 'Irshad Malik ko laaye, he's keen to come back.'

This was early 2000. 'Tell me a connection,' I said. 'Tell me a way.'

'I have told you,' Firdous said. 'Ab aap dekhe.'

Then I heard that Irshad was going off to London in 2004, where he would seek asylum. But by that time, I had left the government; I was in the PMO, and had left when Vajpayee lost power. For whatever it's worth, if I had been in a position to bring him back, I would have. When I met him a decade later in London, we chatted for an hour and a half, and in that time he said so many things. He is a wealth of information. But I also realised when I met him that he was better off in London than he could ever be in Kashmir.

The other thing, which really ought to have happened but has not, is the return of Salahuddin himself. After Majid Dar's assassination Salahuddin showed an inclination to return to

Kashmir: contact was even established which only confirmed his serious intent.

Over the years after Dar's return, Salahuddin showed great keenness to return, though some people in the Valley were not willing to trust him. In fact, he had shown an interest long before, sometime in 1995, in a conversation to, of all people, Syed Mir Qasim, the Congress chief minister of J&K from 1971 till 1975 (when Sheikh Abdullah took over).

I was interacting quite a lot with Mir Qasim from 1994 to '96, because Qasim was a great supporter of Farooq Abdullah and I was working on getting the political process revived in the militancy-hit state. Qasim would tell me, we must keep talking. 'Sab se baat kariye,' he said. 'Doctor Saheb ko khush rakhiye.'

And Qasim told me one day that he got a call from Salahuddin.

I was taken aback. What did he say?

'Qasim Saheb, hame mat bhooliye,' Salahuddin apparently said. 'I have heard that you are getting everyone into the dialogue. If you are initiating dialogue please don't forget me.'

Then there is the story of Salahuddin's son.

One of Salahuddin's big concerns was his son, who had qualified for medical college admission, but in Jammu, not in Srinagar; possibly the grades required for admission for Srinagar were higher. But the boy and his father were desperate that he somehow get into Srinagar. So Salahuddin reached out to everyone, and he spoke to my IB colleague, K.M. Singh, who was in charge of the IB's Srinagar unit (a post I held from 1988 to 1990).

K.M. also had a good equation with Farooq Abdullah: they reached out to one another often, they understood each other, and they trusted one another. K.M. went to the chief minister with the proposal, and said: 'Sir, yeh ek kaam kar dijiye.'

Farooq agreed—which in itself is a story that repeatedly takes place, that of Farooq's ultimate nationalism, particularly when issues of national security are involved. Many people doubt Farooq, even prime ministers such as Narasimha Rao and Vajpayee, but those of us who saw Farooq up close and over a period of time, knew that of all the Kashmiris, Farooq was the one Kashmiri who was always there for India. He said time and time again that Kashmir's accession to India was final and irrevocable, the only Kashmiri to do so.

Salahuddin's son got the admission, and Salahuddin called K.M. up and said: 'I'm eternally grateful to you.'

Words like that should be capitalised on, but unfortunately we never did. We could have brought Salahuddin back, he was willing, but it was just a matter of when to bring him in. One of those things where timing was on a razor's edge. Perhaps we wasted too much time. By the time this matter of his son's admission happened, I was no longer in R&AW but in the PMO, where the focus was the 2002 elections rather than bringing individuals back, even someone as big a deal as Salahuddin. Just imagine what a big thing it would have been in Kashmir if Salahuddin had returned and begun a dialogue—for, after all, he was a political person.

After I left, however, R&AW did not show the same interest in Kashmir. Whatever excitement there was in R&AW over Kashmir was because of me, and the baggage I had accumulated and carried over from the IB. I was able to do a lot because I had a good equation with my batchmate who was the IB chief, Shyamal Datta.

By 2001, Salahuddin was ready to come back, and I advocated it hundreds of times. Possibly the chief after me, Vikram Sood, had other interests; and his people might have thought that since I was handling Kashmir generally from the PMO, there was no need for them to get involved. C.D. Sahay, who was chief after Sood, should have had every reason to be interested but somehow it was one of those things that never happened. I never intervened beyond a point. That's one of the things about the spy agencies—once you're out, you're out, and for good reason, considering the sensitivity of the work we do.

One of the things Irshad Malik harped on was that there are still 2,400 Kashmiris in Pakistan, most of whom are married and settled. Out of those, about 2,000 are unhappy with their meagre existence and the hostile environment. The rest have done well for themselves and are happy. All of them were kids when they went, but that was twenty-five years ago. We could do very well by bringing that disgruntled 2,000 back. They want to come home.

Omar Abdullah as chief minister had spoken of a rehabilitation programme, but we in India haven't been able to work it out. It shows our lack of confidence. So go ahead, tell those Kashmiris: we're not interested in you, it's no big deal to us if you rot there. Yet you can't do that either.

I was on a TV news show after I left the PMO, possibly in 2005 or 2006. Some fellows came to my house and said: 'Hum Kashmir pe aapka interview lena chahate hain.'

'Kya interview lena chahate ho?' I asked.

'Kucch baatein hain,' they said.

'There's nothing to talk about.' I was ready to put down the phone.

'Salahuddin bhi hain iss interview mein,' they said.

So I said: 'Okay, I'm ready.'

There was Salahuddin from Pakistan, there was a young and articulate journalist from Srinagar, and there was me. We talked, and the interesting part of that conversation was about dialogue, so I said: 'Salahuddin Saheb should also think about dialogue.'

In response, he said: 'Hamare liye toh table pe jagah hi nahin hain.'

I assured him there was space at the negotiating table for him. 'Table pe toh bahut jagah hain, Salahuddin Saheb,' I said. 'Table pe hamesha jagah hoti hain.'

'Lekin hamare se toh koi baat bhi nahin karta,' Salahuddin replied.

So I said: 'Salahuddin Saheb jaante hain baat kaise hoti hai, that's not a big issue.'

And he laughed.

But Salahuddin keeps sending messages. Even now I get messages. There are guys who come to me and say that the fellow wants to come back. And I pass this thing on to the government. I presume someone follows it up, but I have no idea. The thing is really, more than anything, how much clarity, time and effort you are willing to put into an operation like this. Only then will they come to you.

Yet twenty years later, our friend is still there, stranded in Pakistan.

8

'THIS MOVEMENT IS AN EXPERIMENT AND IT WILL PASS': A.G. LONE

Pakistan's failed gamble in Kargil also had an impact on the separatists in Kashmir, as it did with Majid Dar. One such man was Abdul Ghani Lone, the lone veteran politician among the separatists. In the late autumn of 1999, a few months after Kargil, Lone returned from a trip to America, via Dubai, a changed man. In Dubai, he had a meeting with the ISI's number two man, Maj. Gen. Jamshed Gulzar Kayani. Lone told Major General Kayani: 'It is time for a dignified exit for Kashmiris', from their movement.

The ISI official was dismissive, as ISI officials always were—they never wanted to hear what the Kashmiris thought, they only wanted their plans executed—and so when Lone returned to India, I sought him out.

It might surprise a lot of people but when I spent two years in Srinagar on an IB posting from 1988 to 1990 I never got to meet Lone. It was a grave omission because those days we were obsessed with the Farooq–Rajiv relationship and Lone had sidelined himself from the mainstream. When I thought about it later on I asked myself what the hell I was doing in

Srinagar. In all honesty, at that point I was spending most of my time with Farooq Abdullah, the National Conference and the Congress, and one didn't move very much beyond that. It was also my brief from my then boss, M.K. Narayanan, to keep Farooq on the right side of Delhi so a lot of focus went there.

It took me maybe five years to understand that the business of Kashmir is much bigger, that it is not just the Abdullahs—though they are key to the whole thing—and that there is more to it.

There had been opportunities to meet Lone Saheb. In Srinagar there was a business community of Punjabis—not just Sikhs, but Hindus as well—who left along with the Kashmiri Pandits in the exodus of 1990. Being a Punjabi I had friends in this group. Some would say, 'Do you know Lone Saheb?'

'No, I don't.'

'Aap hamare saath taash khelo, Lone Saheb taash ke bahut shaukeen hain.'

'What does he play?' I asked.

'He plays rummy with us.'

Obviously, Lone was fond of gambling.

The fact of the matter was that Lone Saheb was a proud Kashmiri of humble origins, and at heart he was a liberal—as were many Kashmiris of that era. He liked his drink, he used to go to Srinagar Club, and he played cards with his Punjabi friends. There was an inspector-general of police in J&K, Amar Kapoor, who died in service of a heart attack and he was a buddy of Lone's.

In fact, someone suggested that at one time Lone might have been an atheist and a communist. While researching this book, I met an expatriate Kashmiri in London, an educationist named Abdullah Raina, about whom there is more in the next chapter. Raina said that there used to be something in Kashmir called the 'No God Federation', and that Lone Saheb was a member.

I checked with Lone's son Sajad about this, and he claimed that this was just a lot of Jamaati propaganda. 'Was there such a thing?' I asked.

'Yeah,' Sajad said. 'It was talked about, but Dad was not a part of it. He was not an unbeliever.'

'All right,' I said. 'Was he a leftist or a rightist?'

'Yeah,' Sajjad said. 'He was a leftist, he was a socialist.'

As Raina put it, Lone was a different type of person from what he became and what many think he was. He started his innings long ago; born in a village in Kupwara in May 1932, Lone obtained a law degree from Aligarh Muslim University, and it was during his early days as a lawyer that he was drawn into politics. As he told Pakistan's *Newsline* magazine in an interview in 2001 (published after his death in 2002), there was a judge in whose court in Handwara he argued many cases; that judge drew him aside one day and said: 'If MLAs are trying to intervene in cases, it is due partly to the fact that there is no one to oppose them. You are the first person from your area to have educated himself. You are an advocate now. You must come to the rescue of your people.'

Lone thus joined G.M. Sadiq's Democratic National Council. Sadiq was to become the last prime minister of Kashmir, and the first chief minister, heading a Congress party government from 1965 till his death in December 1971. He was a Marxist with a reputation for honesty, which was a rare quality in public life. Lone was impressed with Sadiq's honesty and his argument that it was futile to fight the mighty government of India. 'Instead, he argued that we should become part of the system and persuade India to recognise that people in Kashmir cannot be ruled by force,' Lone later said.

Lone joined the Indian National Congress, and entered the J&K assembly in 1967, when Sadiq was the Congress chief minister, and two years later was made a junior minister. Many Kashmiris blame Sadiq for the erosion in Kashmir's autonomy; and even Lone (much later) blamed his former mentor: 'In 1964 the biggest blow to our autonomy occurred during Sadiq's government.' The big blow was the change in nomenclature, from prime minister to chief minister, and from Sadr-e-Riyasat to governor. Sadiq also enacted laws that circumvented the Article 370, which served as a bridge between J&K's autonomy and the Indian Constitution.

Ironically, Raina told me that when Lone was the state's health and education minister under Sadiq's successor as chief minister, Syed Mir Qasim, in 1972, he went to Bombay and apparently said that Article 370 was an emotional barrier between J&K and the country, and should be abrogated. (This was reported in *Current*, the periodical run by D.F. Karaka.)

Again, I checked this with Sajad, who said his father might have been misquoted; that he might have said something like 'Throw it in the sea' or 'To hell with it', etc. Interestingly, Sajad did not say that this episode did not happen.

In 1973, Lone left Mir Qasim's cabinet. 'I finally came to the conclusion that the system was trying to cow me down, that I couldn't contribute anything to my cause,' he told *Newsline* magazine many years later. 'I believed then, as I do now, that India cannot retain this territory by force. If India had any chance to retain Kashmir, then India would have to convince the people.'

Then came the 1975 accord between Sheikh Abdullah and Prime Minister Indira Gandhi, and Sheikh Saheb took over the J&K government from the Congress. Though Lone was still in the Congress, Sheikh Saheb took him in 'as a special talent'. Lone believed that the Sher-e-Kashmir could convince his people to leave behind their reservations about joining India. However, he also believed Mrs Gandhi would never give Sheikh Saheb a free hand to rule, so in 1976 he issued a statement saying Mrs Gandhi ought to detach herself from the local Congress party, and allow it to join the National Conference, to strengthen Sheikh Abdullah's hands. For this, he was expelled from the Congress.

Lone was still part of the NC but 'came to the conclusion that the old man didn't have the guts and courage to do anything', as he put it with reference to Sheikh Abdullah, in the same interview. 'He had lost his fire. He was now rather afraid of New Delhi. After being in jail so long, he was also under pressure from his family at the time.' Lone parted ways with the NC and fought the 1977 assembly election on a Janata Party ticket. He won. However, in 1978 he left the Janata Party and founded the People's Conference (PC), dedicated to the restoration of 'internal autonomy' in Kashmir.

To be fair to Lone, any outsider who has joined the National Conference has not found it easy to survive there, as we saw with Firdous Syed in chapter five. As Nizamuddin Bhat, an MLA from Bandipore, put it: 'Lone joined the main provision store with great fanfare but ultimately had to set up a grocery store across the road, the People's Conference.'

Though Lone was busy with the PC, he came back into the limelight following the 1984 dismissal of Chief Minister Farooq Abdullah by Jagmohan on the orders of Mrs Gandhi. Farooq's replacement (and brother-in-law) G.M. Shah, who split the NC but was looking for further support in the assembly, offered Lone the post of deputy chief minister.

Lone refused. To him, this whole episode was 'anti-people'. Not surprisingly, during the next two years, Lone and Farooq grew closer and stuck together, to the extent that Farooq's mother, Begum Abdullah, once publicly said, 'They are my two sons.' This bonhomie lasted until the end of 1986, when Farooq and the then prime minister, Rajiv Gandhi, entered into a political accord. It was a big disappointment for Lone, and he and Farooq parted company.

Gradually at this point, as Kashmir drifted towards separatism, so did Lone. He and his party would still be part of the political mainstream over the next two years, contesting the 1987 election to the 87-seat assembly. At that time, Farooq Abdullah joined hands with the then Mirwaiz, Moulvi

Mohammed Farooq (father of the current Mirwaiz), in what was known as the 'Double Farooq' accord. The two Farooqs wanted to rope Lone into this, and Mirwaiz Moulvi Farooq even suggested to Lone that if their parties, the PC and the Awami Action Committee (AAC), joined hands, they could be to the Congress-NC what the RSS was to the BJP.

In desperation, Mirwaiz Moulvi Farooq even suggested to Farooq Abdullah that Lone be taken back into the NC and be appointed general secretary. To which Farooq said: 'I agree, Lone will make an excellent general secretary, but who will control Lone?'

Lone was also offered a part in the MUF, the opposition combine that took on the NC–Congress in the 1987 election, and which won four seats amid the charges against the ruling parties of rigging. Lone did not join the MUF, since they could not reach an agreement on the number of seats he would contest. Hence the PC contested on its own, and did not win any seats. Lone later said that had they reached an agreement on seats, the MUF–PC would have won twenty seats despite the rigging. In the event, militancy began and the Kashmir movement gathered momentum, and Lone's involvement in separatism deepened.

His house became a hiding place. One young militant, Yasin Malik of the JKLF, used to visit him frequently. In fact, Yasin, who was wanted for the murder of four Indian Air Force personnel, among others, was finally arrested in August 1990 from the house of Zahoor Watali. Zahoor was the brother of A.M. Watali, the DIG whose house was attacked in one of the first militant events, in September 1988. Zahoor came from the same village as Lone; their families were close; and Zahoor was Lone's man Friday—and his contact with the ISI.

The violence and street demonstrations had taken centre stage in 1990, and in that brief span that Jagmohan was governor, during his second tenure there was a general sweep of separatist politicians including former members of the MUF

such as Syed Ali Shah Geelani and Prof. Abdul Gani Bhat. Lone
was arrested in March 1990, and was in jail for over two years.
He was released in the late summer of 1992, and upon release
he had a brainwave: of setting up a conglomeration of all
separatist outfits, which would be called the All Party Hurriyat
Conference, Hurriyat meaning freedom.

He discussed the idea with the ISI. After his release in 1992,
he travelled to Saudi Arabia, where he met a Brigadier Saleem
and broached the idea. It was not a very pleasant encounter.
'I'm not used to interacting with people in uniform,' Lone told
Brigadier Saleem. 'I've been a minister in Kashmir, we've had a
democratic system there, however flawed.'

'You'd better get used to meeting people in uniform,'
Brigadier Saleem said. 'Because we call the shots.'

Lone's relationship with the ISI would always be rough.

Lone rose to his highest prominence in the Hurriyat. He was
the one true politician in the Hurriyat, and the rest of the
Hurriyat leadership envied him for his political skills and
sagacity. Since it included nearly thirty outfits with differing
aims—some were for independence, some were for accession to
Pakistan, and some even wanted Kashmir to join a global
caliphate—Lone suggested that as a first step they put aside
their differing aims and focus on the basic issue: that Kashmir
was a disputed territory. 'Let us first persuade the Indians that
they should concede that Kashmir is a disputed territory and its
future is yet to be decided,' Lone told his colleagues. 'Once they
do it, then comes the question of how we will solve the issue of
this disputed territory.'

The only other person who had long political experience,
though he always operated from the margins, was Syed Ali
Shah Geelani. Not surprisingly, when the Hurriyat was formed,
and during the early years, the two of them were close. It was
only over time that they developed acute differences: Geelani
insisted their movement was a religious movement, whereas
Lone would say, no, it was a political movement.

Indeed, when the Lashkar-e-Toiba business began in a big way, people like Geelani used to say, 'Yeh hamare mehmaan hain.'

'They are not our guests, these Taliban and all,' Lone would respond. 'We don't want them here, they're not our guests, people coming here and killing Kashmiris.'

This was a sore point between the two.

When the 1996 assembly election was announced after a long spell of governor's rule, Lone probably felt that separatist politics was what would still dominate in Kashmir. People like Muzaffar Hussain Baig, who was the state's advocate general in the late 1980s (and who would in 2002 join the People's Democratic Party and become the deputy chief minister) joined Lone's party, the People's Conference. Lone's impression was probably reinforced by the fact that the National Conference, which had been targeted by militants in 1990, was invisible. So he approached Farooq to urge him not to participate in elections.

Farooq was apologetic. 'Can't back out,' he told Lone. 'I've given Delhi my word.'

And as our friend in Pakistan, Irshad Malik, later told me, the 1996 election was a masterstroke that broke the back of militancy. Had Farooq not agreed to participate—had the election not been held—militancy would have continued another ten years, perhaps. (This was not the same, however, as saying that Kashmiris were politically satisfied.) As it was, militants were coming out from the cold, Kashmiris were going to elected politicians to sort out their daily complaints. And then, of course, the Kargil war happened, which was a big jolt to Kashmiris both in Pakistan and at home, for there seemed to be a misalignment between Pakistan and the one country that could make things happen, the USA.

Lone went on a long trip in 1999 and he visited America. He returned in November, around Diwali, and then made a couple of statements that sounded pretty reasonable. The Americans had probably made it clear to him that the militancy was bunkum and that they weren't going to support it any more.

Lone was crucial in the Hurriyat if we wanted to move forward politically with the separatists. Therefore, when he began speaking reasonably, it looked like a great opportunity. It was time to reach out to him.

I had met Lone in jail several years back, but that's never the same thing. Frankly, I didn't know him then, and he may not have even remembered my face. So I told one of our officers, a tall fellow, 'Go pick up Lone Saheb and bring him here.'

'How?' the officer asked.

'What are you asking me how, you know where he lives, go get him.'

So the officer went with a basket of fruit to Lone and said, 'Saheb wants to meet you.'

Lone was a smart guy. He understood.

In the beginning, I would talk to him, but he said nothing. Zero. He probably didn't trust me, as I was the R&AW chief.

Lone gradually opened up, but even then he spoke little: very measured, few words, but everything he said was meaningful. He was a typical politician, the only one among these separatists. He was a bit like Vajpayee; Vajpayee used to speak even less. He understood politics. In Kashmir he was regarded as one of the smarter politicians, maybe the smartest after Farooq; maybe even smarter. He was in that league.

Nonetheless, he responded positively, and we continued a dialogue, right until the end in 2002. He would talk about politics and the movement and dialogue. He was quite happy talking. He was honest enough to acknowledge that the gun had ultimately failed, and that Kashmiris needed to move on. Lone was totally fed up with Pakistan.

One of the interesting things Lone said was that he thought the movement was a sort of an experiment, and that he didn't expect too much from it though Kashmiris would emerge wiser out of it. It was a fascinating insight, I felt.

One day in November 2000, Lone visited and said: 'I want a passport, I want to go to Pakistan.'

'Lone wants a passport,' I told Brajesh Mishra. 'De dijiye, kya hai.'

He got his passport within two days.

Lone needed a passport because he had fixed the marriage of his son Sajad, then a businessman in Dubai, to Asma, the only daughter of the JKLF chairman, Amanullah Khan. It was a big deal in Pakistan, as it involved the coming together of two political families, and it was well attended by VIPs. It was also the focus of the international media because on 19 November, the first day of the wedding when a 'rukhsati' was hosted by Amanullah Khan in Rawalpindi, Prime Minister Vajpayee announced a unilateral ceasefire for Ramzan, to begin from 26 November. Lone hosted a reception the next day, in Islamabad, where this ceasefire was the talk among the guests.

A few days later, Lone met Pakistan's chief executive, Gen. Pervez Musharraf. The General asked him, 'How are things in Kashmir?'

'Don't worry about Kashmir, look after Pakistan,' Lone apparently replied. 'Your radicals will bite the hand that feeds them.'

Musharraf responded by laughing.

Years later, in the interview to *Newsline* magazine mentioned earlier in the chapter, Lone recalled his meeting with Musharraf. 'We spent more than an hour and a half together,' Lone said. 'He was interested in discussing Vajpayee's announcement and whether India was open to genuine dialogue. I think it is unfortunate that Musharraf came to power as a military dictator . . . if the Indians cooperate, Musharraf is still the best man on the Pakistani side with whom the Indians can deal on Kashmir. He is a practical man. He can reach a settlement on Kashmir.' This is what every Kashmiri leader except Geelani but including Omar Abdullah, who met Musharraf, was to say.

It is very significant that Lone came to the conclusion that Musharraf could have settled with India on Kashmir, while we in government were still wondering whether or not to trust this soldier. Years later, in 2014, while addressing his last press conference as prime minister, Dr Manmohan Singh would bemoan the fact that they had almost clinched a deal.

Lone also spoke to Musharraf about 'ownership' of the Kashmir issue. 'We said to the Pakistanis that they should try their level best to help Kashmir get out from being an Indian possession, but in doing so they should not express a preference for any option,' Lone said. 'Otherwise, they would create problems for our freedom struggle.'

In fact, Lone went to the dinner party hosted in his honour by the Jamaat-e-Islami in PoK, where he asked the Pakistanis if they had a hidden agenda. 'Would you also like to take us over and occupy our land?' he asked. He explained that his question was in relation to the ceasefire offered by Vajpayee, to which Kashmiris had to have their own response. It was also related to foreign militants: 'They are welcome so long as they come to help us,' Lone said. 'But they must not take up the role of the "owners" of the movement.'

One group of folks who probably did not like his questions was the ISI. As it was, it was annoyed with the way he was cold-shouldering the outfit.

For instance, ISI chief General Mahmud invited Lone for dinner. Lone dilly-dallied and then finally he did not go. It was a rebuff the ISI did not forget. In fact, the ISI began to believe that Sajad was the evil influence on his father; that maybe Sajad was in contact with the Indians. For his part, the elder Lone thought that Mahmud was too much of a hawk, and said the ISI chief was 'cracked'. After retirement, Mahmud grew a beard and joined the Tabligh Jamaat. A colleague of his described him as a gone case.

That was not the last time that Lone met Musharraf; the General, who was now president, held a tea party for the Hurriyat leaders in New Delhi, while he was on his way to Agra for a summit with Prime Minister Vajpayee in July 2001.

At the party, Lone is supposed to have said: 'We're tired, we're exhausted, we can't carry on like this. You're only getting Kashmiris killed.'

To which Geelani objected. 'We're not tired, we will never be tired,' he said. Everyone stared at Geelani, and what he was implying: that Kashmiris should continue to get killed.

By the time the Agra summit happened, I had already shifted to the PMO. My brief was no longer external intelligence, and when I asked for the agenda I was told it was Kashmir but in particular the 2002 assembly election. Since I had a lot of time at the PMO I was meeting Lone more and more, and I spoke to him about the coming election.

'Yes, I understand that elections are important,' he said. The 1996 poll was a clear example.

'Look,' I said. 'The PM wants totally free and fair elections.'

'Yes,' he said. 'Free and fair. It is the right way forward.'

It got to a point where I said, 'Will you help us?'

'How?' he asked.

'You could contest,' I said.

'My time is over, but I will help you,' he said. 'Don't ask how, let the time come.'

Now there are people who think that Lone was looking to participate in the 2002 election; that he wanted to be chief minister; and that he was shot dead because the Pakistanis thought he might participate in elections. It is a lot of bunkum. He never, ever gave any indication that he wanted to participate. The notion that he wanted to be chief minister is also silly; as no one, not least Mufti Sayeed (who got the job), thought that anyone other than Farooq Abdullah would become chief minister.

What he would say is that for elections, we would have to look for younger people; 'I'm too far gone now,' were his words. He was hinting at the next generation, and also at Mirwaiz Umar Farooq, then the head of the Hurriyat.

Lone felt that he had been through too much. He would turn seventy that year, and after all that he had stood for and spoken against, to be part of an election would be a total turnaround, which, at this stage, he could not do. He was willing to help in the democratic process, but without getting involved. 'I'm with you,' he'd tell me. 'This is a good idea and we will help you indirectly.'

The other thing was that he was thinking of his political legacy. He had a daughter, Shabnam, and two sons, Bilal and Sajad. Shabnam was the brightest of them; Bilal was an easy-going fellow who liked his golf; and Sajad was making merry in Dubai, possibly working in a disco. Lone decided it was going to be Sajad who would carry his legacy forward. Lone would hint this and say, 'You guys should look after him.' Perhaps he had a premonition of the threat to him, and worried.

Lone was fond of his daughter, for she was a lawyer, she was working, she was serious, and she had political ambitions; quite a contrast to the boys who were having a good time. The problem was Shabnam's lifestyle choice, and Lone, despite his liberalism, was quite upset with it. She had a relationship that Lone opposed and they had a tiff, after which she left.

Bilal, who is happily married, was not ambitious; he was happy being a part of the moderate Hurriyat after his father's death. It was a division that the family decided after Lone's death, that Bilal would be inside the Hurriyat and Sajad would stay out and take care of the party. That is where his father left him, and that is where he has continued. It's a fair distribution of labour because in the Hurriyat you just need to be there and attend meetings, but if someone is to move the party forward then that man is Sajad. Hence, he got his father's political legacy.

By March-April of 2002, Chief Minister Farooq Abdullah

got wind of Lone's contact with the PMO, and it worried him. During this period he sought Lone out.

'I have no objection to Hurriyat participation in the election,' Farooq said to me. 'Why doesn't Lone join us, we'll take him willingly.'

This was quite a turnaround from his reaction to Mirwaiz Moulvi Farooq's suggestion to take Lone in the NC as general secretary; obviously Lone's contacts with the government of India disturbed Farooq. It is said they held a secret meeting at a rest house in Kokernag. Sadly, soon after, Lone was killed. Politically, Lone and Farooq were made for each other but unfortunately they never stayed together long. However, there was sufficient mutual regard. In early 1990, when reports were filtering in that militants were taking shelter in Lone's residence in Srinagar, I approached my colleague M.N. Sabharwal and suggested we raid Lone's place. Sabharwal, who then understood the dynamics of Kashmir better than me, said, 'Relax. I will need to consult Doctor Saheb.' He never got back to me.

Lone tried to convince the Hurriyat of the relevance of the election. He told them that militancy had a limited shelf-life which was long over. Yet he could not convince them. First, because they were well-behaved ISI followers who did not step out of line. Second, as Lone called them, they were like the nawabs of Oudh who depleted their wealth yet carried on like royalty; the Hurriyat had also got what they could out of militancy till there was nothing left, and yet they carried on. The Hurriyat argued back that election was a flawed idea which would only make them part of the Indian system. The Hurriyat was not convinced.

Then there was the new force of the PDP, led by Lone's old colleague and friend, Mufti Sayeed. They grew together under Sadiq and Mir Qasim, and both were ministers in the latter's cabinet. According to Sajad, however, Mufti was Lone's friend, but Lone never trusted Mufti. The elder Lone, in fact, considered Farooq ten times more reliable.

Mufti wanted a tie-up between the PDP and the PC, as the parties had complementary influence: Lone held sway in the Kupwara–Baramulla belt in north Kashmir, while Mufti's stronghold was south Kashmir. Yet it never materialised. In fact, after Mufti took over as chief minister, he offered Sajad a ministership if he joined the PDP–Congress government, but Sajad turned down the offer.

And then Lone met the ISI for the final time, in April 2002.

On 18 April, Lone accompanied Asma, his daughter-in-law, to Dubai as she was going home to Pakistan and at the time there were no direct flights from India. Also en route to Dubai were his man Friday, Zahoor Watali, and Mirwaiz Umar Farooq. In Dubai they met Sardar Abdul Qayoom Khan of PoK; Ghulam Nabi Fai, the ISI's Kashmiri in Washington, DC; and Syed Nazir Gilani, heading a British NGO called J&K Council for Human Rights; all of whom were there to attend a Kashmir Peace Conference of those who wished to end the violence and resolve the dispute politically. In fact, at the meeting, Lone asked Sardar Qayoom to urgently request the Pakistan government to withdraw jehadi groups from Kashmir.

He also took the opportunity to meet the new ISI chief, Lt. Gen. Ehsanul Haq. His family was against his meeting the ISI, as they felt he was walking into a trap.

Nonetheless Lone went, and at this meeting complained against the Hurriyat's political handler, Brigadier Abdullah, which is an old and popular cover name for ISI officials. As mentioned in the chapter with Firdous Syed, the ISI used to handle Kashmir with a military wing and a political wing, each headed by a brigadier. Lone had a problem with his particular Abdullah.

'Lone Saheb, we will change him immediately,' Lt. Gen. Ehsan said.

The new political handler was the military attache at the Pakistan High Commission in New Delhi, Javed Aziz Khan, and he was given the code name of Brigadier Rathore. (Now retired, he continues to advise the Pakistan government on Kashmir.)

Brigadier Abdullah apparently did not take kindly to being shunted out. He may have ordered the hit on Lone, and it was possibly not a conscious decision by the ISI chief.

As it was, Lone's encounters with the ISI were never really good due to his allergy to the military. Even talking to the ISI was like banging your head against the wall: the officers would listen to your every argument, would smile, nod, and then go back to what they originally said.

Thus, going to Dubai was Lone's fatal mistake. In Pakistani eyes, he was too much of an Indian, too far gone. The ISI more than anything dreaded the general mainstreaming of Kashmiris, led by Lone.

Lone had spent about a week in Dubai. From there he went to London, where he spent two days, and on to Washington, DC, where he met National Security Advisor Condoleezza Rice; Fai was also at this meeting. In fact, Lone handed Rice a note on Kashmir. His wife Hanefa and Bilal joined him in Washington.

Lone then returned via the east, as he wanted to show Hanefa around Singapore. He travelled to Kuala Lumpur, from where he was to go to Singapore, and stayed the night, but he then got an urgent summons from Mirwaiz Umar Farooq. The young Mirwaiz wanted Lone to cut short his visit and attend the twelfth anniversary of the assassination of his father, Mirwaiz Moulvi Farooq.

So the Lones never went to Singapore. Instead, on 18 May, they arrived in Delhi, and on 20 May they reached Srinagar.

The next afternoon, according to his driver Rashid, Lone said his afternoon namaaz, left his home in Sanat Nagar, and at around 2:15 p.m. arrived at the Idgah for the 'barsi'. The rest of the Hurriyat leadership except for Geelani was already on the dais: Mirwaiz Umar Farooq, Professor Abdul Ghani Bhat, and Moulvi Abbas Ansari. They all made speeches, and the unusual thing that day was Lone did not make a speech. In between every speech, a group of boys in the crowd would shout pro-Pakistan slogans.

The last speech was by the Mirwaiz. As he wound up, at around 4:30 p.m., someone started shouting something about a grenade.

The leaders decided to exit, and as Lone was descending from the stage, about twenty shots rang out.

The crowd ran helter-skelter, so no one could get a look at who the gunmen were. Rashid, who had parked Lone's car about 60 yards away and had a view of the stage, pushed through the pandemonium, but by the time he reached Lone, he was dead.

Lone's two PSOs had also been shot. Though Lone had been shot multiple times from the front, the PSO who died had been shot from the back. The other PSO was taken to hospital.

Driver Rashid loaded the two bodies and took them to Sanat Nagar. When he reached, Lone's wife was on the first floor; she ran downstairs and began weeping. Neighbours and local shopkeepers also came. Abdul Ghani Lone was no more.

Sajad was overcome. As he later wrote in a local newspaper: '[I] lifted the shroud and there he was—my Dad—lifeless, stone cold, eyes closed, hair curled back, in a state of eternal slumber. My Dad's journey of life had ended.' He went ahead and named the killers. 'I was filled with anger and out from my mouth came the infamous statement blaming the ISI for my father's killing. I was unmindful of the TV crews and their cameras. And in the evening it was across all the TV screens.'

And when Geelani came to Lone's place, Sajad told him to get out.

Then Sajad's mother, Hanefa, took him aside. 'I've lost my husband, I don't want to lose my son,' she said. 'I will not allow a second dead body with bullets in this house. Calm down.'

Hanefa told her son to retract his charge against the ISI, which he did. The next day Geelani was allowed to participate in the funeral procession. A few days later Sajad wrote an article in which he said, 'even grieving is dangerous in Kashmir because it can lead to further loss', explaining why he backtracked. Yet it never left Sajad's mind. He wrote an article in the *Tribune* on 29 December 2011 titled 'In the Land of the Mutes', in which he wrote: 'Death comes in multiple ways, and so does mourning, thanks to the leaders who have managed to learn to extract profit from the enterprise.' It was clearly a reference to Geelani.

Prime Minister Vajpayee gave a statement saying that Lone was killed because he was working for peace, and that his killing was a setback to that process.

You may recall Mohammed Sayeed Malik, the journalist who was Mufti Sayeed's eyes and ears during the Rubaiya kidnapping. He wrote an obit for Lone, in which he said: 'Lone was martyred for being courageous and forthright. As a statesman he had the vision to move forward rather than being bogged down, not marking time. Unfortunately we are caught in an agony in which no one knows who killed who.

'The monster of death has haunted Kashmir for so long . . . We have suffered a lot and continue to suffer. Kashmiris are still in doubt whether the killer is dead or roaming about. Unless Kashmiris think independently there is no hope of moving forward. This is what Lone taught Kashmiris.'

One of the ironic fallouts of Lone's assassination is that once he had said that the Hurriyat would break over his dead body; and a year after he died, it broke.

The ISI used to credit R&AW with splitting the Hurriyat, but actually it was the ISI which split the Hurriyat, for it wanted to build Geelani up. A further irony is that in 2014, the ISI was still trying to get the three Hurriyat factions to re-unite, but that looked unlikely, as the moderate Hurriyat people are not too enamoured with Geelani.

In his interview to *Newsline* magazine, which was published after his killing, Lone had spoken of the need for the government to engage the Hurriyat: 'On one side there is the APHC that says that Kashmir is a disputed territory . . . On the other side is the Indian government that says: "Kashmir is an integral part of India and accession is final." . . . The APHC reflects the view of the main political forces in Kashmir that differ with India on these crucial questions. Therefore, the APHC and the government of India are the two main parties that face each other. So, if there is to be a dialogue to narrow down the differences or to find a solution, it must be the Hurriyat and the government of India that enter into discussions.'

In the end, when the Hurriyat began talking to the government—to Deputy Prime Minister L.K. Advani—it just followed what Lone suggested earlier.

As for the People's Conference, there were a lot of people who were close to Lone but who drifted away because they didn't know how to deal with Sajad's huge ego. He's in a hurry to be chief minister, and like other youngsters in Kashmir, he doesn't like to sit and listen to advice. He has a political legacy and a future. Following his much publicised meeting with Prime Minister Modi, Sajad has arrived on centre court. Now it is up to him to demonstrate his mettle; whether he has it in him to reach the top. It will also make Bilal wonder where he stands now. One day Sajad visited and I asked about his friends. 'I have two handlers, both of whom are in touch with Pakistan,' he said casually. 'One has joined the NC, the other has joined the PDP.'

According to Sajad, his father realised that Kashmiris had a duality of temperament, in that each would say one thing to you and something else to another person. In that, Abdul Ghani Lone believed that the Kashmiris' worst enemy was the Kashmiris themselves.

There exists a threat to Sajad, to Bilal, and to others. Lone's killing was one of many in the 'dirty war' that Pakistan waged in Kashmir—that some officers were tempted to retaliate to, as I will mention in the next chapter. Take Mirwaiz Moulvi

Farooq, whose barsi Lone was killed at; or Majid Dar, who was killed after Lone, but delayed only because the reaction to Lone's killing was far stronger than the ISI anticipated.

Or the killing of Hurriyat leader Prof. Abdul Ghani Bhat's brother; this deeply alienated Prof. Bhat from Geelani. Indeed, Geelani began to be called Amir-e-Jehad; some began to call him Bub Jehad. Kashmiris used to call Sheikh Saheb Bub, which translates to Dad.

9

SPY Vs. SPY

The one person I never met while I was R&AW chief was my Pakistani counterpart, the ISI chief, a position held by two successive people during my tenure: Gen. Ziauddin Butt and General Mahmud, who was burned by the fact that in 2000 we turned Majid Dar around. It's not that I was overly keen to meet the ISI chief, but it is strange that I met the CIA chief, the Mossad chief, the Russian intelligence service chief—and even the inscrutable head of the Chinese secret service.

Meeting other chiefs was a part of the job. One needed to maintain liaison with other services. What didn't make sense was never liaising with the ISI chief. The CIA and the KGB never stopped talking to each other even during the worst days of the Cold War; it is documented that during the Cuban missile crisis at the height of the Cold War, US president John F. Kennedy and Soviet premier Nikita Khrushchev were writing and talking to one another. Whereas we, at the drop of a hat, stop talking to the Pakistanis.

After I left the government altogether I continued to advocate this in the various track two dialogues between India and Pakistan that I joined (these are non-official meetings of retired

With President Zail Singh at my son Arjun's wedding in 1994. I was deputed to accompany him on his trips abroad from 1982 to 1987. It was a great learning experience.

With the feisty Farooq Abdullah at the IB centenary celebration in Srinagar in October 1988. On my left is M.K. Narayanan, Director Intelligence Bureau from 1987 to 1990. He was my mentor and boss at the IB.

Receiving the President's
Police Medal from PM
P.V. Narasimha Rao.

A rare photograph of
then IB and R&AW chiefs,
Shyamal Datta and I, at
the PM's residence during
the most crucial day
of the Kandahar crisis,
30 December 1999.

With Dr Farooq Abdullah and my wife Paran at our 25th wedding anniversary in December 1991.

Shabir Shah and Ghulam Hassan Mir with Yousuf Tarigami, the lone CPM MLA from Kashmir, and I as onlookers at Junaid Qureshi's wedding.

With Prime Minister
Atal Bihari Vajpayee at
the R&AW headquarters
in 2000.

Vajpayee's entry
in the visitors'
book at the
Minar-e-Pakistan
created much
goodwill and
euphoria.

With CIA chief
George Tenet in
Agra, June 2000.

With Director Louis Freeh at the FBI headquarters, working out counter-terrorism cooperation, September 2000.

With Deputy Prime Minister L.K. Advani during a conference of police chiefs.

Majid Dar's interlocutors led by Fazl Haq Qureshi with Union Home Secretary Kamal Pande and senior officials of the MHA, Srinagar, 3 August 2000.

The Mirwaiz leaving the PM's residence after talks in 2004.

With former ISI chief Asad Durrani during one of our many 'happy hours' in a track two meeting in Istanbul, October 2014.

With the King
of Bhutan, Jigme
Singye Wangchuck,
in Thimphu,
October 1999.

Brajesh Mishra was
principal secretary
and national security
advisor to Vajpayee,
making him one of
the country's most
powerful bureaucrats
ever. He was also a great
person to work with.

Rajesh Pilot at
my son Arjun's
wedding. Pilot was
a dynamic minister
and proactive on
Kashmir.

At the track two meetings in Lahore (above) and Bangkok (below) in January-February 2010. In no particular order, among the prominent personalities at the meetings were: (above) Shaharyar Khan, former foreign secretary of Pakistan; Babar Ali, prominent Pakistani businessman and philanthropist; Bharat Bhushan, senior Indian journalist; Gen. Mahmud Durrani, former national security advisor of Pakistan; Salman Haider, former Indian foreign secretary; Mani Shankar Aiyar, politician and former diplomat; Suhasini Haider, senior journalist; (below) Humayun Khan and Aziz Ahmed Khan, former Pakistani high commissioners to India; G. Parthasarathy, former Indian high commissioner to Pakistan; Sherry Rehman, Pakistan Peoples Party leader and later ambassador to the US; Gen. Ehsan-ul-Haq, former ISI chief; Vikram Sood, former R&AW chief; and Sagarika Ghose, senior journalist.

soldiers, academics, bureaucrats, journalists and others which help in generating out-of-the-box ideas to better bilateral relations that can't otherwise be taken up at official meetings). It wasn't as if a R&AW chief had never met the ISI chief—in the late 1980s, one of my predecessors, A.K. Verma, had two meetings with his counterpart, Lt. Gen. Hamid Gul. Thus it wasn't a heretical idea, and could hold some benefits. I even wrote a paper about it with former ISI chief Lt. Gen. Asad Durrani, whom I often met at meetings of retired intelligence chiefs.

The Pakistanis have been keen to meet. During my tenure at R&AW, we used to forever be getting these messages from friendly intelligence agencies: why don't you meet the Pakistanis, they are keen to meet. Sometimes we would hear it from the Saudis; sometimes from the Iranians; and sometimes from the Sri Lankans. And once, someone even as innocuous as the South Africans said: why don't you and the Pakistanis talk? The thing was, the Americans and the British would stay out of all of this though they were the ones who actually wanted this meeting of the secret services. It must have been one of their ways of trying to get things going.

One day I went and told the national security advisor. 'Sir, yeh messages aate rehte hain,' I said. 'Mil ke toh dekhte hain, isme harz kya hai. Dekh hi le.'

'Nahin-nahin,' Brajesh Mishra responded. 'Abhi time theek nahin hain.'

Perhaps he thought I wasn't hawkish enough to be talking to the Pakistanis.

Eventually, the R&AW chief was dispatched to meet the ISI chief to firm up details for the ceasefire that Pakistan announced in November 2003; C.D. Sahay and Ehsanul Haq met in July–August of that year, and according to Sahay, it really helped the situation in Kashmir as infiltration plummeted in October 2003; along with the successful and fair 2002 assembly election in J&K, it led to the deputy prime minister starting a dialogue with the separatists in January 2004. The ISI also acknowledges that timely intelligence provided by R&AW about a likely Jaish-e-Mohammed attack may have saved President Musharraf's life in 2004. Musharraf himself is said to have acknowledged it. Incidentally, two of the Jaish militants involved were hanged in Pakistan after the attack in a Peshawar school in December 2014. And there was another meeting, between Sahay's successor P.K. Hormis Tharakan and his counterpart Ashfaq Pervez Kayani, who later became the army chief.

Letting the R&AW chief and the ISI chief meet is an idea that makes sense. There's no question of a hidden agenda, and in any case we know each other's agenda—it is simply each other. From the Pakistani point of view, if the intelligence chiefs meet then the leaders can also meet; the army chiefs could meet and then you could have a summit meeting, for one thing follows another.

Also, if I go by Asad Durrani's way of thinking—which is how intelligence people think—then intelligence chiefs can do so much for their governments and their leaders which can remain non-attributable. It always helps the political process.

In fact, making one of R&AW's Islamabad posts an open post on a reciprocal basis would be a good idea.

An open post is one where the host country knows you're an intelligence man and that you're there for cooperation and collaboration. As opposed to the open post, of course, is the undercover posting, which is supposed to be secret and unannounced. In New Delhi, the CIA has an open post, as does the British MI6; their representatives interact with our agency people here. We have open posts in Washington, DC, in Moscow, in New York and in Paris.

Yes, Paris sounds odd since there isn't much to do there, and there was a move in my time to give it up. We had been asking for more undercover posts, and the geniuses at the Ministry of External Affairs said if you want any new posts you'll have to cut down on existing ones. One of our bright guys suggested we give up Paris. Though I had never served in Paris and was leaving the organisation in six months, I felt Paris should not be lost; it was a good reward for service rendered to the organisation. And now with the current shift in the global security scenario it would seem the retention of high level intelligence liaison is absolutely essential. However, I was aghast at the suggestion to close down Paris.

Pakistan, on the other hand, is no ball. It's not an easy posting; there is watertight surveillance, much of it open and meant to scare off fellow Pakistanis, even those who just want to socialise. One of our guys—who did good work there—mentioned an incident where he invited several Pakistani acquaintances to lunch at a restaurant in Islamabad. It was a fun lunch, but afterwards when the guests came outside, they found a whole bunch of plainclothes men standing beside their motorcycles, waiting for them; and all of them stood in menacing poses with their arms folded. Each of the guests looked deflated, not looking forward to the prospect of being grilled about their meeting with the Indian.

Many diplomats, including some of ours, have even been physically manhandled by their Pakistani hosts. And to top it all, often the posting has been filled arbitrarily—you just pick somebody and say, go to Islamabad, which led me to suggest that Islamabad should be declared an open post. It would not only make life comfortable for the person posted there but also yield greater output if we were interacting directly with the ISI. Since we don't talk to Pakistan, how can we 'open' anything; the status quo continues. Such is the mindset and obsession with Pakistan that we retract even from so-called ISI agents. This has been an opinion about postings in the recent past, which led me to tell the chief of the moment that the Islamabad posting is a waste and that there should be an open post.

This is something that would be very hard for a lot of people to swallow but let's face it, the most important work R&AW does is in the neighbourhood, besides maintaining its relationships with Washington and Moscow. There is no point in looking at Tokyo or Johannesburg, for instance. And in our neighbourhood our most important relationship, if it were to get started and institutionalised, would be the R&AW–ISI one because it is out of this relationship that you could get positives. Also it would rid us of the 'hauwa' of the ISI. We make it out to be much bigger than it is. As a former militant commander who spent considerable time in Pakistan told me, 'There are some very fine officers in the ISI, but no one of Doval's intellect or C.D. Sahay's operational acumen.' I have found them not very different from us except that they are from the army, which calls the shots in Pakistan, the reason why ISI is called a state within a state. During my visit to Karachi in 2011 a TV channel asked me what I thought of the ISI and I said I would love to be DG ISI.

Other relationships are merely cosmetic. Take the relationship with the CIA, for instance: you meet them, have a meeting where you follow a script saying this is what we are doing, this is what is happening. And they reciprocate with their worldview. But none of it gets you anywhere, because in the end, every country, every agency has its own agenda.

Hence if both India and Pakistan could get past their cynicism and their huge distrust, there's a lot that the two intelligence agencies could do together.

Such is our mindset and obsession with Pakistan that we shy away even from so-called ISI agents; that's what makes handling Kashmir so much more difficult. Their agents should be first targets. Whatever they could do we could do better. We had the upper hand because Kashmir and Kashmiris were a part of India. Even Kashmiris living across have needed our help. Double agents are the best agents; the business of intelligence is about sinners, not saints. And that is where the ISI scores over us professionally; they never give up on a target even if reckoned to be the most Indian. That was how they assiduously pursued Sajad Lone despite his participating in the 2000 elections when

Geelani wanted his party, the People's Conference, boycotted by the Hurriyat. That was how they got Majid Dar's wife to Pakistan despite killing her husband and maiming her for life.

Instead, we have to work through others, like the Americans. In chapter two I mentioned the meeting with CIA chief George Tenet, who was easy to get along with; at a dinner the night he arrived held at my official residence, he knocked back a few glasses of whisky and made a big show of what a pal he was. (He and his wife invited Paran and me to accompany them to the Taj Mahal the next day, in his private jet; we went, but in our own R&AW Gulfstream.) Tenet had come and told me that we needed to check General Musharraf out ourselves, and that Musharraf was somebody with whom you could do business. Remember at that time we still had the bitter aftertaste of Kargil. You could say that this was one of the steps that led to the India–Pakistan summit the following summer at, by coincidence, Agra.

Similarly, we had another American drop in: the head of the CIA's Counter-Terrorism Centre (CTC), Cofer Black. Black was a veteran CIA hand whom al-Qaeda tried to assassinate when he was the head of station in Sudan from 1993 to '95. He was also blamed by the 9/11 Commission for not informing the Federal Bureau of Investigation (FBI) of the entry into the US of two of the plane hijackers, who were under CTC surveillance along with other members of al-Qaeda.

Cofer Black had come to India to visit Brajesh Mishra, and he was passed along to R&AW. We had a formal meeting with some of my guys, during which he asked for a private one-on-one with me. During this chat, he said that his agency was putting heavy pressure on the ISI to reduce the violence. He then said that we, meaning the Indian agencies, had to reciprocate and not indulge in any violence. So I told him: 'Us? We never do such stuff.'

There were several times, though, when we were frustrated with the violence; particularly when we were working out a relationship with someone in Kashmir, and that person would get bumped off by the ISI. It happened with too many Kashmiris, and in the previous chapters I have mentioned Abdul Majid Dar and Abdul Ghani Lone. Each time someone was killed by the Pakistanis there was huge frustration and there were discussions, at times, of the need for a tit-for-tat policy. But it remained only an informal discussion because no government in Delhi would approve of it. That the 'Bub Jihad' is still alive and kicking despite all the mayhem that he has been responsible for is a tribute to our liberal traditions. Whether or not this helped us in Kashmir is a debatable matter. I am of the firm belief it did because, as Mufti said, making Geelani a martyr would be counterproductive. Farooq would have been quite happy and willing to roll him down the Jhelum.

The issue of retaliation came up also in the context of harassment of our diplomats in Islamabad. In early 1990 when there was extreme tension in J&K, both MEA and R&AW favoured more aggressive surveillance of Pakistani diplomats in Delhi. But from the counterintelligence viewpoint it would be counterproductive. Following someone when he knows he is being followed may be a crude deterrent but serves no intelligence purpose. For the same reason I believe making public the taped conversations of Musharraf and Aziz Khan during the Kargil war, whatever political purpose it served, was a mistake. It dried up a crucial channel of information.

Even the talk of killing Dawood Ibrahim—the underworld don who is said to have masterminded the 1993 serial bombings in Mumbai, and who subsequently fled Mumbai and is said to be hiding in Pakistan—has taken place outside of the government and has not been sanctioned by any government of the day.

Hence in Kashmir, although counter-insurgency operations have exacted a heavy toll, and though there are many takers for bumping off unsavoury characters, we have not adopted a policy on extra-judicial executions. As Lone Saheb's son Sajad once said to me in a pique, justifying why it was too risky for a Kashmiri to cooperate with India rather than Pakistan: 'What's the most you can do, throw us in jail? The ISI-walas will shoot us dead.'

That brings up the question that if we didn't have a tit-for-tat policy to kill, then how did we get people on our side. And the simple answer is: selling peace through a sustained dialogue. There is no better way. People may find it difficult to believe that the reputed Mossad chief, Efraim Halevy, who incidentally was my contemporary and whom I met in Tel Aviv in 1999, was a firm votary of dialogue. He understood that the Palestinian militant faction, Hamas, could neither be demolished nor cowed down and that talking was the only way out. That is what some sensible people do and that is what we did: talk, talk and talk almost endlessly. In the end it is all about human relationships; little gestures, like a surprise birthday cake, go a long way in building friendships. Operations require sensitive human judgement and a feel for the quarry.

When I left the government in 2004, once the NDA lost power (I didn't resign due to any political affiliation but due to what I thought was propriety; it will come up later in the book) I was made the villain of the NDA's Kashmir policy by several who thought I was throwing around money too freely, bribing my way through Kashmir. People in the IB, my former organisation, and higher-ups apparently told Kashmiris, 'Dulat has spoilt you.' Maybe. But for more than the last ten years since I left the government, Kashmiri leaders including separatists still visit me regularly when I have little more to offer than tea and sympathy.

Using money to win people over is perhaps the most effective tool at the disposal of intelligence officers not just in Kashmir, and not just all over the subcontinent, but all over the world. Most agents are paid agents. If in Kashmir, for instance, you find someone who is working for the ISI, you just offer a lot more money than it does. Perhaps he will be afraid of getting killed by the ISI but at the very least you have neutralised him. Corrupting a person by giving him money is not only a lot more ethical than killing him, but a lot smarter in the long run. And no one has yet come up with a better way of dealing with Kashmir. Money in Kashmir goes back a long, long way.

The most important R&AW posts, apart from Islamabad, are basically tourist spots in the east and west where money and secrets frequently change hands. On a visit to an important North African country in the summer of 2000, the intelligence chief said that London was the headquarters of international terrorism. I was taken aback but most intelligence agencies recognise that London remains the hub because dissident groups from all over the world have congregated there. To their credit they keep people under strict, if discreet, watch.

Once word of our talking to Kashmiris got out, expatriates also got into the act. The first to arrive were the three from London. There is a story of three Kashmiris in London— Abdullah Raina, Khurshid Hassan Drabu and A. Majid Tramboo—who came visiting India in January 1994. Drabu and Tramboo were immigration barristers. Tramboo was from a well-known business family in Kashmir and he had married a Pandit girl from Amritsar. Raina was an educationist who had spent twenty-five years teaching at Sopore degree college, where he was a contemporary of Hurriyat leader Prof. Abdul Ghani Bhat and of Saifuddin Soz, previously a courtier of Farooq Abdullah but later a member of the Congress party; when Raina emigrated to London, he and his wife got jobs as teachers. These three men set up in London what was called the Kashmir Council for Human Rights, of which barrister Tramboo was the general secretary. In sync with the general change of mood among Kashmiris in Kashmir and in Pakistan, the diaspora Kashmiris were also concerned about the destructive violence that was going nowhere, and they had also decided that enough was enough; something needed to be done politically.

Raina, Drabu and Tramboo figured it was better to go to

Pakistan first and see what the thinking was there, as also seek Pakistani clearance. They landed in Islamabad and stayed at the Holiday Inn, and inevitably met the ISI: Brig. Faisal Dar, the head of the political wing of the Kashmir desk, and the chief, Lt. Gen. Javed Ashraf Qazi. The ISI guys, unsurprisingly, cut to the chase and asked them to be Pakistani agents in London, telling them to do something similar to what Ayub Thakur was doing for the ISI.

Ayub Thakur was a nuclear physicist who was born in Shopian in the Valley, and who had been stripped of Indian citizenship just a few months earlier because he was an ISI agent in London. As a lecturer at Kashmir University in the late 1970s, he was also a leader of the Islami Jamiat-e-Talaba and organised protests against India in 1980 for which he had to spend time in jail. After that he migrated, first to Saudi Arabia, where he taught for six years, then to London. In London he set up the World Kashmir Freedom Movement (WKFM). In the years after 9/11, the USA's FBI would identify Thakur's outfits as being funded by the ISI.

When the ISI suggested that they return to London as its agents, Raina, Drabu and Tramboo declined saying that they were quite clear that they wanted to remain neutral. The three said they only wanted to deal with Kashmir, and that they were not interested in Pakistan and jehad, etc. 'We are agents of the Kashmiri people, not of Pakistan or of India,' they told the ISI. They were simply looking for a breakthrough that would lead to forward movement in Kashmir.

The three arrived in Delhi and approached us in the IB's K-group, saying exactly the same thing they said to the Pakistanis: 'We are well-wishers of Kashmir,' they said. 'We are told the government of India is thinking of reviving the political process. Maybe we can help, we know some of these people.'

They wanted permission to meet the separatists who were in jail: Abdul Ghani Lone, Syed Ali Shah Geelani, Yasin Malik and Shabir Shah. We said, sure, go ahead.

Raina, Drabu and Tramboo met Lone and Geelani in Tihar
Jail, and both of them suspiciously asked: 'How come you've
been allowed to meet us?' They gave some cock-and-bull about
going as friends, and they all chatted. Then the three met Yasin,
who was at the All India Institute of Medical Sciences (AIIMS)
due to his cardiac problem; and they went to Jammu, where
Shabir was incarcerated. They also visited Srinagar and talked
to a bunch of people.

When they returned, they recommended that Yasin should
be released. They said that Yasin and Shabir were positive, but
Yasin was extremely positive, that he was reasonable and
cooperative. Then they went to Pakistan, where they probably
reported what happened here.

Raina, Drabu and Tramboo were back in Delhi that
September, by which time Yasin had been released (and Shabir
was on the verge of being released). The three said that Yasin
needed support—we'll get to Yasin in detail, later in the book—
and that he ought to be strengthened. They again visited Srinagar,
they talked to people, and when they returned they spoke of
money.

As I said, money is an effective tool, but in this case the
question of money caused a falling out between the three
British Kashmiris. Drabu eventually became an immigration
judge, and after retirement he became an advisor to the Muslim
Council of Britain, which he had helped found. As for Raina, I
met him again in 2014 in London, where the old fellow came
looking like Father Christmas, white beard, white hair, white
everything.

Gradually, Tramboo went astray as far as we were concerned
and crossed over totally to the ISI. He set up a Kashmir Centre
in Brussels, doing what Thakur did in London (and what
Ghulam Nabi Fai did in Washington, DC). Tramboo also
eventually became an immigration judge. I heard from him in
2011, when his wife had a bereavement in Amritsar, one of her
parents had passed away. Tramboo was trying to get a visa and

get her home; so out of the blue after so many years, he called me up. I happened to be in London holidaying so I spoke to the high commission there, and I spoke to friends here in Delhi, saying give the lady a visa even if you can't give that bloody Tramboo because he's on the blacklist. She didn't get a visa; there's a limit to what you can get done once you're out of the system. Tramboo called me four or five times and I had to stop taking his calls. He sent a message through someone that he never thought Dulat would not take his calls.

Money in Kashmir goes way back, even to Sheikh Abdullah's time. After all, why was Sheikh Abdullah dismissed as prime minister of J&K in 1953? One of the allegations in the Kashmir conspiracy case framed against him and Mirza Afzal Beg and twenty-two others in 1958 was that he was getting money from Pakistan. Obviously much of this case must have been padded up, I don't know how much, but it couldn't have been padded without the germ of truth that the Sher-e-Kashmir had contact with Pakistan, and had money coming in from there. While in jail, Sheikh complained that Kashmir had been corrupted by Delhi bribing people to keep them in power.

Sheikh Saheb was in jail for eleven years and then he was released for 'diplomatic reasons', as the court was told. He and Prime Minister Jawaharlal Nehru reconciled and the latter sent Sheikh Saheb to Pakistan to see if a solution was possible. Nehru died while Sheikh Saheb was in Pakistan and not long after he returned he was again thrown in jail. This time, Prime Minister Lal Bahadur Shastri's government said that Sheikh Abdullah had had contact with the CIA.

Thus, since Sheikh Saheb's time, anybody who's been on the right side of Delhi has been getting money from Delhi. It's as simple as that.

Even the former governor of J&K in the early 1980s, B.K. Nehru, a cousin of then prime minister Indira Gandhi (his grandfather was Motilal Nehru's elder brother), says in his memoir, *Nice Guys Finish Second*, that when Chief Minister

Farooq Abdullah was sacked in 1984 (by B.K. Nehru's successor Jagmohan), the new government was formed by spending a lot of money. G.M. Shah, Farooq's brother-in-law (who sulked when Farooq was made CM after Sheikh Saheb's death because he felt he should inherit the political legacy), needed thirteen defectors from the National Conference. The money went in an IB bag, and was distributed by a big businessman who used to be a Congress MP, Tirath Ram Amla. They used to call each packet of money a 'bullet'. B.K. Nehru says that Shah was forever running out of bullets, and demanded from Mrs Gandhi more and more bullets.

If this was happening in 1984, then why would the Congress party itself act so innocent about spending money thirty years later? When I went to Srinagar in May 1988, one of the first things I learnt was about the relationship between Kashmiri leaders and money.

Yet if money is in play, then the corollary is that the agent goes to the highest bidder. Indeed, Kashmiris are a heavily layered people, and it is not out of character for a Kashmiri to be in touch with either India or Pakistan (or even both) at some point of time. It's not easy to decipher the Kashmiri psyche, or even to win Kashmiri confidence: centuries of foreign rule, from the Mughals to the Afghans to the Sikhs, have made them natural agents. By now, it is in their DNA.

When I was posted to Srinagar in 1989, I used to hear stories of the earliest IB guys posted to Kashmir, because of whom, as well as the exploits of long-serving IB chief B.N. Mullik, the IB is made out to be much bigger and more sinister than it actually is; that the IB is the real authority in Kashmir; that it controls everything. When I reached Srinagar, it was something to feel kicked about, but it also weighs heavily on you because nobody trusts you. I met Mullik only after I joined the organisation, long after he had retired. He struck me as a saint rather than a spook. Nonetheless, Mullik laid the foundations of the modern-day Intelligence Bureau.

On the other hand Pakistan has always had a lobby in Kashmir; it has always had control over somebody or other in Kashmir. That lobby today is the All Parties Hurriyat Conference, which is a Pakistani creation. The control over the Hurriyat may have loosened a bit when Musharraf and Vajpayee were making tentative steps towards peace but tightened again with insecurity returning to India–Pakistan relations, and somebody or other getting killed for it.

Our idea as mentioned earlier was to reach out to as much of Kashmir as possible. The irony these days is that Delhi has stopped paying attention to Kashmir despite its importance to us nationally; whereas the Pakistanis, who have frankly realised that they have lost out in Kashmir, still have assets there who are totally committed to them. There's nobody in Kashmir more committed to India than Farooq Abdullah, but there seem to be a lot of people in India who simply don't recognise that and are readily dismissive of him.

The ISI strategy now in Kashmir is very clear—it is not going to lose control of the separatists. So it is quite simple: to solve the problem in Kashmir you have to work on the separatists and win them over.

In that the ISI has handed India with several advantages: according to our friend and former militant Firdous Syed, the Kashmiri movement degenerated into a mercenary war due to Pakistan's ill-treatment of Kashmiris, and due to ISI arrogance. Foreigners were used, as were criminals. Kashmiris have suffered. Now it is such that everyone is perceived to be either an ISI agent or an IB/R&AW agent. Kashmiris have learned to adapt; and at times they out-bluff both sides. But at the end of the day, ISI arrogance has been greater than Indian arrogance and this has helped us in Kashmir. That is not to say that we did not have our frustrations or could get done whatever we wanted. As a Kashmiri separatist once said to me, whether in flattery, jest or frustration: 'Aap ne toh badi hamdardi say pechana tha Kashmir ko . . . lekin . . . yahan ki siyasat ka haal na poochiye:

ek tawaif hai tamaashbeenon main.' (You demonstrated great empathy in understanding Kashmir ... but ... politics in Kashmir is like a nautch girl in the midst of spectators deriving vicarious pleasure from her plight.)

On balance, with regard to Pakistan and Kashmir, it was a pretty satisfying stint at R&AW and my time was winding down. It would have been nice to have been a chief like Mullik or R.N. Kao, the first R&AW chief, who was in the saddle for eight years; there is so much that could be done. I had only a year and a half, and it took me six months to get used to the whole thing and for the guys there to get used to me. By the time you settle down and get into the groove, time's up.

The British have a good system, where their MI6 chief has a five-year tenure, and in most cases a knighthood on superannuation. It goes with the job. I met the Spanish ambassador while I was writing this book, and he said their chief also has a five-year tenure. The trouble with our system is that if someone gets five years, what happens to the other guys, of which there are so many, looking at a chance at the top job. So I suppose as a compromise two years isn't bad, particularly if you happen to have grown up in the intelligence community.

While there was a lot of resentment when I joined R&AW because I was an outsider and I didn't know anyone save a few (I knew C.D. Sahay from before, for instance, as he had a posting in Jammu and was kind enough once to invite me to dinner when I visited), when I left things seemed to be okay. There was no grievance; quite the opposite, for after I left I was once asked to do a cadre review for R&AW by Brajesh Mishra; C.D. Sahay, chief after Vikram Sood, who had succeeded me, had been pressing for it. 'He's got time,' Brajesh Mishra said about me. 'He'll head the cadre review committee.'

There were two others from R&AW on the committee. We met on and off, discussing things and there were a couple of points we were in disagreement on. Sahay kept pressing me to finish, and I told him it would get done once we arrived at an agreement on those points.

I mentioned in chapter two the root of the problems at R&AW: the mismatch within the agency between people from different backgrounds. R.N. Kao and his deputy K. Sankaran Nair never gave a way to resolve it, and as a result there was all kinds of groupism and demoralisation, mainly between the IPS officers and the non-IPS officers. The cadre review was basically an attempt to work out a compromise to this groupism.

Our report was almost ready but I had not signed it or presented it, and a youngster on the committee, who was from the RAS, said it was not fair. 'I will add a dissenting note,' he said.

'If you want to add it, you're welcome to,' I said. 'But I would advise you not to. It won't take you anywhere and somebody somewhere will one day hold it against you.' And they did.

After Sahay retired, his successor P.K. Hormis Tharakan, asked me to do a review of my cadre. With the change in thinking in the government he wanted a change in my thinking too. More 'balance' as he called it. So I made a few amendments and returned the report to him. The fact is that there was a feeling in R&AW that the RAS was being discriminated against and that a non-IPS officer would never make it to the top. In that sense my successor Vikram Sood (from the Indian Postal Services) brought a breath of fresh air and hope for the RAS even if it was shortlived.

Interestingly, Brajesh Mishra was inclined to bring in another outsider to head the organisation after me. One day, a couple of months before my superannuation, when I was pressing him to decide on my successor, he said, 'How would you react to an outsider?' 'Don't do it, sir,' I said. 'How can you say that? You were an outsider,' he countered. I said, 'Exactly. I know what it is like, that's why I'm saying it. It's not fair either to the officer or the organisation.' Brajesh never raised the matter again and Vicky Sood became chief and a good chief too.

Cabinet Secretary Prabhat Kumar once asked me: 'Dulat

you have served in both the IB and R&AW, how would you rate the two organisations?' I said to him, 'Institutionally there is no comparison—the IB is far older, more cohesive and solid but man to man, person to person, R&AW is just as good.' This brings me to the larger issue of R&AW's role and existence as an intelligence organisation. What ails the organisation, in my view, is its own inability compounded by the government's ambivalence in charting a clear course for it. Therefore internal debates and bickering continue and inevitably flow into the public domain, confounding the existing confusion. Rajiv Gandhi had once said that intelligence organisations could not be treated like the rest of the bureaucracy. It is time the government settled these issues once and for all—who better to do it than Prime Minister Modi.

The ultimate compliment to R&AW was paid by the former ISI chief, Asad Durrani, at one of our track two meetings when he said, 'R&AW is as good as the ISI if not better,' adding with a chuckle, 'What we do brazenly you achieve by stealth.'

In November, a month before I retired, Brajesh Mishra asked me to accompany him to Beijing for an official visit. He got me an invite to meet my counterpart, whom I had already met once before, during an official visit in May.

The Chinese give a good dinner—Brajesh Mishra and I were taken to a vast, empty restaurant and we were given some vile, horrible paint-remover to drink, which we declined—but when it comes to talking business they do not answer in a hurry. 'Very good idea,' my Chinese counterpart said to a suggestion I made about Indian-Russian-Chinese intelligence cooperation. 'We need time to think about it.' On everything they said, good idea, let us study it. Except terrorism—every time we mentioned it, the Chinese became tense. It is a growing problem for them.

(The Russians, on the other hand, where the trilateral cooperation suggestion originated, are filled with bonhomie. When I visited Moscow, my counterpart landed up at my guest-house in the morning with a bottle of vodka.)

Anyway, it was a good visit and I knew Brajesh Mishra enjoyed the trip. More than once he told M.K. Narayanan that while the agencies were doing well R&AW was more productive than the IB, and Narayanan of course complimented me though I'm not sure he was happy at R&AW being rated higher than the IB. Despite this tide of goodwill from the national security advisor, I was totally unprepared for what happened on 24 December 2000 (remember, on my previous Christmas Eve as R&AW chief, IC-814 was hijacked).

That afternoon I got a call from Ashok Saikia, the establishment officer in the Prime Minister's Office, saying that he had to fix my contract.

'Contract for what?' I said.

'Contract for joining the PMO,' he replied. 'I can't believe you don't know.'

I knew nothing of the sort, so it was all the more reason, he pointed out, that I go over and meet him.

There was nothing extraordinary in the contract, and it was the same as Brajesh Mishra's, in that unlike other government servants who serve at the pleasure of the president, we were to serve at the pleasure of the prime minister. (This is why I decided to quit after the government fell.)

Apparently, my induction had been discussed by the prime minister and his principal secretary three months earlier, in September, when Vajpayee was in Mumbai for his knee operation.

'I just met Brajesh Mishra yesterday and he didn't say a word to me,' I said.

Just then Brajesh walked into the room.

'Thanks for the job,' I said. 'I was just telling Ashok that you didn't tell me about it even yesterday.'

He had a good laugh.

I was surprised, because I was looking forward to retirement, to be free of all of this, to just chilling out. Instead, come 1 January 2001, I was going to be working from the PMO.

10

FROM COLD WAR TO HIGH POLITICS

Less than a week after joining the PMO I received a call on the RAX, which is the government's secure phone line for senior officials and ministers. On the other end was a woman's voice; the call display showed it was coming from the prime minister's residence, at 7 Race Course Road (RCR). I was foxed.

'Welcome to the family,' she said.

It was Namita Bhattacharya, known by her nickname Gunu, and she was the prime minister's adopted daughter.

'Now that you're here, we're reassured,' Gunu continued. 'Please look after the two old men. They're your responsibility.'

She was not only referring to her 76-year-old father but also to his 72-year-old principal secretary and national security advisor, Brajesh Mishra; but in any case, what she said was not as important as the mere fact of her reaching out to me. I was touched, and thanked her for calling.

The PMO in Vajpayee's time was one big happy family, and had a relaxed atmosphere. Of course, part of it was the kindness that the prime minister showed me in the five and a half years that I was with him—two in R&AW, and three and a half in the PMO—but it was also his family who made me feel like one of their own.

In this, Gunu was the anchor as she was the hostess of the house, and she always met me and my wife warmly. The same went for her husband Ranjan: he was an obviously smart fellow who was said to have wielded enormous clout though up close he came across as humble. He and I got along well and occasionally played golf together, just the two of us.

In fact, it was Ranjan who once told me: 'Brajeshji trusts and relies on you more than even Shyamal,' he said, referring to my old batchmate Shyamal Datta, DIB, who was widely known to have freer access to the top and was much closer to the family. Shyamal was the one who got me to R&AW and had me appointed chief. In any case, at least five to seven of us had a nice, comfortable relationship even with the family.

Vajpayee would, at least once in six months, invite all the families from the PMO for a meal or a dinner. You would get good food and a good drink: it was a supremely relaxed affair.

The first PMO lunch that I attended, though, was not the prime minister's but Brajesh Mishra's at his residence in Safdarjung Lane. It was soon after I joined R&AW and I wondered who would be at the principal secretary's lunch. I was expecting thirty people or so but when I reached there were 150 people including the prime minister. 'Bloody hell,' I thought, seeing the politicians in attendance and thinking this was to be a formal affair. It turned out to be like any garden party: drinks were served freely, there was no hypocrisy. Unfortunately, for reasons I never understood, Brajesh Mishra never had a party after that. But the prime minister's parties for the PMO continued regularly.

Along with the partying there was also work. When I joined the prime minister's office on the first day of 2001, I asked Brajesh what I was supposed to do. 'Anything you like,' Brajesh said. 'But we want you to focus on Kashmir.'

Though the brief was not yet specific I was content because

I had spent a lot of time on Kashmir and it was what I enjoyed doing.

A few days later we had a longer chat and I asked, 'Okay, what in Kashmir?'

'Elections are coming up next year,' the principal secretary said. 'We want as much participation as possible, as many people as you can get in.'

'Okay,' I said.

'And try and get these separatists in,' he added.

What more could one ask for? Kashmir had always been my favourite subject and now I would be devoting all my time to it. What added to these three and a half years being a great experience, possibly the best period in my career, was that one saw everything from close quarters.

There were people who had problems with my brief on Kashmir, be it when I headed R&AW or when I was in the PMO. Why was I meddling in Kashmir, it was an internal matter? But Brajesh Mishra encouraged it, and even when I was in R&AW he would tell me, every three-four months: 'Bhai, woh Kashmir pe PM ko thhoda brief kar dena.'

The IB was not very happy about my meddling, but it carried on throughout my stint in R&AW and the PMO, and only ended when Dr Manmohan Singh came to power and M.K. Narayanan took over as his national security advisor; Narayanan made it clear to the R&AW people that they would not meddle in Kashmir. Sadly, a lot of Kashmiris were then dumped by R&AW, and many of them are dissatisfied today.

Those who cribbed about my involvement were technically correct but the fact of the matter was: they weren't doing anything. So what was the problem with my doing something in Kashmir? As I said, Brajesh needed to stop me if that was the case, and say, look at Pakistan instead. But he encouraged me to handle Kashmir when I was in R&AW and got me to the PMO to specifically deal with it. I was officer on special duty but unofficially referred to as advisor on Kashmir in the PMO.

Whatever little our problems may have been Shyamal Datta and I got along famously (I was after all beholden to him for my job) and the IB and R&AW had a great relationship.

Brajesh Mishra in that regard was a great boss. He gave the brief, but how I did it and when I did it, he never interfered. I was free to do things my way. We had hit it off back when I joined R&AW, and from there it only got better. He made me feel comfortable and complimented the organisation on a couple of occasions.

Occasionally he might say, 'you're overstepping something', or 'you're becoming too prominent'. For instance, there was a time I went to Srinagar and a major Delhi paper splashed a story on its front page that I had gone to Kashmir to conduct 'golf diplomacy' with the separatists and other Kashmiris. Actually, whenever I went to Srinagar during those days I played a lot of golf, and if anyone asked it was a good cover story. Of course I did not go just to play golf but to meet someone or discreetly take care of some governmental business. When I returned to Delhi and briefed Brajesh Mishra, he told me that I had become too prominent. 'Take it easy for the next three weeks,' he said. 'I don't want any news.'

In our PMO there was no doubt who the boss was—which has not been the case in some other PMOs. Here, Brajesh virtually ran the government for the prime minister; he was everything. No wonder he is regarded as one of the most powerful principal secretaries ever to serve a prime minister. And of course he was India's first national security advisor. With so much power he eclipsed even the cabinet ministers.

Everyone who worked in the PMO and who worked with him never complained about Brajesh Mishra. He was good with people, he was clear-headed, quick on the uptake, quick on deciding, he knew how to get things done and he never wasted time. You could be sitting with him, and if you overstayed by two minutes or he was to meet someone else, he would tell you, 'Someone's waiting, I'll talk to you later.'

And yet Brajesh Mishra was an extremely relaxed person, though paradoxically he found it difficult to relax. He loved his drink and smoked a lot, which was bad for him. The doctor stopped him but he would still smoke three or four cigarettes. He was not a social namby-pamby drinker. He drank everywhere and he only drank his Scotch. Also, he would talk about how, when he went to New York, the first thing he wanted to do was go and listen to some jazz. He loved jazz and often spoke of the jazz clubs in New York, which he frequented when he was our permanent representative to the United Nations from 1979 to 1981.

At the same time, however, you would never see him in anything but a safari suit (or a suit in winter). It was amazing. I travelled with him a few times, once to Israel, once to China, and even on the flight where there were just the two of us, he would not even take his tie off at night to sleep. On an El Al flight from Bombay to Tel Aviv, for instance, he took off neither his jacket nor his tie. I found that funny. (For the record, the only time I wore a safari suit was for a brief while during my posting in Kathmandu; safari suits had just come into vogue, invented by the Chinese, I think.) His wife used to joke about it: 'Can you ever imagine him in a T-shirt?' she asked me. 'He never gets out of his safari suit.'

Unlike other bureaucrats, Brajesh Mishra did not like to be seen strutting around. He didn't encourage politicians to come and meet him unless it was the one or two he was comfortable with: Arun Shourie and Arun Jaitley, who in any case couldn't offend him in any way. He didn't like politicians and he didn't attend political functions, even if the prime minister was going. Brajesh and Vajpayee had an understanding: you run your politics and I'll run the government. And they got along amazingly.

Which was not the case with the most powerful ministers in the government. It's strange that the most senior ministers in the government did not see eye to eye with Brajesh Mishra, be it

Home Minister (and later Deputy Prime Minister) L.K. Advani or Foreign Minister Jaswant Singh. And it didn't seem to bother anybody, least of all Vajpayee, who of course was an accomplished politician and had a good equation with Jaswant Singh and even with Advani.

Brajesh Mishra was very democratic and sometimes I wondered why at times he would waste his time. 'Everyone is entitled to his say, so let him have his say,' he would tell me.

For instance, a new organisation was carved out of R&AW's Aviation Research Centre (ARC) called the National Technical Research Organisation (NTRO), modelled on the USA's National Security Agency. The ARC director was to head the NTRO, and there was a lot of friction between R&AW and the NTRO; as it happened back in 1968 between the IB and the R&AW, they were arguing over cupboards, chairs, officers. I don't know why it had to be created, the ARC was doing fine.

There was a big flap about how many airplanes the NTRO would get. I told Brajesh, 'Sir, take a call, end this nonsense.' But he was very open about it, very democratic, willing to listen. He gave everyone time and a hearing. And things got sorted out.

If he didn't want to see someone, he would palm that person off to me. He didn't suffer fools. And if he had to put off a call on something, he would say, 'I will have to ask the PM about this,' which was his standard line, popular among his own colleagues.

In the PMO I was free to meet the prime minister whenever I wanted; even if I wanted to meet him every day I could, but I did not need to nor would he have wanted to meet me every day. He never refused an appointment nor would Brajesh meddle or ask why I was going to meet the PM. All appointments were listed on his table and he would merely note that you had a meeting that particular day. He might have occasionally asked: 'Koi khaas baat hai?'

On normal days Brajesh Mishra interacted with the prime

minister every evening. Vajpayee functioned out of his residence and rarely came to his South Block office, so if any of us had to meet him we had to go to RCR. In Brajesh's case it was not a question of him briefing the prime minister because they knew each other so well. It was a question of sitting down and discussing a matter. So at the end of every day Brajesh would leave office at about 6:30 p.m.—he didn't sit late, like a lot of people do—and he would go to RCR, where he would spend his time depending on how much time Vajpayee had. He probably wound up and reached home at 8:30 to 9:00 p.m. most evenings.

You might wonder how the government functioned at all in this easygoing manner, but the truth is, in our country the government functions on its own and in Vajpayee's time it functioned smoothly despite the fact that there was a coalition government. Vajpayee managed the coalition very well: he was good with people, he was good with words, and above all he had a sense of humour.

Once, for instance, there was a time when the railway minister, Mamata Banerjee, was sulking. She was a moody person who could be very difficult to get through to. I witnessed one example of Vajpayee's people skills at the airport. Mamata had stormed out of a cabinet meeting, and then Vajpayee went on a trip abroad. I was still in R&AW then and in those days we had to go and stand in line at the airport to either see off or receive the prime minister—more on his return than his departure—in case he had a brainwave or something and you were required.

At the airport the officials were lined up on one side and the politicians on the other side. For the politicians it was purely optional who went. But on this occasion Mamata was at the airport and she was first in line. As Vajpayee came in she bent down to touch his feet, as was her habit. He caught her hand and gave her a hug. That ended all problems with her party, the Trinamool Congress. Vajpayee could do that.

Vajpayee was not only a very astute politician but a poet and philosopher as well and an unparalleled orator. I had the privilege of first hearing the great man in 1978 while posted as first secretary in our embassy in Kathmandu when as foreign minister Vajpayee spoke at a function of the Nepal–Bharat Maitree Sangh starting with 'Jis desh ke kanker, kanker me Shankar ho—' which sent the crowds into raptures. Vajpayee mesmerised the packed house; most of the Nepalese women came out with moist eyes. Not only in Kathmandu but everywhere he went and spoke as in Lahore in 1999 and Srinagar in 2003 he held the crowd in thrall.

Vajpayee fulfilled Plato's ideal of the perfect state in which 'philosophers were kings and kings philosophers'.

My only reservation was that Vajpayee took his time in deciding things, particularly in important or crucial matters. You would never be able to tell that from meetings, which he never allowed to meander uselessly; he would sit there, munching his samosa and jalebis, but ensured the meeting was quick and business-like and over. If he had to say something or make a remark, he would do so; otherwise it was thank you very much.

Perhaps his decisions now took a long time because of Kargil, etc., and he had to face that criticism. Vajpayee the foreign minister who went to Pakistan, when he was much younger, and Vajpayee the prime minister were two different people.

Nonetheless, Vajpayee was never one to allow himself to be led by the bureaucracy. The bureaucracy anticipates things and tries to be 'his master's voice'. In Vajpayee's government, however, you never felt an unnatural swing to the right; it was like any other government. Indeed, it was a friendlier government, a happier one, and I don't think the bureaucracy had a better time than during Vajpayee's time, though there might have been the odd guy who felt he was being discriminated against because he was with the Congress or some such thing.

For instance, if you leave it to bureaucrats, things like

relations with Pakistan will not improve no matter how much you may personally want to improve them—a clear example is Dr Manmohan Singh's ten-year tenure as prime minister. When Vajpayee took the bus to Lahore, it was not a bureaucratic decision; it wasn't a whim either, but it was a decision 'driven' by the prime minister himself, with the supporting homework being done by the bureaucracy. And who would have thought that within two years of Kargil, Vajpayee would invite and talk to General Musharraf.

In his 'pure politics' approach of not being led by his bureaucrats, Vajpayee to my mind showed several similarities with his predecessor, P.V. Narasimha Rao (recall that Vajpayee headed a thirteen-day government in 1996 after the Congress government led by Narasimha Rao lost power). The two of them were keen on a breakthrough in Kashmir, and in this both were willing to look beyond Farooq Abdullah: in the mid-'90s, Narasimha Rao placed his hopes on Shabir Shah, while, as we shall see in the next two chapters, Vajpayee favoured Omar Abdullah over his father.

The other similarity that people talk about is that both Narasimha Rao and Vajpayee were nudged along in their Pakistan and Kashmir initiatives by the Americans. Though those who argue this seem to make a logical case for their assertion, I never saw anything that suggested this nor do I have evidence that such was the case with either prime minister. Perhaps this suggestion comes from those quarters who are themselves unwilling to credit these prime ministers with original thinking.

Narasimha Rao was, like Vajpayee, a smart strategist and must be given credit for a couple of things. For one thing, after the shock of the militancy erupting in 1990, whatever opening we in the government made—talking to all Kashmiris, no matter who they were—the credit goes to Narasimha Rao. His approach was not at all hampered by any baggage. There was a time when separatists or Kashmiris going to the Pakistan High Commission would be harassed by the police and agencies. In

May 1995, Pakistan president Farooq Leghari came to Delhi for a South Asian Association for Regional Cooperation (SAARC) summit and he invited the Hurriyat leaders for a meeting. We at the IB did our best to try and dissuade them; the result was that two went, two didn't go, one reported sick, and Moulvi Abbas Ansari landed up at 2 p.m. for an 11 a.m. meeting, saying that he had gone shopping and had got lost in an auto-rickshaw coming to Chanakyapuri, which is the diplomatic enclave. It was comical.

'What's the big deal?' Narasimha Rao asked. 'If they want to go there, let them. It's not a big deal.'

This opening-up started in Narasimha Rao's time. Before that, anyone who visited the high commission was suspect. They'd be searched or frisked or whatever it is, and followed. So all that stopped. Narasimha Rao said, nahi, aane dijiye jaane dijiye. Why are we doing this? There is no need.

Perhaps it was because Narasimha Rao wasn't too impressed with intelligence work (or the officers that brought him intelligence). Part of it might have been because his predecessor as Congress prime minister, Rajiv Gandhi, was impressed by the intelligence community, and his tenure is remembered as the best it has ever been for Indian intelligence. But it was mostly due to Narasimha Rao's notion of intellectual superiority, and the attitude that there was nothing new that the spooks could tell him.

In any case, Narasimha Rao, who had overseen the 1992 assembly election in Punjab after which the Khalistan movement lost much of its steam, was determined from 1994 onwards that democracy be revived in J&K. This governor's rule business will not do, he apparently felt, referring to the arrangement in J&K from 19 January 1990, when Farooq Abdullah resigned following the appointment of Jagmohan as governor. We have to get back to the political process. If you want to normalise Kashmir, that is the only way.

And in Narasimha Rao's mind, reviving democracy did not

mean going back to the Abdullah family. He did not see that as moving forward. He was one for talking to the Kashmiris, and if he could rope separatists or even militants into the political process, then that would be dream fulfillment. On this job, he deployed his young telecommunications minister (and from 1993 to 1995, the junior minister for home affairs), Rajesh Pilot, and the DIB, D.C. Pathak.

Rajesh Pilot had already had some involvement with Kashmir during Rajiv Gandhi's time, when he was a junior minister in charge of surface transport (1985–89). At that time, Pilot was a sort of message carrier between New Delhi and Farooq Abdullah, and he assisted Rajiv Gandhi in the 1986 Congress accord with the National Conference. That's how I got to know Rajesh—I used to meet him after I was posted to Srinagar, and we got along quite well. I found it easy to talk to him.

The only thing was, Governor K.V. Krishna Rao could not stand Pilot. General Rao was a former army chief who was appointed to the J&K Raj Bhavan for a second stint in May 1993, succeeding Gary Saxena (a former R&AW chief who would also do a second stint, from 1998). Gary was a great man manager: though an intelligence services man, he got along well with Kashmiris and with the army. He could have, in my opinion, helped a Kashmir initiative from Raj Bhavan in Srinagar, had he been asked.

Krishna Rao's importance, perhaps, was that he had a great relationship with Farooq. It was a sort of father-son relationship that the General said formed because he was the corps commander in Jammu from 1974 to '78, when Sheikh did the accord with Indira Gandhi and then took over as chief minister.

Besides not liking Pilot, Krishna Rao was also allergic to the home secretary, K. Padmanabhaiah. In another smart move, Narasimha Rao set up a Department of Kashmir Affairs that he himself headed; the secretary was Padmanabhaiah, and this gave Kashmiris encouragement that their matter was being handled at the highest level of government. To his credit,

Padmanabhaiah also visited Kashmir several times, which is more than what can be said about other home secretaries.

Padmanabhaiah and Rajesh Pilot, though, were on the same wavelength. This brings up an interesting story. Pilot was very close to K.P.S. Gill, the Punjab police chief credited with leading the fight against militancy from the front, and in 1996 he wanted to send K.P.S. to Kashmir as governor. K.P.S., however, preferred to go as director-general of police. There was a vacancy, so Pilot got the ball rolling. But as soon as Krishna Rao got wind of it, he immediately filled the vacancy by appointing an officer he was not fond of, M.N. Sabharwal. Just to pre-empt these guys. Such were the fun and games in Kashmir.

Narasimha Rao was a veteran at balancing out people. In March 1994, for instance, when India was under a lot of pressure internationally because of Kashmir, there was an important meeting in Geneva, Switzerland, of the fiftieth session of the United Nations Commission for Human Rights; a few months earlier, in 1993, US assistant secretary of state Robin Raphel had questioned the finality of J&K's accession to India; at the same time Pakistan prime minister Benazir Bhutto said the Kashmir dispute was an 'unfinished business of Partition'. Both statements had come during a high-profile standoff between the army and JKLF militants at the Hazratbal shrine on the outskirts of Srinagar. Narasimha Rao's brainwave was to send to Geneva a delegation headed by the leader of the opposition, who at that time was Vajpayee, and which included Farooq Abdullah. India presented a united front to the world on Kashmir, and this helped relieve the pressure internationally.

However, whatever balancing Narasimha Rao might have done, Rajesh Pilot was key to the Kashmir breakthrough. The prime minister knew that this was a youngster who spoke his mind; who was open, frank and ambitious; and who had a future, perhaps even as prime minister. Narasimha Rao's thinking did not always match Pilot's thinking—in fact, he wanted to go much slower than Pilot did, and thus did not fully trust him, often using the senior home minister, S.B. Chavan, to slow him down. Pilot was prepared to do at that time what no other person was prepared to do: take a little risk and talk to Kashmiris. Which is how I got into this whole business of talking.

Thus there were two parallel tracks: we in the IB had begun talking to Kashmiris, and when Pilot got wind of it, he didn't want to get left behind. On the political plane he started his own channel. In fact, Pilot deserves credit for being the first political interface with separatists and militants, long before Advani as deputy prime minister began talking to the Hurriyat in 2004. This sort of interface was a lot hairier then—Pilot's car was shot at on a couple of occasions in Srinagar—but Pilot was meeting Kashmiris, having them hang around at his house, letting the youngsters know that this was a point at which you could come in.

The IB didn't want to be left out of the loop, so the DIB, M.K. Narayanan, asked me to tie up with Pilot. Everything happened almost simultaneously: if we were talking to X and Y, and we thought we would talk to Z later, Pilot would already be talking to Z and his people. There were no secrets with Pilot, who felt this was all in the national interest, and who tried to rope in a Kashmir-knowing team of bureaucrats like Wajahat Habibullah, an IAS officer who was fond of JKLF leader Yasin Malik.

The JKLF boys got along with Pilot and a lot of that gang was always hanging out at Pilot's house, though I never saw Yasin at his place. (As a minister he could not go visit anyone in jail. That was our job.) They were close to him and they liked his openness. Unless you have some empathy for Kashmiris, and some time and patience to listen to their bitching, you won't understand a thing of what is going on over there. Pilot was willing to listen, and was willing to say, if that is so, what can we do for you? There was nobody in Delhi more sympathetic to Kashmiris or to their cause, in the government of India, than Rajesh Pilot.

We were always talking about what we could do, how we could move things forward. Once Pilot asked me on the matter of unemployment: 'Can you think of anything we can do for these Kashmiri boys?'

'Sir, there's so much you can do,' I said.

'I've been talking to some corporate honchos,' he said. 'I've been wondering whether I can get them jobs abroad, in Dubai and all that.'

It struck me as not a bad idea. What he was saying was that not many people were willing to accommodate Kashmiris here, at that point of time, so he was looking at options outside India, and he mentioned Dubai.

'I've also spoken to some business people in Bombay,' he added. 'I'm hopeful something will happen.'

We spoke during crises, as mentioned in chapter three, during the al-Faran hostage situation. And Rajesh spoke of the prime minister. 'This old man is too sharp, too bloody smart,' he said once. 'Calls me and tells me, "Home Minister, how are you?" Makes me feel I'm the home minister and then uses Chavan to undercut me.' He understood the whole game with the wily Narasimha Rao.

Pilot was simple, down-to-earth, straightforward; he was ambitious, no doubt, and he must have thought that Kashmir was a good opportunity. Even after Narasimha Rao's government left, Pilot's interest continued; even when he was out of power there were Kashmiris at his place. If he had not died in that tragic accident, in May 2000, he would have gone places.

Pilot never forgot that he was an air force officer and had his friends and links there. At his parties and get-togethers you would always find air force officers there; it was normal for the Air Force Marshal Arjan Singh to be there. At his daughter Sarika's wedding—his son Sachin married Farooq's daughter Sara, but that was some time after Pilot had passed away—I was surprised to find that we were invited, along with a lot of other people, but that there were no politicians. 'I don't see any politicians,' I remarked. 'When is madam (Sonia Gandhi) coming?'

'I haven't invited anybody,' Rajesh said. 'If I invite one then I've got to invite the whole lot, and I don't need them here. I have invited only friends.'

He was that kind of a guy.

Pilot had an exceptional relationship with Farooq. It cooled a bit when, in 1999, Farooq voted in Parliament for the NDA government and against the Congress's motion of no-confidence; the NDA fell, but returned to power later that year. Perhaps Pilot expected Farooq to vote the same way that the other NC MP, Saifuddin Soz, did. The following year Pilot died.

Ironically, when Sara and Sachin married, Farooq did not attend the wedding—even though it was the wedding of his favourite daughter. It was not very courageous of him, and when I asked him how he could have done this, he had no answer. (Incidentally, Omar did not go, even though he was in Delhi). Farooq did not disapprove; he was a liberal, and besides, Omar had married a non-Muslim, Payal.

In any case, I visited Pilot's place a few times after he died and once the crowds had disappeared. I sat with Sachin, who had just come back from the US, where he was studying at the Wharton Business School of the University of Pennsylvania, and I asked him: 'When are you going to take up your Dad's mantle and join politics?'

'No, no, not me, Uncle,' he said. 'This is too much for me.'

'It's in your genes,' I said. 'You're capable.'

Once he got into politics, I found Kashmiris coming and visiting Sachin. Perhaps it was the Sara connection, but it had to do with his family. People had a lot of regard for Rajesh Pilot.

In our talking to separatists and former militants, things progressed with Shabir Shah to such an extent that by 1994, Narasimha Rao was dreaming that Shabir would enter the democratic process. He was his big hope. But as we saw in chapter four, Shabir was not up to the task, and in November 1995, the night before Narasimha Rao went to the African nation of Burkina Faso, when he asked me whether Farooq was the only option, I had to convey to him that no separatist, including Shabir, was ready to climb aboard. The National Conference had been putting pressure on Delhi giving some political package which it could sell to the electorate before elections. So I told the prime minister: 'Yes, it's like that.'

Narasimha Rao was so keen on Shabir that when I reached the stage of talking to him, the prime minister asked me to meet the finance minister, Dr Manmohan Singh. I went and met him. He asked me what it was all about, so I told him we were talking to some Kashmiris, some separatists. Singh's query was whether Farooq knew about this. 'I'm not sure if the PM has briefed him,' I said. 'But maybe Farooq doesn't need to know everything.' This made Singh uncomfortable, though he did meet Shabir. The whole idea had been to make Shabir feel that the engagement was getting serious; that Narasimha Rao was keen on him. But Shabir did not take the bait.

Famously, while in Burkina Faso, Narasimha Rao announced that he was ready to grant autonomy to Kashmir, and that 'sky's the limit'. Though many people thought he was saying this for the benefit of Farooq Abdullah (which will bring us to the NC's autonomy resolution in the next chapter), at the back of Narasimha Rao's mind was Shabir Shah. The prime minister was thinking, if this is what the separatists want, or if they want to be reasonable, then here is the space for us to talk, and here is the space for accommodation. Shabir would have got political concessions, for Narasimha Rao was interested. But Shabir missed the bus.

By the time the 2002 election rolled around, it was too late for Shabir. Like Narasimha Rao, Vajpayee also wanted a break from the past and he too wanted to look beyond Farooq Abdullah. But whereas Narasimha Rao's dream was to have a separatist like Shabir Shah join the political mainstream and take control of Kashmir, Vajpayee's notion of a break from the past was different. In looking beyond Farooq Abdullah he too wanted a generational change, but closer to home. His dream was Omar Abdullah.

11

VAJPAYEE CHOOSES OMAR

Omar Abdullah is Farooq's only son, born in England while his grandfather, Sheikh Saheb, was still in jail (his mother Mollie is English). Though he came from a political household—to the extent that when he graduated from Lawrence School in Sanawar, he enrolled at Sydenham College in Mumbai and lived at the residence of his father's political buddy, Sharad Pawar—he entered the corporate world, working for the Oberois for five years or so; it was in this job that he met his wife Payal.

The years after Farooq won the 1996 assembly election—thereby taking the wind out of militancy by providing a working democratic political system in the state again—were a heady time. He had his most trusted bureaucrats helping him administer J&K, he and I drew very close, and in this milieu he and his wife began to think of his political legacy. Farooq suggested to Omar that he enter politics and his wife Mollie was also agreeable. After all, politics was in Omar's genes.

An opportunity opened up very soon, when the United Front government fell in November 1997; the Lok Sabha election was held in February and March the following year, and Farooq encouraged Omar to contest. It was a logical first step for the handsome young man, as he would get a kind of acquaintance before the inevitable encounter with the hurly-burly of politics.

Not all in the family welcomed Omar's entry into politics. In particular, Farooq's elder sister Khalida was extremely distressed. To her family, it must have seemed like dejá vu.

Khalida was the eldest of Sheikh Saheb's five children; his other daughter Suraiya was the youngest. Khalida was also her father's favourite. When she was only fourteen, back in 1948, she was married off to a man twice her age, Ghulam Mohammed Shah, otherwise known as Gul Shah. He was a National Conference loyalist and in Sheikh Saheb's Emergency Administration in the immediate years post-independence he served as the controller, food and civil supplies. When Sheikh Saheb returned to power after two decades of imprisonment, Gul Shah served in his state cabinet as a minister in charge of important portfolios such as food and civil supplies, transport, works and power. To some, including Gul Shah himself, it seemed he would inherit Sheikh Saheb's political mantle.

What Gul Shah perhaps did not count on was that after the 1977 assembly election, in the final five years of Sheikh Saheb's life, it was the latter's wife, Begum Akbar Jehan Abdullah, whose power grew. She wielded a lot of influence in Sheikh Saheb's last days. She became a member of Parliament after Sheikh Saheb returned to power in 1975, and during his final years, there were many rumours of corruption in his government that dented his image as a statesman, and somehow many of those rumours could be traced back to the Begum and her coterie.

Begum Abdullah was old school, and an extremely charming and elegant lady, but she didn't talk much. She was careful about what she said. During my days in Srinagar, whenever I heard her, she showed great respect for the Nehru–Gandhi family, but in whatever she said she was definitely part of the older guard, the more conservative part of the National Conference.

Begum Abdullah's favourite was their eldest son Farooq, who had studied medicine in Jaipur and then went to England to train and then practise (where he met his wife Mollie, and where his son Omar was born). Farooq had returned and his mother felt that he should inherit his father's political legacy. This inheritance was a matter of concern since Sheikh Saheb was not in the best of health—and even Prime Minister Indira Gandhi was seized of the matter. After all, Kashmir was an important border state, and although Pakistan had been defeated in 1971, extra care had to be taken with regard to the governance of India's only Muslim-majority state.

Indira Gandhi thought about it at length, and by 1980 she had decided that it would be best for all concerned if Dr Farooq Abdullah succeeded his father. He seemed to be the more trustworthy option. Perhaps she was swayed by Farooq's modern outlook, his foreign exposure, and his ease with English as well as with Kashmiri and Urdu. Perhaps his happy-go-lucky image did not threaten her. After all, Gul Shah had been active with the Plebiscite Front during the years that Sheikh Saheb was under arrest. She let Sheikh Saheb know that her preferred choice for his successor was Farooq.

Gul Shah might have been a smarter politician than Farooq, but he was widely regarded as a bully. Another factor that might have swayed Sheikh Saheb was the fact that Gul Shah ill-treated Khalida; she would come home and complain to her parents about it. Thus ultimately it was Begum Abdullah who tilted the balance, and Farooq was appointed the president of the National Conference in August 1981. Sheikh Saheb passed away in September 1982, and Farooq took over as chief minister. Gul Shah felt cheated; he had had a long innings in politics, and he was senior to his brother-in-law both in age and in politics. So he left the government, and in due course, the National Conference. Khalida's family and Farooq's family drifted apart.

As chief minister, Farooq hobnobbed with opposition leaders such as N.T. Rama Rao, Jyoti Basu, Parkash Singh Badal,

Sharad Pawar, and A.B. Vajpayee. This impertinence was not what Indira Gandhi had expected. She had a new governor, Jagmohan, appointed, who dismissed Farooq and replaced him with Gul Shah, who led a splinter of the NC which was called the NC (K) after his wife. (In 1988, his party's name changed to the Awami National Conference.) Gul Shah's tenure is remembered for the heavy hand with which he put down dissent, and for which he came to be popularly called the 'curfew CM'.

Farooq patched up with Mrs Gandhi's son Rajiv and in 1986 he returned to power. Gul Shah was out in the cold, and Begum Abdullah decided that the two families should patch up. Even when Farooq Abdullah became chief minister, his mother ran a kitchen cabinet though by 1988 it was not as powerful as it had once been. Farooq, for his part, would 'mummy' her and keep her in good humour, but she did not meddle too much in day-to-day affairs. Of course she did not approve of what Gul Shah had done but she could not go against her daughter either. It was a difficult tightrope walk. But though she was often around when you visited Farooq's residence, she never spoke while her son was speaking. They were very close.

Begum Abdullah began inviting Khalida to the chief minister's home, where she lived. Khalida visited regularly, and her son Muzaffar Shah, whom everyone called Muzy, came along. By 1988, Muzy had drawn close to Farooq, all the time saying Mamu this and Mamu that. Farooq grew fond of the boy. After all, Omar was away at school and the thought of Omar entering politics did not enter anyone's head at the time. Muzy was around.

The rapprochement grew steadily and I once even saw Gul Shah at Farooq's place, sometime in 1997, so I asked the chief minister if things had become okay with his sister and her husband. 'Haan-haan, theek hai,' Farooq said. 'Politically we can't align with each other, but the family relationship has settled down, it's fine.'

By this time, Muzaffar was expecting some kind of political concession, and he had begun to eye a seat in Parliament. When it became known that in the 1998 election (Kashmir chose three representatives to the Lok Sabha, from Srinagar, Anantnag and Baramulla) Omar would be contesting, Khalida's family again felt short-changed. It was the early 1980s all over again, when Gul Shah lost out to Farooq; this time his son lost out to Farooq's son.

Khalida's family must have seen Muzaffar as a proper politician, whereas Omar had spent his formative years outside the Valley; not only that, Omar spoke haltingly in Kashmiri. Khalida's family let it be known they felt that the fact that Omar's mother was English would hurt the party politically; and then there was the fact that Omar was married to a girl who was neither Kashmiri nor Muslim.

But nothing they said could stop Omar from becoming member of Parliament. The inter-family rivalry and hatred, which had been on the mend, deteriorated; and the people around each of the families only fuelled these negative feelings. Since Muzy always thought he should get something, being Gul Shah's son and all, I approached Farooq sometime in 2001— when the idea was gaining currency that Omar should take charge in Kashmir—to suggest sending Muzy to Parliament. But Farooq expressed helplessness: 'We can't have so many family members in these positions,' he said.

In the case, when elections were held again in 1999 Omar was re-elected, and because he had voted for Vajpayee's first NDA government in the no-confidence motion sponsored by Sonia Gandhi's Congress party earlier that year, the NDA decided to induct him into the new council of ministers, making him the youngest in Vajpayee's cabinet. (NC MP Saifuddin Soz, in that vote of no-confidence, was persuaded by Congress leader Rajesh Pilot to vote against Vajpayee; this angered Farooq, who in any case had no love lost for the Gandhi family, and Saifuddin Soz had to leave the NC. He then joined the Congress party.)

Omar's tenure in the commerce ministry was marked by good reports about his performance, and he also seemed to feel comfortable in Delhi. It was while he was in the commerce ministry and I was at R&AW that a crisis emerged. This was the J&K assembly's discussion, in June 2000, of the report of the State Autonomy Committee (SAC) recommending greater autonomy to the state.

As mentioned before, the J&K assembly election took the steam out of militancy. The main reason was that the National Conference participated in the election. The National Conference participated because Farooq Abdullah agreed to participate (recall that Abdul Ghani Lone had tried to dissuade him from participating); while he was away from the Valley, the NC had stopped functioning and gone into hiding. Farooq got the NC going again; it was nothing without him. At the same time, Farooq realised that if his party was going to be the alternative to separatism and militancy, then he was going to have to do something for his people—or at least make the right noises. The 'peace with honour' that Shabir Shah and others could not give Kashmiris, he would give them. After all, Narasimha Rao had said, from Burkina Faso less than a year ago, that so far as autonomy was concerned, 'the sky's the limit'.

Thus, promptly after the assembly election, on 29 November 1996, the state government set up the State Autonomy Committee with the following terms of reference:

- To examine and recommend measures for the restoration of autonomy to the state of Jammu and Kashmir consistent with the Instrument of Accession, the Constitution Application Order, 1950, and the Delhi Agreement, 1952.
- To examine and recommend safeguards that be regarded necessary for incorporation in the Union/state Constitution to ensure that the Constitutional arrangement that is finally evolved in pursuance of the recommendations of this committee is inviolable.

- To also examine and recommend measures to ensure a harmonious relationship for the future between the state and the Union.

The committee had nine members, including Dr Karan Singh as the chairman; he resigned in July 1997, and the NC's Ghulam Mohiuddin Shah took over in his place.

The committee tabled its report in the assembly in April 1999, and in it recommended the restoration of the 1952 Delhi Agreement, in which the only things that the Union would be in charge of would be defence, external affairs and communication. It also recommended that Article 370 of the Constitution, which grants special status to the state, be made a 'special provision' in the Constitution instead of 'temporary provision'.

While this was tame compared to the azaadi demand of militants, it was anathema to the BJP and its ilk, which have always stood for the abrogation of Article 370 and putting J&K at par with other states in the Union. The NC had always walked this tightrope, with Sheikh Saheb adept at wording political matters in such a way that satisfied both Kashmiris and Delhi. Farooq, looking ahead to the 2002 assembly election, knew he had to deliver on his promises well in time, and so, on 19 June 2000, the assembly was convened for a week-long special session to discuss the committee's report and pass a resolution accepting it.

The NDA was not happy about the turn of events. 'What is your friend up to?' Brajesh Mishra asked me.

I spoke to the chief minister. 'There is a little concern here, everyone is asking about the resolution.'

What Farooq told the top IB man in Srinagar, K.M. Singh, was that he had contested the 1996 election because the government of India wanted him to contest, and at that time he had told the government that he needed a plank to fight an election. Autonomy had been that plank. His committee had in fact been discussing the matter with Governor Gary Saxena while preparing the report; and now another election was coming up, so his government had to do something about autonomy.

Furthermore, Farooq said to me, ever since the report was tabled, he had been pleading with New Delhi to also appoint a committee, which could have a couple of cabinet ministers on it. He seemed to imply that such a committee could be an eyewash, but at least it would keep autonomy in play, to help the NC in the 2002 elections. However, there was no response to his suggestion from the NDA, and left with no choice, Farooq was forced to move this resolution in his assembly.

'Why are you worried?' Farooq asked. 'Everybody has to be kept happy. Tell them not to worry, the resolution won't get passed. Kucch nahin hoga.'

Events apparently overtook the chief minister and the resolution was passed by the J&K assembly. Again Farooq thought it was no big deal and he sent the resolution to the Union home ministry, knowing fully well that the home ministry headed by the NDA's resident hardliner, L.K. Advani, was not going to do anything with the resolution. He figured the NDA government would just kick the can down the road, giving him both an escape route and an election plank.

But New Delhi was not happy at all. Members of the NDA government were upset, and a cabinet meeting was immediately called. It summarily threw out the resolution, saying it was not acceptable.

Farooq was infuriated. The NDA government was not playing politics when he needed it to, for his own party's well-being; it was almost symbolic, as if it were being more hardline than was necessary, shutting the Kashmiris out, without so much as a conversation. The Delhi–Srinagar relationship became strained.

Farooq threatened to resign, but more than that, he threatened to pull out of the NDA coalition. Omar was summoned to Srinagar, and there was on 10 July 2000 a meeting of the NC MLAs. The meeting discussed what the next step should be. The atmosphere was very tense, both in Srinagar and in New Delhi. The meeting carried on the entire day, and the MLAs decided to continue the following day.

But the next morning, on 11 July 2000, Begum Abdullah died of a cardiac arrest. The lady was eighty-four years old. And this unfortunate event fortunately saved the day. K.M. Singh called up and said, 'Please help, this is an opportunity.'

I went to Brajesh Mishra. 'Farooq has lost his mother,' I said.

'Haan-haan, Advaniji jaa rahe hain,' he said.

'Maybe something more than Advaniji,' I suggested. 'Maybe the PM should go.'

Brajesh Mishra looked at me. 'You really think so?' he asked.

'Yes, I think so.'

'Okay,' he said. 'Let me speak to the PM.'

Vajpayee, not surprisingly, said, theek hai, jayenge.

'In that case,' I said, 'I would also like to go.'

'Sure,' he said.

The delegation included Defence Minister George Fernandes, Advani, and the prime minister. When we reached Srinagar, the VIPs took their time in coming out, so I was off the aircraft ahead of everyone. When I stepped onto the tarmac, the first thing that happened was that Omar Abdullah hugged me. People might have thought it unusual because Omar was not normally given to displaying emotion, but on this occasion he was relieved to see us.

The strain over the autonomy resolution had rattled him completely. At that time he was not dreaming of, or even distantly dreaming of, becoming chief minister. He just didn't want to lose his job and his life in Delhi. So when he saw me, he realised the prime minister had also come, and he knew that this gesture would end all talk of snapping ties and save the day.

And it did. Farooq was extremely touched by the prime minister's thoughtfulness at coming to his mother's funeral. The resolution controversy died, along with Begum Abdullah.

It did, however, plant the seed of doubt about Farooq Abdullah in the NDA government's mind, and possibly pushed Vajpayee into looking beyond Farooq for cutting the Gordian knot in Kashmir. While this seed was growing in his mind, I left R&AW and reached the PMO.

As Omar was Farooq's son and I was fond of him, I looked out for him. In the PMO I heard that the prime minister, during his next trip abroad, was taking such-and-such minister along. I went to Brajesh Mishra. 'Why don't you take Omar on one of these trips?' I said. 'He looks good and he's a Kashmiri. It gives him good exposure and it also sends a positive signal.'

Brajesh Mishra was agreeable and on the next trip, Omar went along. Then he went again. And again. Vajpayee had a chance to watch Omar from close quarters, and he struck him as a bright young fellow. The more Vajpayee and Brajesh Mishra saw Omar, the more they liked him. They moved him to the external affairs ministry, which was a sort of promotion, where he was the junior minister.

Another episode which solidified Vajpayee's positive feelings was a dinner that Omar hosted for the prime minister at his residence on Akbar Road. It was an exclusive dinner for the prime minister and his family: the PM was there, his foster daughter and Ranjan, Brajesh Mishra and myself; there was Omar, his wife Payal, Omar's in-laws and Farooq.

There was a high table at which everybody sat except Brajesh, Ranjan and I, who were drinking at the bar outside. It was a personal, private dinner, the PM with his family meeting Omar's in-laws, and reinforced positivity all around.

And the germ of the idea that Omar and Farooq should be switched, with Omar taking charge in Kashmir and Farooq settling down in Delhi, may have been planted during this time.

Between the prime minister, Brajesh Mishra, and I'm sure Advani was involved in this, they decided to suggest Farooq Abdullah an inducement to leave Kashmir: they decided to offer to make him the Vice-President of India.

12

VAJPAYEE'S 'BETRAYAL' OF FAROOQ ABDULLAH

These facts are well-known: in 2002, Vice-President Krishan Kant was on course to become the eleventh President of India. Such promotion to Rashtrapati Bhavan was a tradition and the six previous vice-presidents had gone on to become president. Vajpayee and Sonia Gandhi were agreeable to Kant's candidature—he was one of the Congress party's original 'Young Turks' and later a member of the 1977–1980 Janata Party government—and his name had been announced as such. Several members of the NDA government like Home Minister L.K. Advani, however, remembered that along with Madhu Limaye, Kant had been responsible for the fall of the Janata government over dual membership in the Rashtriya Swayamsewak Sangh (RSS). So they opposed Kant. Vajpayee then had to propose longtime civil servant and Tamil Nadu governor P.C. Alexander as the NDA's candidate, but the Congress vetoed the idea. Ultimately A.P.J. Abdul Kalam became president and proved to be the most popular one India has had. Two days after Kalam was sworn in, a broken-hearted Kant passed away, the only vice-president to die in office.

What is not widely known is that Vajpayee had offered
Farooq Abdullah the vice-presidency. The offer was made when
it was assumed that Kant was going to be the president. It made
sense in the informal formula that politicians followed: to
balance out the two high offices with either a north-south or a
majority-minority combination.

The offer was made at my residence, by the prime minister's
principal secretary and national security advisor Brajesh Mishra,
later reaffirmed, according to Farooq, by the home minister,
L.K. Advani, and of course the prime minister himself. Farooq
was elated. His life ambition had been to one day become
President of India, and this was the penultimate step to that
goal.

It did not happen and it was the great tragedy of Farooq's
life. It was a betrayal.

There were two ways of looking at it, of course. One is that
it was an outright betrayal. Farooq has time and again been let
down by various people in New Delhi. Such people have argued
that Farooq is frivolous, that he is unreliable, that he can't be
trusted, or that they just didn't like him. For instance, Narasimha
Rao fantasised about sorting out the problem in Kashmir by
looking beyond Farooq at Shabir Shah because Rao simply
disliked Farooq. Recall that his only question to me before he
left for Africa was whether or not Farooq was necessary for the
revival of the political process.

If Vajpayee did not like Farooq it would be different from
Narasimha Rao's distaste. After all, Vajpayee and Farooq had
a lot in common. Vajpayee attended the opposition conclave
that Farooq as chief minister organised in Srinagar in 1983.
The two were also of a similar kind: the kind that loved fun and
the good things in life. The irony is that Rao, in 1994, had a
brainwave and deputed both Vajpayee and Farooq to Geneva,
to an important meeting of the United Nations Commission for
Human Rights, where India was under great pressure for its
dealing with the movement in Kashmir. It was ironic that a man

like Farooq, thought to be unreliable, was sent to defend the country at a UN forum.

Vajpayee, as we saw in the previous chapter, saw the autonomy resolution as a disappointment even if it was a compulsion for Farooq, who had come to power promising greater autonomy and would have to face an election the next year; for Vajpayee, who ran a coalition government, balancing his allies and his own Nehruvian instincts with the hardliners in his party was never easy, as the Gujarat riots in 2002 proved. The autonomy resolution only added to the pressures on Vajpayee. His not liking Farooq or thinking that Farooq was unreliable would have been linked to this episode. Or it was deep down dislike that came to the fore with this episode.

The other way of looking at the betrayal would be that Vajpayee, ever the Chanakya, played a bigger game when he offered Farooq the vice-presidency. He liked what he saw in Omar, and he wanted to switch the father-son combination by bringing Farooq to Delhi and putting Omar in Srinagar. It was a masterly political play. It whetted Omar's appetite, and when Farooq's current term as chief minister ended he never became chief minister again, even though he was publicly willing to do so in 2008.

True, many people are offered high office and then circumstances prevent it from happening. With Farooq, however, many forces in Delhi worked against him, unfairly. I wonder if, as such people say, Farooq is unreliable then who the hell in Kashmir is reliable?

Is it a coincidence that the one Kashmiri that Pakistan never tried to approach—because he was too unpredictable, that is, he was too much his own man—was Farooq Abdullah? And that the person with the highest bounty on his head ever since militancy hit full stride was Farooq Abdullah?

Earlier in the book, it's been mentioned how Farooq made the introduction to hijacker Hashim Qureshi; how Farooq came through with a favour for Syed Salahuddin, the Pakistan-based Hizbul Mujahideen preacher who has for long wanted to come back to India; and he introduced to the Rashtriya Rifles a rural folk-singer named Kuka Parrey, who went on to lead a force of counter-insurgents, the Ikhwan-ul Muslimoon, which was one of the army's successes. Farooq also was vehemently against releasing terrorists in his jails in exchange for hostages in both the Rubaiya kidnapping and the IC-814 hijacking, a position many have advocated as national policy. Farooq has never cited any of his actions that were of national security importance to make a case for himself, either privately or publicly. And yet he is called unreliable by vested interests in Delhi.

One of Farooq's defining moments could be Independence Day, 1989. He was the chief minister, Gen. K.V. Krishna Rao was the governor, and I was the IB man there. For just over a year, militancy had taken root and risen with bomb attacks and targeted killings. Because of the steadily increasing level of violence, it was a 15 August like no other. The ceremony was at the Bakshi Stadium, and during the governor's speech we could hear bombs go off somewhere outside. Yet the governor kept speaking.

When Farooq's turn came he made a moving speech. Essentially what he said was that Kashmir was an integral part of India and that it was not going anywhere, it would remain a part of India. It may sound routine for those sitting outside of Kashmir, but at that time, when the tide for azaadi in Kashmir was building up, when the mood and atmosphere was such that no one would publicly speak on behalf of India, Farooq's speech stood out.

At that function the chief minister was to inspect the police guard of honour. The director-general of police, Ghulam Jeelani Pandit, had arranged a jeep to take Farooq from the podium, where the guests of honour sat and where the speeches were made, to the guard lined up further away. The idea was that with security at risk, Farooq would take the salute in the jeep and return to the podium. Yet when the jeep reached the guard, Farooq stopped the jeep and hopped out. He then did a better slow march than Pandit had done in inspecting the guard. It was impressive. That was Farooq.

Additionally, a few weeks later, in September, Farooq was at the Hazratbal shrine, built by his father Sheikh Abdullah not only to house the Moi-e-Muqqadas, a relic of the Prophet Mohammed, but as a base since the Jamia Masjid in downtown Srinagar was the base of the Mirwaiz and his pro-Pakistan supporters. Farooq looked at the crowd and he warned it against getting into militancy. 'Bahut bura hoga,' he told them. 'Barbadi laoge, tumhari ma-behene loot jayengi.' He warned them that violence would only bring ruin to Kashmir, and it was prescient. Yet no one listened.

The irony in all of this is that Farooq became chief minister because he was Delhi's preference. Mrs Indira Gandhi was anxious that he take over from his father, Sheikh Saheb. According to B.K. Nehru, the governor of J&K at the time, she even went and met Sheikh Saheb when he was ill and had not taken a decision on whether it ought to be his son-in-law, the political veteran Gul Shah, or his son, whom many believed to be non-serious. Farooq was a member of Parliament in Delhi and Mrs Gandhi apparently went and said, 'Sheikh Saheb, don't you think it's time we brought Farooq to Srinagar?'

Farooq, however, was not comfortable with the Nehru–Gandhi family from the very beginning. If you take his family's point of view, the whole post-1947 relationship of Kashmir with New Delhi is one of lack of trust. Sheikh Abdullah, also known as Sher-e-Kashmir, led Kashmiris against Maharaja Hari Singh. When Independence came, Hari Singh was to choose between the two new countries, India and Pakistan, but he dithered and Pakistan tried to force the issue by sending in irregulars and troops in October 1947. This forced Hari Singh's hand, and he signed an Instrument of Accession to India with the last British viceroy, Lord Louis Mountbatten, assuring him it would be conditional on a plebiscite.

It suited Sheikh Abdullah to be part of India. He was close to Prime Minister Nehru and not to the founder of Pakistan, Mohammed Ali Jinnah, because of the differing philosophies of the two men, in a way a reflection of the philosophies of the new countries. Also, Kashmir enjoyed a special status within India, in charge of its own affairs except defence, foreign affairs and communications, with Sheikh Saheb as J&K's prime minister. For Nehru Kashmir was important as it would demonstrate to those Muslims who had not gone to Pakistan that India would take care of them.

But Nehru came under great pressure from those who came away from Partition believing that no one required any special guarantees. Thus there were a series of moves to erode the special status and make J&K like other states in the Union. Sheikh Saheb felt repeatedly betrayed, and in 1953 he was toppled and jailed. The promised plebiscite was never held. That there were trust issues is thus hardly surprising.

Sheikh Saheb was thrown into jail for a series of long stretches spanning twenty-three years. He went free only after he entered into the 1975 political accord with Prime Minister Indira Gandhi. He did so only when he saw India defeat Pakistan in war in 1971, leading to the division of Pakistan and the creation of a new country, Bangladesh. And he went ahead with the accord only after his son Farooq, who had qualified as a physician in England and had there married Mollie, went to Pakistan in 1974 and sounded out the leadership; Zulfikar Ali Bhutto told him to go ahead, as Pakistan was in no position to help the Kashmiri cause for political justice.

What the 1975 accord also did was settle any doubts that Farooq may have had. Thus, from the beginning of his political career Farooq has consistently and repeatedly said that Kashmir's accession to India is final and irrevocable.

Before Sheikh Saheb died he had inducted Farooq into his cabinet, and so in 1983 Farooq became chief minister of J&K. They were heady days and one of the things that Farooq did was host an opposition conclave in Srinagar which got Indira Gandhi all worked up. The sad thing was that she and Delhi in general did not seem to see the positive side of this conclave, which was that if Indian opposition leaders were going to Kashmir and if Farooq was getting involved in such activity, it was only helping in the mainstreaming of Kashmir. And that has been India's number one priority and ultimate aim in Kashmir since it joined the Union in October 1947.

But Indira Gandhi did not see it that way. She wanted Farooq out. Her cousin, B.K. Nehru—who in his book *Nice Guys Finish Second* has pointed out that Farooq was the first nationalist to head J&K; his father was certainly not a nationalist, and the others who became chief ministers were simply opportunists—did not play ball so she had him replaced with former bureaucrat Jagmohan. Jagmohan immediately dismissed Farooq, and this set the tone for Farooq's politics. Later, in his book, B.K. accused her of putting party and personal interests above the national interest.

The first I had heard of Farooq was when he entered into a political accord with Rajiv Gandhi in December 1986. I was on one of my assignments as the security officer for a presidential visit to Belgrade, the capital of the erstwhile Yugoslavia. Someone brought Giani Zail Singh a copy of the *Times of India* and said: 'Dekho Gianiji, ki khabar aayi hai.'

The great news he wanted to tell the president was that Farooq and Rajiv had reached an accord. Gianiji being Gianiji said: 'This is the beginning of the end of Farooq Abdullah. He will meet the same fate as Longowal did in Punjab.'

Harcharan Singh Longowal, as mentioned in the first chapter, died within a month of signing the Punjab accord. While Gianiji was not saying that Farooq's death was imminent, what he was saying was this: as a regional party why would you want to hobnob with the Congress? It was, in the estimate of the shrewd president, tantamount to political suicide and was no doubt one of the reasons that Kashmiris rejected mainstream politics for militancy a short while later.

202 | KASHMIR: The Vajpayee Years

I was transferred to Srinagar from Bhopal in 1988, and despite the entreaties by Arjun Singh, who had again in February 1988 become the chief minister of Madhya Pradesh, I went ahead with my transfer to Srinagar. While I was going, the DIB, M.K. Narayanan, called me in and said: 'Please make sure that Dr Farooq is kept in good humour, that our relationship with him is okay and that he's on our side. Please see to that.'

I came out of the DIB's room and went to his special assistant, who also happened to be my friend, Ratan Sehgal. 'Ratan,' I said, 'I thought Farooq was a good guy from whatever I heard. Is there a problem?'

'No, I don't think so,' said Ratan. 'But Rajiv (Gandhi) is very keen that we have a good relationship with Farooq.'

That was basically my brief. The way that Prime Minister Rajiv Gandhi looked at it, Farooq was the key to Kashmir. It is surprising that this simple truth eluded others.

Ironically, in the years after the Rajiv–Farooq accord, while I was in Srinagar, and while militancy gathered momentum, I did not see much bonhomie in the relationship between the two. I still recall that the two families, the Abdullahs and the Gandhis, went on a holiday together to snowbound Gulmarg once the accord was done. There was a lot of fanfare: both were English-speaking, both had foreign wives, they got along famously. Yet there was uneasiness. I think Rajiv and Farooq were not in love with each other, and that they had a decent, civilised, gentlemanly working relationship. One reason this worked is that Narayanan went out of his way to make it happen.

Farooq, after the accord, whenever he came to Delhi, felt he wasn't getting time with the prime minister; that he couldn't meet the PM when he wanted to. On the other hand, Rajiv felt that there were others who could deal with the chief minister of J&K, and that's how the young, up-and-coming minister Rajesh Pilot came into play: Rajiv felt it would be enough to interact with Farooq through Pilot. But this attitude would piss Farooq off.

There was an occasion in 1988 when I got a message from the IB headquarters in New Delhi, saying, 'Your chief minister hasn't been to Delhi for a while and the home minister wants to know why the CM is avoiding him.' Buta Singh was the home minister.

'Buta Singh was remembering you,' I said to Farooq.

'Who the hell is Buta Singh?' he exploded. 'Why would I want to meet him?'

'What happened?' I asked. 'What's the big deal?'

'When I go to Delhi and when I want to meet the prime minister, I'm kept waiting and I'm told he doesn't have time for me,' Farooq said. 'Why should I have time for your home minister?'

He would eventually be mollified, but this was Gianiji's point: once a regional party hobnobs with the Congress, it may not be a hostile relationship, but it will never be comfortable for the smaller partner.

I was first introduced to Farooq at a farewell party that the chief minister threw for my predecessor in Srinagar, K.P. Singh. More formally, though, I came to meet him in May 1988, when I took charge and I had to call on the chief minister.

It was not easy getting to Farooq, especially after my experience of meeting Arjun Singh whenever I wanted, or having had a good equation with President Zail Singh. For ten days nothing happened and I felt irritated. I inquired with my private secretary that I had asked for a meeting with the chief minister, so what happened? He said, 'Haan, saheb busy ho toh kai bar time bhi lag jaata hai.'

So I called up some colleagues, including the then advisor (home) to the state government, O.P. Bhutani, and the deputy inspector general (DIG) of the criminal investigation department (CID), M.N. Sabharwal. I told them I wanted to meet the CM but I wasn't getting to see him; I made it a point to say that I was coming from Madhya Pradesh where I got to meet Arjun Singh almost as soon as I wanted, and that he never kept me waiting. I was called home the following day.

I was wondering: how do you address the great man? Dr Abdullah? Chief minister? I asked Bhutani, who said Doctor Saheb is good enough. That sounded too much as if I was referring to him in the third person, so I usually called him 'Sir' and got away with it.

I arrived at his house on Gupkar Road and he walked out and shook my hand as if we were great buddies. He then said, 'Come on, get into the car. I'm going to Delhi.' He got in behind the driver's wheel, I got into the seat next to him, and the security detail in the car behind. And we drove to the airport.

Farooq loved driving, still does; he doesn't let anyone else drive. As he drove we spoke about a few things. The conversation was extremely pleasant, surprisingly so. This was the thing with Farooq: he could make you extremely comfortable (and when the time came, he could make you feel extremely uncomfortable). Once we reached the airport he said we'll continue this conversation when I return, and then he hopped onto his flight. His security guys dropped me back.

The trick to dealing with Farooq was to never tell him what he should do. Anyone who suggested or hinted that they could take him for granted would find out how wrong they were. Otherwise he was a great person to deal with. I never had a problem. He understood that I was the IB guy, and that if he could get a level playing field with Delhi through me, then what was the problem with talking to an IB guy?

Farooq always stressed on one thing: please report the truth to Delhi. He even said this publicly. In October 1988, the IB was celebrating its centenary, and as part of the celebrations, there were get-togethers in various outstations. Srinagar also had one such get-together where the DIB arrived with some officers from headquarters. We had the chief minister and the governor and some other ministers and people. It went off quite well. Farooq gave a speech and said the same thing: I expect the Intelligence Bureau to report correctly because otherwise you are doing a disservice to the country, to New Delhi, and to the government here, whatever it may be.

The IB had a sinister reputation in the Kashmiri mind. Part of it was because since Independence, the IB had basically been running Kashmir, advising the home ministry and reporting directly to the prime minister on whatever happened there. Nehru was particularly keen because he was ethnically a Kashmiri, and Kashmir had become a dispute with Pakistan in the United Nations. B.N. Mullik was quite active in Kashmir, and he mentioned as much in his memoir, hinting that he had a significant role to play in the 1964 recovery of the Moi-e-Muqqadas (there were riots in Kashmir when the relic disappeared).

If anyone in Kashmir had to abuse a political opponent, they would call him an IB agent.

The Abdullah family also felt that a lot of their problems were due to Kashmiri Pandits, who held disproportionately powerful positions in the government under Nehru and Indira Gandhi; the Abdullahs felt that Kashmiri Pandits carried lots of tales back to Delhi, and were thus highly untrustworthy. The IB, in J&K, had a fair amount of Kashmiri Pandits. One should not forget that when Sheikh Abdullah was arrested a conspiracy case was filed against him. It was put together by the IB. It went on for a number of years but nothing came of it. Thus, there was a feeling that these IB guys were up to no good. Sheikh Saheb even said once, I will see to it that these guys are packed off from here.

In my relationship with Farooq I think there was a distrust to begin with of Delhi and of the Intelligence Bureau. Over time, he figured that the IB was okay and that he could deal with it; his relationship with me also evolved naturally and it was fairly good though I couldn't claim that Farooq was a buddy of mine. There was a certain amount of respect; I saw a positive side of Farooq even though a lot of people were highly critical of him, all the time. But the way I saw it he was a leader of some standing, and without Farooq, there was no National Conference.

But not long after I took over, the first incident that defined the modern era in Kashmiri militancy happened, on 31 July 1988, when a bomb went off at the Srinagar Club, next to the Amar Singh club. Though Farooq always wanted to know from us what was going on, he always knew what was going on; he had numerous sources of information, which is not surprising considering how dominant his party, the National Conference, was in the Valley for all those years. And not long before this incident, Farooq told a public meeting in Anantnag that Kashmiris needed to be careful as things were getting bad. He said something near 100 militants had infiltrated into the Valley.

Immediately Delhi pricked up its ears and asked me, where has your chief minister got these figures from? So I asked Farooq: 'Sir, you mentioned that 100 militants have come in.'

'Did I?' was his response. 'So what?'

'Sir,' I said, 'Delhi's asking.'

'So let them ask,' he said.

I went to the chief secretary, Moosa Raza. As it was, Moosa's time with Farooq was exciting because he just didn't understand Farooq and didn't know what to make of him.

'Sir,' I said to Moosa Raza, 'CM has said there are 100 militants here but we don't have any such information and now he's said this and Delhi's getting all excited.'

'Don't worry,' Moosa said, looking worried. 'I know he says these things and we often have to later contradict him. What I'll do is that from now on I'll give him some points from which to speak or to refer.'

The next time Farooq had a public meeting, Moosa went along and gave his chief minister a piece of paper with five or six points written down. Farooq put the slip in his pocket and began speaking. After a while, Farooq was back to saying whatever he felt like saying; so Moosa, who was sitting in the front row, frantically began to point with one finger to his pocket, gesturing that the chief minister should reach into his own pocket and pull the slip out. Farooq looked at Moosa and

Moosa's finger. He then continued without ever referring to that slip of paper. As I mentioned, Farooq never liked being told what to do.

During those years in Srinagar when I got to know Farooq, I saw that he was not non-serious, as many people claimed. The fact of the matter was that he did not suffer fools and he did not waste time on fools. Also, he did not like negativity. When militancy was hotting up, the police chief, Jeelani Pandit, got on Farooq's nerves because he would every day go to his chief minister with a list of bad news, of terrorist incidents. Farooq wanted to hear about militants getting caught or about a police plan to combat militancy. So Jeelani Pandit got the sack and was replaced by J.N. Saxena, who had been my predecessor K.P. Singh's predecessor in Srinagar.

The other thing was that there was no hypocrisy about Farooq. Early on, after my first few interactions, I wanted to call on him. 'What is this "call on you"?' he said. 'Come home and have dinner.'

There was one other couple there and as soon as we sat down Farooq said, 'Will you have a drink?'

'Sir,' I said. 'If you have a drink then I'll have a drink.'

'Of course I'll have a drink,' he said.

I was once asked that since I knew so many Kashmiris, could I say how many liked to have a drink? I replied that I could say who liked his drink, but I couldn't say who didn't. That's how the Kashmiri is. And that's how Farooq is: he loves doing everything and people talking about it. He does not hide who he is. Being a doctor he was always careful about his health and his drinking was restricted to entertainment with friends.

Farooq was also very much a family man. I joined in May 1988 and in March my wife and I had to send our daughter off to boarding school since there was no place to send her to school in Srinagar. She went to Sanawar, where Farooq's son Omar was the head boy. The founders' day at the Lawrence School is early October and Farooq asked me if I was going. I had planned on taking leave to do so, so Farooq said, 'Come with me and tell your department that you're keeping a watch on the chief minister.' Of course I didn't take him up on his offer.

His wife Mollie was very much a part of things and despite all the talk of his womanising, she put up pretty well with him. She was totally apolitical and stayed in the background, busying herself in work at the nearby hospital on Gupkar Road. She was civilised and though she never took interest in politics, if she needed to accompany the chief minister somewhere, she would. No doubt she enjoyed being the chief minister's wife, but she left Srinagar in 1990 when things went out of control. It had become too much for her and she told her husband that it was no place for their girls to go to school. (Omar was already in college in Bombay.) First she spent some time in Delhi, at her mother-in-law's house in Safdarjung Lane; then she left for England.

After Rubaiya's kidnapping, Farooq repeatedly told the new prime minister, V.P. Singh, that he would resign the moment Jagmohan was brought back as governor. The BJP, which along with the Left supported the National Front government from outside, was demanding the deployment of Jagmohan to combat the militancy, which had gone out of control. Farooq obviously had bitter memories of Jagmohan, who had dismissed him in 1984 and had Gul Shah installed in his place. 'Anybody but Jagmohan,' Farooq told the prime minister. Railways Minister George Fernandes assured Farooq that it wouldn't happen, but in the end neither he nor V.P. Singh could stop Mufti, Arun Nehru and Jagmohan from having their way, and true to his word, Farooq resigned.

I was jettisoned then from Srinagar in March 1990, nearly two months after Farooq quit, because the governor thought I was Farooq's man and home minister Mufti Mohammad Sayeed did not disagree. It took two months to replace me because things were so bad in Kashmir that IB officers were reluctant to be posted in Srinagar. As I mentioned in chapter four, R.C. Mehta took up the assignment, and when he reached he asked me if I would introduce him to the former chief minister.

Farooq was still in Srinagar. I rang him up and told him that my successor had arrived. 'You're leaving?' he asked.

'Yes, sir.'

'Oh, boy,' he said. Those were his exact words.

Farooq agreed that I could bring R.C. over for tea but asked me to come an hour earlier. I did and found myself chatting with a relaxed man, a man who spoke in an absolutely open way. And he said something to me that was crucial to understanding his politics.

'I'm not like father,' Farooq said. 'I'm not going to follow my father's politics.'

It was quite an admission because Sheikh Saheb had been the last word in Kashmir. But he had also spent decades imprisoned. 'I don't intend to spend twenty-three years in jail,' Farooq said. 'I've figured out that to remain in power here you have to be on the right side of Delhi and that's what I'm going to do.'

There it was in a nutshell: the simple and straightforward politics of Farooq Abdullah.

He then thanked me and said it was sad that I was going, that it was all a part of the job. Frankly, I was happy to get out of there because militancy had made the stress unbearable. I was relieved to be going.

The irony is that once Farooq decided to resign he got a frantic message from Rajiv Gandhi, conveyed by Rajesh Pilot. Rajiv wanted to meet Farooq before he resigned, because the Congress party did not want Farooq to resign. Pilot came to Jammu and picked up Farooq and flew him to Delhi, but Farooq stuck to his guns and said, 'No, I'm resigning.'

From that day on, Farooq's worth went up many times in Rajiv's estimation, and Rajiv was always saying Farooq, Farooq, Farooq. In March 1990, Rajiv went with Deputy Prime Minister

Devi Lal on an all-party delegation visit to Kashmir, and the Congress president had a lot to say on that trip. He told the media that there was a great mess in Kashmir; that the National Front government did not know what it was up to; and that it was responsible for Farooq's resignation.

Here's another irony: the man with a key role in Farooq's resignation and Jagmohan's appointment was Home Minister Mufti Sayeed. Once V.P. Singh's government fell in November 1990, till Farooq was re-elected chief minister in 1996, Mufti had only one refrain: that there was no other solution to Kashmir but Farooq Abdullah. I remember at least six occasions on which he said this, all reported by the media.

Farooq went to England and would come to Delhi when he thought that something was going to happen. But he was mostly abroad and I met him once, in 1993, at his Sussex home. In the early 1990s, in fact, there were only three constant visitors to Farooq at Safdarjung Lane. One was Shia cleric and Congress leader Moulvi Iftikhar Hussain Ansari (the other two were a professor at Jawaharlal Nehru University in Delhi named Riyaz Punjabi, and A.S. Dulat). Like Abdul Ghani Lone, Iftikhar had been with the People's Conference and done a bit of party-hopping. As Kashmir's top Shia leader he had extensive contacts with the Iranians, who gave him a lot of respect. His cousin, Abbas Ansari, would later be one of the stalwarts of the All Parties Hurriyat Conference.

In those lonely days of the early 1990s when no one would even visit Farooq, Iftikhar was closer to him than even Farooq's fellow partymen. As a mainstream leader Iftikhar was the most outspoken against the separatists and would repeatedly tell me, 'Why are you wasting your time on these fellows, yeh kissi kaam ke nahin.' On this, his and Farooq's thinking matched, except that Farooq understood Delhi's compulsion in reaching out to separatists and was fine with it—so long as it didn't compromise him. Iftikhar, on the other hand, was much more suspicious of our hobnobbing with separatists.

As mentioned, Iftikhar was closer to Farooq at the time than even the National Conference people, because the NC leaders had all but disappeared due to militancy and the threat to their lives. (Several were killed.) With Farooq away from the scene the party was hollow. For all the talk of it being a cadre-based party spread all over the state, it was nothing without Farooq. It was demoralised, and the only person flying the party flag in Srinagar, besides Farooq Abdullah on Gupkar Road, was Syed Akhoon from Budgam. Otherwise, there was no NC. There was only Farooq.

We were trying to get the NC back in business in the early 1990s, telling its leaders that it was high time they came out of hibernation and began getting politically involved. This was particularly so in 1994 and '95, when separatists like Shabir Shah and Yasin Malik were released and talking peace and Delhi was talking politics. The NC leaders would always respond: 'You get our leader back and then we'll talk politics.'

By then Farooq also got wind that change was in the air and that he was needed in Delhi, so he came back and stayed instead of returning to England.

There is a telling anecdote that concerns a London-based Kashmiri named Dr Siraj Shah, director of a human rights group called Kashmir Watch. Several expatriates were getting involved in 1993–94 and trying to get things resolved in Kashmir. Like Narasimha Rao, Dr Siraj was also hooked on Shabir Shah, believing him to be the ultimate solution to Kashmir. Perhaps he had heard on the Kashmiris' network that the government of India was more interested in Shabir.

So Dr Siraj met Shabir a few times, and then one day approached me and said, 'I've had enough of him.' He had become disillusioned with Shabir and thought the separatist to be a waste of time and money. 'Can you introduce me to Dr Farooq Abdullah instead?' Dr Siraj asked me.

The three of us had breakfast together and Dr Siraj came away impressed with Farooq. 'This is the right man for Kashmir,' he said to me. 'Why are you wasting your time on these other idiots?' he added, in reference to the separatists.

Dr Siraj said even he wanted to come back to Kashmir. 'When are elections going to be held?' he asked.

'Doc, you won't fit in here,' I said.

'No, I'm familiar with Srinagar,' he said. 'I've lived there all my life.'

'What about your European wife?'

'She can stay in London,' Dr Siraj said, without missing a beat. Now I'm told he dumped her and married an English girl.

The point was that Kashmiris of all hues, whether abroad or here, found Farooq indispensable to Kashmir. Indeed, till Farooq returned in 1995 and revived his party, there was no political mainstream in Kashmir. Which is why Irshad Malik—the militant whom I wish I had brought back to India when I was R&AW chief and who is now in London—said that the 1996 assembly election was a masterstroke, because it revived the political process and broke the back of militancy. It could only revive the political process because Farooq jumped into the fray, which he had reservations about right till the last moment; in fact, he did not participate in the 1996 Lok Sabha election in June, because the NC had not made up its mind about taking part. A lot of effort went into persuading Farooq to agree to take the plunge.

Farooq's party, of course, won the assembly election and was invited to form the government. A week before the swearing-in he was busy mustering his troops and we met for lunch at the Taj. 'Doctor Saheb,' I said. 'I'm told that in 1983 when you formed your first government you had only a handful of ministers and it made a huge impact. Why not do that again, keep the cabinet small, and afterwards you can expand it?' He agreed.

The swearing-in ceremony was held in the Sher-e-Kashmir auditorium and was attended by the Congress president, Sitaram Kesri, along with other opposition leaders. I also went, and I took along my IB colleague Ajit Doval, who was being posted in Srinagar and whom I wanted to introduce to the new chief minister. It was a moving ceremony. While he was being sworn in, the audience stood up and gave him a standing ovation. He became emotional. He was on stage and he began calling people on stage, 'tum bhi aajao', and in the end around twenty fellows got sworn in.

Among them was one non-NC member: Iftikhar Ansari, who was in the Congress party. During the ceremony, Farooq asked Kesri: 'Inko hamare saath aane dijiye.' Such was the goodwill that Kesri immediately agreed, and said, 'Inko National Conference mein le lijiye.'

Another irony is that Farooq and Iftikhar parted company over cases of corruption that were lodged against Iftikhar; the cases involved a scam in the cleaning of the Dal Lake. The two fought against each other in the parliamentary election of 2009, and in his campaign, Farooq took a few cracks at his former friend. 'Thankfully Iftikhar is not a woman or you can imagine the number of husbands he would have had,' Farooq said on the campaign trail, lampooning Iftikhar's past party-hopping.

Iftikhar passed away in September 2014, while this book was being written. I went to see him in May; he had been suffering from cancer and had gone to the US for treatment. 'Your friend is going to lose,' he said.

'He is your friend too,' I said.

'That he is, I acknowledge,' Iftikhar said. 'But he doesn't.'

'Are you serious about his losing?'

'He will lose,' Iftikhar said. 'But even so, Farooq's place in history is assured.'

When Farooq returned to power, H.D. Deve Gowda was the prime minister and Farooq was most comfortable with him. There was no meddling in J&K's affairs and that was the best thing from Farooq's point of view. There was no panic in Delhi when Farooq's government set up the State Autonomy Committee because for somebody like Deve Gowda, who came from a state, and whose government was a United Front of regional parties, discussing how to expand a state's autonomy was the most natural thing in the world.

Those were also the best years I had with Farooq. It had to do with the fact that when I returned to the IB headquarters in 1990, the normal course of things would have been to go on to other assignments. I started on that track, but thanks to my DIBs, Joshi and Narayanan, I headed the Kashmir group for eight years, till I joined R&AW. Perhaps Farooq felt that unlike other officials I wasn't a guy who had disappeared from the scene. We would thus meet often, either when he was in Delhi or when I went to Srinagar, and had many a drink together. Those were the days he relied on me.

Once Farooq complained that he was being pressured by Delhi to get an outsider as chief secretary, and that the Union home secretary, K. Padmanabhaiah, had handed him a slip of paper with several names on it. One of the names was of a fellow who like Padmanabhaiah was a Maharashtra cadre IAS officer. I asked Farooq, 'Sir, what is this, do you want an outsider?' Farooq admitted that he wanted the J&K cadre IAS officer Tony (Ashok) Jaitley, so I tore up the slip and said get him only.

Then Tony came to Delhi and met me at the India International Centre one day. Why don't you come down to Kashmir, the boss would like you there as DG, he said. I wasn't interested because I had done my stint in Kashmir and I wasn't really a policeman's policeman. 'I'm basically an intelligence man,' I told Tony. 'I don't know if the force there will accept me.' So I didn't go but it didn't matter. Farooq and I had a relationship that whenever he had a problem, he would turn to me. It made many people uncomfortable. Soon after he took over as CM, Farooq wanted a change of his police chief. 'Why would you want an outsider?' I enquired. 'Sabharwal knows the force and they are comfortable with him.' 'Maybe,' he said, 'But I am not. Please get me a new chief.' So I suggested

Gurbachan Jagat, a 1966 Punjab cadre officer with all the experience of dealing with terrorism. Jagat made an outstanding DG and went places after that, ending up as governor in Manipur. Farooq supported him at every step.

During this time he also helped me with my golf game. I had learned golf in Srinagar, from an old pro at the old course on Maulana Azad Road, which was burnt down during militancy. The golf club was a place for great kebabs and I also knew a couple of people in the air force and in the army who were keen on golf and who got me to learn.

After Farooq returned as chief minister in 1996 I would play with him. Of course he's a 4 or 5 handicap whereas I had a handicap of 24 or so. I never lugged a golf set up there, he had three-four sets lying at home and would give me one. Farooq loved his golf and any time he could squeeze out he would be on the golf course. He used to teach me, saying this is what you're doing wrong, this is what you're supposed to do. I used to tell him I was spoiling his game, but he was patient. He was a good teacher and I picked up a few things from him.

And it was in those days that one day, Farooq and I were sitting together on a flight from Jammu to Delhi, with his principal secretary, B.R. Singh, sitting behind us. Farooq suddenly turned around and told Singh that only one thing remained on his agenda, and that was to get Dulat to the Raj Bhavan as governor. I laughed. That will never happen, I told him. This story was to be repeated many times and my response always was the same: it won't happen. And for once Farooq was wrong and I was right.

Inevitably, the United Front government fell and the BJP-led NDA came to power. Sonia Gandhi had taken over the Congress with the departure of Sitaram Kesri, and though Farooq had never quite been buddies with Rajiv, with Sonia the equation was absolutely non-existent. When she pulled down Vajpayee's one-year-old government in 1999, Farooq did not side with her.

Farooq was determined not to go with the Congress and he was ready to go with the BJP because he was probably thinking ahead to the 2002 election, and in his thinking the BJP at the Centre during the election was preferable to having the Congress in power in Delhi. He thought the BJP was a lesser evil. On top of which was the lack of equation with Sonia. While he was chief minister, on at least four occasions when he came visiting Delhi and I met him at J&K House, I would say, 'You come to Delhi to meet everybody, but why don't you meet madam?'

His reaction was usually, 'Why should I?'

But siding with the BJP did not help Farooq. Vajpayee wanted to switch between father and son; Omar had been pampered by Delhi and Vajpayee thought he was just ripe to go to Kashmir as chief minister. It would be a good time to get Farooq out.

Farooq was given a lollipop: that he would become the Vice-President of India. The prime minister told him so. The home minister told him so. Brajesh Mishra told him so, at my house: 'Doctor Saheb, why don't you come to Delhi?'

Around May, however, the whispering in Delhi began. Farooq as vice-president? He's not serious! We don't know if he will sit in the Rajya Sabha. Talk went around. And, most significantly, the RSS did not approve of Farooq Abdullah.

In early May I was in Srinagar and received a message that the chief minister wanted to meet me. The time given was 11:00 and I took it for granted that I had been called home, but then I was told, 'No, Saheb ne office bulaya hain,' which is very unlike Farooq. I went to the office and he sat me across the desk and said: 'Do you believe that these guys will make me vice-president?'

'Why not?' I asked.

'I don't believe it, that's why I'm asking you.'

'What do you believe?' I asked. 'Sir, you've spoken to the home minister about this, haven't you?'

Farooq said yes.

'You've spoken to the prime minister about this?'

'Yes.'

'If both have given you their word then you will be the next vice-president,' I said.

'But I don't trust them,' Farooq said. 'I don't trust Delhi.'

The moment Krishan Kant was out and Alexander in, Farooq's fears were confirmed. 'They can't both be minorities,' he reasoned about the two constitutional posts.

He was proved right. Dr Kalam out of the blue became president and Farooq had to be ditched. The NDA leadership had obviously said to Farooq whatever they had said, but they were not sincere about what they said, and it did not bother any of them to go back on their word. Farooq was ditched and that was that.

That was the end of Farooq Abdullah.

Later that year his party lost power in J&K and when it did return to power, Omar was leading the government. For Farooq, however, 2002 proved a terrible year. He did not get the vice-presidentship; then there was a lot of talk that he would be taken into the cabinet as a Union minister. After the elections, I asked him, 'What happened, why did you refuse a ministership here?'

'Which ministership?' he asked.

'Weren't you offered a ministership?'

'What rubbish,' he said. 'Nobody's offered me anything. But now that you are talking of ministership, at least get me a house. I don't even have a house in Delhi.'

Even that he did not get. Omar had been allotted a house on Akbar Road—where Vajpayee and his family had once had dinner—so Farooq was told: your son has a house, why do you need one?

Not surprisingly, Farooq was cut up at that point of time. He was disgusted and he might have thought I was a part of the conspiracy but never showed it, though he might have held it against me. I know that I was absolutely taken by surprise.

By now, the story with Farooq is pretty much over. By the time the 2014 assembly elections were to be announced his health was not good and he was in London for a kidney transplant. While he was a minister in the UPA government, he went on record in an interview to journalist Saeed Naqvi and said outright, 'Delhi doesn't trust us.' Imagine, a minister of the Union saying that—in Delhi.

Delhi has wasted Farooq. For instance: Pervez Musharraf was once invited to one of the Delhi media's conclaves after he stepped down from power, and Farooq was there. Farooq went up to Musharraf, offered his hand and said: 'Mujhe Farooq Abdullah kehte hain.' The point here is that Farooq is one Kashmiri leader whom the Pakistanis are wary of, and whom they would never approach directly. If the Pakistanis could buy everybody in the Valley, the one person they would still be unsure of would be Farooq Abdullah. Pakistan never messed with Sheikh Abdullah after 1975 because he was too big. Farooq was not only big but unpredictable, something which even Delhi never understood.

Since 1997, the Sindhu Darshan festival has been celebrated annually in Leh; it is a festival that L.K. Advani worked hard to bring into existence to worship the Indus river. On 1 June 2000, it was celebrated with great pomp and even Vajpayee came for the inauguration. Of the three people who spoke on that occasion—Vajpayee, Advani and Farooq—Farooq was easily the best orator. Farooq, incidentally, has also been to the Vaishno Devi temple near Jammu. And whenever he lands up at cultural functions in Kashmir, he is sure to sing a few ghazals—and bhajans.

Yet when it comes to the Republic Day and Independence Day awards and honours, Farooq has never figured. He hasn't even got a Padma Shri, whereas one of the Ikhwanis—the counter-insurgents who are not much considered heroes in Kashmir—received a Padma Shri a few years back. It's simple, someone recommended it, the Ikhwani got it. People laughed.

There were times when Sheikh Abdullah's name was recommended for a posthumous Bharat Ratna, but he was turned down. Farooq should have at least been given a Padma Vibhushan by now. He's not even considered for a governorship or an ambassadorial assignment.

Farooq is the tallest and most meaningful Kashmiri leader. His nationalistic and secular credentials can never be doubted. He was the first chief minister to adopt the Prevention of Terrorism Act (POTA), which some people in India say is a law that has been misused disproportionately against Muslims— and Farooq adopted it despite being the chief minister of India's only Muslim-majority state. Yet the UPA did not even consult him on Kashmir even though he was a member of the cabinet. It is not surprising that he went on record to say that Delhi did not trust Kashmiris. It is not surprising that he felt bitter when betrayed over being made the Vice-President of India. And this feeling of betrayal would carry over to the 2002 assembly election, when he lost power and suspected it to be a conspiracy of the government of India.

13

WAR AND PEACE

Between the autonomy resolution in the J&K assembly and the vice-presidential election in August 2002, several events happened which had their role in Vajpayee's master plan for cutting the India–Kashmir–Pakistan Gordian knot: the 2001 Agra summit, the 9/11 attacks on America, and the attack on our own Parliament and India's subsequent military mobilisation along the western border. After this series of events coincidentally came the 2002 J&K assembly election, which would prove to be another milestone.

Vajpayee and Brajesh Mishra had tasked me with overseeing a completely free and fair J&K assembly election, if possible with the participation of separatists. I had been talking to the separatists individually, some for years, some like Abdul Ghani Lone as recently as during my tenure at R&AW. The only separatist I never spoke to was Syed Ali Shah Geelani, who was in touch with an aide of mine. Getting them into the electoral process was another matter altogether because they were so tightly controlled by Pakistan—remember that when Lone began making reasonable noises he was shot dead—but the brief had been given, so I got on the job.

I used the opportunity of a public lecture to make the case for involving 'more people'—a way of saying those outside the mainstream, namely the separatists—and the case for continuing talking. In February 2001 I went to Jammu to deliver the Amar Kapoor memorial lecture. Kapoor was an IPS officer of the J&K cadre and from the 1964 batch, a year senior to me, and as mentioned earlier, a pal of Lone's who got along equally well with Farooq. He was an amiable person and had earlier served with us in the IB. He had been the additional director-general of police four years earlier when he died suddenly of a heart attack; this lecture was instituted in his memory. I was still in R&AW when I accepted an invitation to deliver the lecture, which was called 'Kashmir, the way forward'.

Governor Gary Saxena was a former R&AW chief and he insisted I stay at Raj Bhavan. This is the time that on the way to the lecture I went to the chief minister's residence, because Farooq was presiding over the function, and I unsuccessfully pleaded that former militant Firdous Syed be given another term as a member of the legislative council.

The lecture also did not go down well with Farooq and the National Conference, because I talked about dialogue and involving the separatists. The NC was always wary of Delhi trying to replace them by separatists. The concern that Narasimha Rao was actively courting Shabir Shah might have been one of the factors that tilted the scales for Farooq to participate in the 1996 assembly election. Our dialogue with Lone, as mentioned earlier, also made Farooq anxious before the 2002 election.

I made mention of Lone and his statements during his recent visit to Pakistan for his son's wedding and on his return; Lone had realised the futility of the gun and the ruin it could bring to Kashmir. I referred to him as 'Lone Saheb'.

Thus, a few NC people did not stay for tea though they did not go so far as to stage a walkout during the lecture. They were not happy. 'Yeh Lone kab Lone Saheb ban gaye?' one of the NC fellows asked me.

'It was only out of respect for age,' I said. 'He's older than me.'

Gary Saxena read about it in the papers the next day. He understood what was going on and he complimented me. 'Tum accha bole,' he said. 'Bara balance kar ke.' Farooq was not happy, though I did compliment him while he sat on the dais.

If a dialogue process with separatists had begun then the government wanted a political face to the process, in the way that Rajesh Pilot was the face in Narasimha Rao's time. The NDA thus appointed the deputy chairman of the Planning Commission, K.C. Pant, as its political interlocutor for Kashmir in April 2001. Pant was a senior politician who had spent his life in the Congress and was credited with successful negotiations with Telangana agitators in the 1970s. He immediately said he wanted to meet the Hurriyat.

The Hurriyat, however, turned him down. The reason which moderate leaders have reiterated from time to time as the occasion warrants is that they want to deal directly with the PMO. At the time Prof. Abdul Ghani Bhat, a member of the Muslim Conference (which was the party that Sheikh Abdullah started before he changed it to the more secular National Conference; it then became the premier party of PoK, led by Sardar Qayoom) and a Hurriyat executive member, said he would not meet Pant unless an agenda for the meeting was made clear and something was given in writing.

Some bright spark in the government immediately put an ad out in the newspapers in Kashmir saying Pant had been appointed interlocutor and that everybody who wanted to talk to him could meet him. This elicited many sniggers in the Valley, and the Hurriyat said no thanks.

Pant had already set his visit for 28 May 2001, and he asked me to arrange some meeting for him. So I called up my old friend Shabir Shah and said, 'Aap toh milo Pant Saheb se, you are the main player here and the biggest leader, so you must meet him.'

Anyone getting an ego massage like that would immediately say yes, and Shabir was no different, but he set a condition: 'I will meet him, but he will have to come to my house.'

I told Pant and he said, 'Woh kaise hoga?'

'Gaadi mein jayenge aap, usse milenge, aise hi hoga,' I said.

Which is what Pant did—he went in a car and Shabir spent some time with him, so his visit wasn't a total washout. Pant then said to me, 'Now you must get him to Delhi to come to my place.'

'Yes,' I said. 'We'll do that.'

Shabir did come to Delhi and to Pant's place, with a lot of TV cameras in tow. But that was the end of that.

A year later Pant was sidelined in August 2002 by the formation of a Kashmir Committee on the initiative of eminent jurist and political maverick Ram Jethmalani, but that too went nowhere as the Hurriyat refused to formally meet the committee because it was not sponsored by the government. This committee hung around till 2004 but in any case was made redundant when in February 2003 former bureaucrat N.N. Vohra was appointed the interlocutor. (Though the Hurriyat also refused to meet him, Vohra was appointed governor when the post opened up in 2008.) Fortunately the six-month respite between interlocutors was when the J&K assembly election took place, in which obtaining broad-based participation was my brief.

Many things helped create the atmosphere for the 2002 election, including Majid Dar's coming back from Pakistan and announcing a ceasefire, Vajpayee's unilateral Ramzan ceasefire in November 2000, and the 2001 Agra summit.

The Ramzan ceasefire lasted six months and when it came to an end in May 2001 the prime minister explored follow-up measures to this successful initiative. Both his foreign minister Jaswant Singh and his home minister L.K. Advani have said in their respective memoirs (*A Call to Honour* and *My Life, My Country*) that the three of them had a meeting in which it was decided to put the Kargil misadventure of two summers ago behind them and invite Gen. Pervez Musharraf over. Advani made this suggestion, he says, following his interactions with the Pakistani high commissioner here, Ashraf Jehangir Qazi.

Again, despite Advani's hardline image, he was the one who broke the ice with Qazi. As the story goes, following the Kargil war, Pakistan was in the doghouse here in India and though the high commissioner went about his engagements he kept a lower profile than usual. At one particular function, Advani and Qazi came face-to-face and the high commissioner was at a loss over how to face the home minister. He was turning away when Advani said: 'Aapne udhar mooh kyon kar liya?' And he met Qazi with warmth.

The two began to meet: veteran television anchor Karan Thapar set up secret meetings (twenty of them, according to Karan) between Advani and the high commissioner. Karan Thapar's story goes back to 1998 (as published in his column 'Sunday Sentiments' in March 2008.) Qazi, a friend of Karan's, needed someone to establish rapport with the NDA government. Karan introduced him to George Fernandes, then defence minister, and the two would meet for dinner at Karan's place and became friends. But Qazi was keen to meet Advani so George set it up and asked Karan to drive Qazi to Advani's residence in Pandara Park late one night. Karan waited outside while Qazi met Advani for 90 minutes. On the second occasion Karan was seen waiting under a street light by Sudheendra Kulkarni, then Vajpayee's speech writer. When Kulkarni saw Karan the latter passed it off saying he was waiting for a friend having dinner at the Ambassador Hotel. Thereafter, Advani's daughter Pratibha suggested that he wait with them (her and Mrs Advani) while the two 'A's met. Possibly no one got a whiff of these meetings. A link developed, which proved useful when Vajpayee was deciding on the government's next move, and whether or not to invite General Musharraf. The feedback was that the general was equally keen to visit, and so an invitation was extended for him to come for a summit meeting in Agra in July 2001. In preparation for the meeting, General Musharraf had himself appointed president in June, so that he was a genuine head of state and not just 'chief executive'.

The summit did not produce anything, and in fact President Musharraf left in a huff, without even stopping at Ajmer Sharif to visit the dargah as he had planned. As has been recorded in not just Jaswant's and Advani's memoirs, but also in the memoirs of the foreign minister, Abdul Sattar, and President Musharraf himself (*Pakistan's Foreign Policy, 1947–2009: A Concise History*, and *In the Line of Fire*), the sticking point came on 15 July, when Jaswant and Sattar exchanged drafts that the other had problems with; basically Musharraf wanted to focus on Jammu and Kashmir, which Vajpayee and the rest of his Cabinet Committee on Security (CCS), whom he had taken along to Agra, were willing to do provided there was equal focus on terrorism—and that did not happen to our satisfaction. Worse, of course, was Musharraf's belligerent press conference the next morning, which pretty much unilaterally declared the summit over.

In his memoir, Musharraf claims that he gave an earful to Vajpayee about someone above the two of them who could 'overrule' and 'humiliate' them both. Advani says this was an indirect reference to himself. Sattar in his memoir first puts the blame on the 'political affairs committee', as he mistakenly calls the CCS, and then writes that they later heard that it was Advani who torpedoed the summit by rejecting a final draft that Jaswant had brought to the CCS. (Jaswant himself claims it was a collective rejection.)

Furthermore, Musharraf claims that Vajpayee sat there 'speechless' listening to him. Obviously, Musharraf was clueless about Vajpayee's ways. Vajpayee's habit was never to utter a word, even in internal meetings, unless he had to; often it was puzzling. When I was the R&AW chief, for instance, there were many times when I spoke to him on the RAX phone and then waited a long, long time for a response, wondering what had happened to the old fellow. And Jaswant in his memoir says that later he asked the prime minister what transpired in the final meeting with Musharraf, to which the prime minister said in Hindi that nothing had happened: Musharraf kept talking and he kept listening. Musharraf the commando could not fathom Vajpayee the Chanakya.

If Advani had torpedoed the summit by vetoing the final draft, the irony would be that it happened due to a tactical error by the Pakistanis, who focused on pleasing only the prime minister. They believed he was their best chance at diplomatic success. Public perception was that if the Pakistanis wanted to do any business here it had to be Vajpayee and not Advani—the hardliner. This is possibly why Agra failed. Had they kept Advani in good humour then perhaps it would not have failed. That they ignored him is ironic considering that Qazi was almost a family member in Advani's home, as some people say.

An interesting story has lately emerged from Musharraf's vantage point. He has apparently told some people, after he lost power and fled Pakistan for first Dubai and then London, that the main culprit was not Advani. The villain as he put it was one of Jaswant's joint secretaries, Vivek Katju. He would have been assisting Jaswant when the draft statement was going back and forth, proposing language changes that would satisfy both sides—as is the job of foreign ministry mandarins. If the Pakistanis feel he had been intransigent in finding common ground before a final draft was sent to the CCS, then how Advani reacted becomes a moot point. Was he the villain that Pakistanis make him out to be? Why would he sabotage something which was his own brainchild? And why did High Commissioner Qazi not use his friendship with Advani rather than putting pressure on the prime minister who, according to Brajesh Mishra, found himself almost alone. Qazi corroborates Brajesh and provides greater insight into what happened in Agra.

Ashraf Qazi told me during a recent visit to Delhi that Advani was the 'architect' of Agra. He said Advani was a wonderful human being so long as you pandered to his vanity; he himself had a great relationship because he was always respectful of Advani. But he added, the Advani of Agra was very different from what he knew of him in Delhi because he had suddenly developed all kinds of reservations. According to Qazi, it all started badly the previous evening when Advani called on Musharraf in Rashtrapati Bhavan and brought up the matter of Dawood Ibrahim. Qazi says, Musharraf was taken aback and said, 'Let us at least get to Agra!' Their chemistry never took off and this was to haunt the Agra summit throughout. Qazi felt that Musharraf the general could still have pulled it off but Vajpayee the politician found himself alone with only Jaswant Singh for support. And Qazi said Jaswant Singh called him twice in Agra to say that the deal was done and yet it never happened.

Perhaps Musharraf regretted the fact that he stormed out of Agra like an army chief and did not act like the president he had become just the previous month. He must have regretted it because it took three years to restart the peace process. As Dr Manmohan Singh said in his last press conference as prime minister in January 2014, he and Musharraf nearly clinched a deal on Kashmir in late 2006 or early 2007. It was a window of opportunity we lost. So had the failure of Agra not stalled things for three years, who knows what might have been accomplished while Vajpayee was in office?

In the end it put too much pressure on the prime minister and one enduring criticism of Vajpayee is that he didn't have the gumption to go the last mile to get something that he really wanted: a positive conclusion to the Agra summit. And when the team returned from Agra, there was huge, palpable disappointment. This is a point that most accounts of the Agra summit have skipped: the feeling of 'so close, yet so far' shared by the two old men running the government.

'Yaar, hote-hote reh gaya,' Brajesh sighed to me, shaking his head at the done deal that came undone. 'Ho gaya tha, woh toh.'

Yet the Agra summit had its positive fallout in Kashmir, for when things are going peacefully between India and Pakistan, then that is when the Kashmiri feels most optimistic, and this helped in the run-up to the 2002 assembly election, because the summit helped in discussions with the separatists. You may recall from the Lone chapter that on his way to Agra, Musharraf met the Hurriyat, and Lone had told him that Kashmiris were exhausted and also tired of being killed (though Geelani disagreed).

The attack on America on 11 September 2001 also had its effect on Kashmir and in paving the way for elections. In the process the militancy suffered a series of setbacks—first when militants like Firdous and Yasin Malik burnt out by 1993 or '94, then when the political process was restored by the 1996 assembly election, and again when Pakistan's Kargil misadventure disillusioned those Kashmiri militants stranded in Pakistan—then 9/11 further clinched the fact in the Kashmiri minds that nothing could be expected from Pakistan.

The events of the 9/11 attack are well known. The NDA government acted fast and openly expressed support. In a statement, the Cabinet Committee on Security expressed its 'great horror at this crime that has been perpetrated and has offered its deepest condolences and sympathy to the people, government and the president of the United States of America'. The government further said that 'terrorism is a crime against humanity and India is committed to fight it'. The focus on terrorism was what India had wanted highlighted at the Agra summit, and now it was America's focus. Kashmir was suddenly, for those around the world who had so far refrained from seeing it so, a terrorism problem above all else.

Prof. Ghani told me that 9/11 was a sobering experience for the Kashmiris. 'Yeh apne ko nahin bacha sakte, humein kya bachayenge,' he said. It was quite a statement for the man who used to be the most pro-Pakistan of the Hurriyat leaders by virtue of being a member of the PoK prime minister's party.

Immediately after the attack, President George W. Bush famously gave Musharraf a choice: 'You're either with us, or against us.' For the military man, whose army had deep links with the Pentagon (and whose ISI chief was sitting in the Pentagon when it was attacked), the choice was a no-brainer, even though it would have serious repercussions in his country, where there was a section of people with sympathy for the man behind the 9/11 attack, Osama bin Laden.

'Who can depend on Pakistan?' Prof. Ghani asked me. 'It can't look after itself, how will it look after us Kashmiris? Now that Musharraf has joined the war on terror, Pakistan is an American stooge. So how will it help us?'

In effect, Prof. Ghani was also saying the same thing that Majid Dar said when he returned from Pakistan: that the tap of terrorism can be turned off by Pakistan any time, and that all the tap required was American pressure. There was thus a parting of ways between Kashmiris and Pakistan: 'They're sponsoring terrorism and also fighting terrorism,' Prof. Ghani pointed out. 'It's a contradiction.'

The setback for us was the 13 December 2001 attack on our Parliament by five terrorists of the Jaish-e-Mohammed, an outfit formed by Maulana Masood Azhar a few months after he had been released by India in exchange for the hostages of the hijacked flight IC-814. It was the first time ever that someone had dared attack our Parliament and it wasn't just an attack on an official building, it was symbolic. As they say, in a democracy Parliament is supreme. It was akin to an attack on the entire country and its political system at one go.

One of the PMO security guards rushed into my room with news of the firing. 'Sir, udhar goli chal rahi hai, MHA mein goli chal rahi hai.'

I did not take him seriously. MHA was just across the road. 'Paagal ho gaya hai kya?' I scolded him. 'Go and find out.'

Moments later he rushed back in and said, 'Parliament mein goli chali hain, attack ho gaya hain.' He said we could hear it from here.

So I opened the window and I heard gunshots.

I barged into Brajesh Mishra's room and said: 'Sir, Parliament is under attack.'

I was expecting a commotion and activity, but the old fellow was having a smoke and watching the attack on television. 'Haan-haan, come and sit,' he said. 'Watch it, it's all here.'

I was too excited to sit, so he reassured me. 'Nobody's gotten inside,' he said. 'They're all outside.'

He was monitoring the attack from his room in a most calm and composed manner. For me, it was one of those rare days that I did not go home for lunch. But at quarter to two, as was his practice, Brajesh Mishra left the building, though on this particular day he went to 7 RCR, where at 3 p.m. the prime minister would address the nation: 'Now the battle against terrorism has reached a decisive moment. This is going to be a fight to the finish.'

The five terrorists were killed but also lost were six Delhi police personnel, two members of Parliament's watch-and-ward staff and a gardener. A week later, the Indian army launched Operation Parakaram and began mobilising troops on the border. By early January five lakh soldiers had been mobilised. (Also, India suspended the Delhi–Lahore bus that Vajpayee had inaugurated. It would restart only in July 2003.)

The Pakistanis were worried, and Musharraf on 12 January 2002 on Pakistan television denounced 'religious extremism', pledged to reform madrasas, and banned the Lashkar-e-Toiba and the Jaish-e-Mohammed. Yet India kept up the pressure, especially after a terrorist attack on an army camp in Kaluchak, Jammu, on 14 May 2002, in which 34 persons were killed, a number of them army wives and children. It was the last straw that broke the camel's back. The Pakistan high commissioner was asked to leave. Earlier on 1 October 2001 the J&K assembly had been attacked which resulted in the death of 38 people, another dastardly attack by the Jaish. Farooq's apprehensions were proving right again. It was only in June that the pressure of two armies facing each other began to ease.

Yet while tension between India and Pakistan always makes Kashmiris insecure, the government used the opportunity of the build-up to ensure that pre-election violence in Kashmir, where the assembly election was going to be held in September–October, was curbed. Thus it was only by October that the forces were completely demobilised to the status quo ante.

While I was in the PMO I was occasionally invited to the National Defence College (NDC) for lectures. The NDC provides a course in strategic learning for defence and civil officials of the level of brigadier or joint secretary and above, and I used to go and brief them on Kashmir. One of my lectures took place after Operation Parakaram, and I found that on that particular day, the brigadiers were being quite aggressive.

'Why did we not go to war?' the brigadiers asked. 'Why are politicians always reluctant to go to war?'

'What makes you think the politicians were reluctant to get into this war?' I asked. 'What makes you think the generals wanted to go to war? My sense is that the generals were not ready to go to war.'

That quietened the military fellows down for the rest of the lecture. Let's face it, armies nowhere like to go to war. It is the last bad option. Since I have been on the Indo-Pak track two dialogue, I keep hearing that the most honest dialogue takes place between retired generals. Logically, militarymen of both countries need to meet regularly.

The army's chief of staff at that time was a brilliant officer, General S. Padmanabhan, who had been the corps commander in Srinagar from 1993 to 1995, and later in charge of northern command. He was the only army chief to have spoken about scaling down the military presence in Kashmir. The rest of them would on one hand say that the situation in Kashmir had improved and on the other say that the Armed Forces (Special Powers) Act, also known as AFSPA, couldn't be removed. While AFSPA gives legal cover to armed forces fighting militancy, it is also on several occasions used by rogue soldiers to act with impunity, and there is always an institutional reluctance to properly look into the allegations of extra-judicial executions or of rape of civilians by individual officers or units.

Thus the ASFPA is a dirty word not just in Kashmir but in the states in the north-east as well. It is another cause of anger against India, and undermines all efforts at trying to mainstream Kashmiris or Manipuris, etc.

Yet the AFSPA is linked to the bigger question of how much power the army is wielding, and the movement in Kashmir has provided the army with an opportunity to expand its presence in J&K. Though the army justifies its heavy deployment by periodically raising the bogie of infiltration, it is not restricted to the border; many Kashmiris feel the army has turned the entire Valley into a cantonment.

One of the ways to mainstream Kashmiris, it goes to reason, would be to reduce superfluous army presence. The moment to have done this was ideally after the 1996 assembly election, when a democratic government was in place. The army had done a damn good job of containing militancy in the early 1990s, but now it was time for the army to be pulled back and gradually withdrawn. The army could have gone back to guarding the border. Doing so would give more space for political activity, which in turn further marginalises the separatist movement.

Yet the army did not want to cede the power it wielded as head of the unified command, and insisted that only it could be in charge; Farooq wanted it headed by his DGP. The compromise was that the name of the set-up was changed to the unified headquarters, headed by the chief minister, who was assisted by the two corps commanders deployed in J&K. Farooq said fine, and then blamed all law and order problems on the army.

General Padmanabhan in 2001 said that the army had done its job, now it was up to the politicians to resolve the matter. Sadly, he was told that generals were not supposed to make political statements. He had the sharpest mind as far as generals go, and he was frank enough to say that the army's job was over, and he was basically told to shut up. (It's a different thing that nowadays the generals make the army out to be indispensable by offering some theory or another about infiltration and terrorism every six months or so.)

The border mobilisation was not the only way in which the government cut off the metaphorical oxygen to militants and separatists in the run-up to the 2002 assembly election. It is a fact that the IB under K.M. Singh not only neutralised sleeper cells in Kashmir but also neutralised hawala transactions. Hawala is the illegal foreign exchange trade, and in Kashmir it is used mainly by Pakistan to fund its assets, be they militants, separatists, or even the odd mainstream politician. The IB had detected twenty cases and the finger pointed directly at S.A.S. Geelani, the Hurriyat hardliner.

Twenty transactions were detected between December 2001 and June 2002, and the IB interrogated one of the suspects who revealed that the money was coming to Geelani through Ayub Thakur, a London-based Kashmiri famous for being on the ISI payroll. The IB provided the details to the Reserve Bank of India and that led to the income tax raid on Geelani in June 2002. The raid took place in so much secrecy that even the raid party had no idea where they were being taken. The only person who had any knowledge of the raid was Chief Minister Farooq Abdullah.

The raids turned up some unaccounted money and foreign exchange, and so Geelani was arrested and sent to jail in Hazaribagh, Jharkhand. A charge under POTA was slapped against Geelani. The government was a bit apprehensive over how the public might react to the arrest, but the reaction was muted. What also became muted was Geelani's usual anti-election propaganda.

Incidentally, POTA remained in force in Kashmir for a total of two years until it was revoked once Mufti Sayeed became chief minister following the 2002 election, as part of his healing touch policy. Mufti incidentally also had Geelani released and taken to Mumbai for treatment before returning him to Srinagar.

It was perhaps a quid pro quo. Mufti, an old Congressman who had left the party to join V.P. Singh in 1987 and then rejoined his original party when it was led by P.V. Narasimha Rao, formed the J&K People's Democratic Party in 1999 to, as he put it, 'persuade the government of India to initiate an unconditional dialogue with Kashmiris for resolution of the Kashmir problem'. Mufti added that the ruling National Conference 'had failed to provide a healing touch to the Kashmiris who have suffered immensely'. Links between the Congress and the Jamaat go back much further. Syed Mir Qasim, the Congress CM who made way for Sheikh in 1975, has acknowledged that the Congress funded the Jamaat in the 1972 election in which the Jamaat won six seats including Geelani's.

The fact of the matter is some people even believe that the PDP was conceived in a meeting between Mufti and Geelani, and the idea was that Geelani's Jamaat-e-Islami and the associated militant group, Hizbul Mujahideen, would help the PDP campaign with canvassing and voter turn-out when the 2002 assembly election happened. But this is not quite correct. The PDP was born basically out of Mufti's lifelong ambition to become CM which he wrongly believed could not be achieved in the Congress. Another architect of the formation of the PDP was Ghulam Hassan Mir. Between Mufti and Mir they believed that another regional party was needed to dislodge the Abdullah family. The talk about Delhi sponsoring the PDP was hogwash.

Normally such a new party would take time building its electoral account but for the PDP the conditions were ripe given an anti-incumbency mood against the Farooq government, which he tried to mitigate by handing over the reins of the party to his son Omar three months before the election; the National Conference's failure to go anywhere with the autonomy resolution (the Union cabinet in Delhi had angrily and summarily rejected it) that it had promised in the 1996 election; and the all-out effort by the Jamaat and the Hizb. Remember, the Jamaat had never made an electoral impact before, and there is broad agreement in Kashmir that even if there had been no electoral malpractice in 1986, the Muslim United Front would not have won more than ten seats or so.

If the PDP had enlisted the indirect support of separatists and militants then our effort was to get separatists to directly participate. As mentioned in previous chapters, Lone had promised to help and both Farooq and Mufti felt that Lone himself would participate though Lone had never given any indication that he would. Farooq even went to the extent of holding a secret meeting with Lone just days before the latter was assassinated. One of the PDP bigwigs, Ghulam Hassan Mir, even said that Lone wanted to be chief minister.

However, after Lone's assassination, the help came in the form of the participation of Lone's party, People's Conference, though its candidates took part as independents. That was a big mistake, for the 2002 election was a huge chance for the party and with the sympathy factor over Lone's killing it could have won around four seats. Sajad then would have been an inevitable and big factor in government making. For once the Hurriyat did not give a call for boycott of the elections which frustrated Geelani, who accused the Mirwaiz of 'honeymooning' (he had just been married) in Paris.

The election was growing and growing. A whole lot of people were filing nominations. This is what the NDA wanted, but it also wanted Omar Abdullah as chief minister.

Farooq had his own view: 'You know he's my son,' he said to me on several occasions. 'He has to succeed me and I would like him to succeed me. But I would like him to first learn the ropes.' Farooq's plan was that Omar would be a minister in his government for two or three years, as an apprenticeship, and then he would take over as chief minister for the rest of the term. Farooq would then withdraw. 'Let him learn,' Farooq said.

Brajesh Mishra, on the other hand, was very clear about going through with the switch to get Farooq out of Kashmir. So when participation grew beyond expectations, he asked me: 'Omar is all right, no?'

'Now why are you worried, sir?' I said. 'Let things take their own course. How will it matter?'

What worried Brajesh was that even people on the fringe of the Jamaat were jumping into the election. Anything could happen. For my part, I talked to Shabir Shah to convince him to contest. We had a long argument as I told him that it was his last chance (though the fact was that he had missed his big opportunity in 1996).

'What can I do single-handedly?' Shabir asked. 'I have nobody else with me. Maybe if I did, I could win three seats. But what's the use? You have already decided that either Farooq Abdullah or his son will be the chief minister.'

'Why do you say that?' I asked. 'You've got it wrong.'

And this later turned out to be the case. The fact is that if you don't want to move forward, you can make the same excuses over and over again.

I also tried to rope Shabir's former militant chief Firdous Syed into the election. He was demoralised after being denied another term in the legislative council the previous year, but I told him that he had enough in him to be a politician and contest the election.

'Where do I contest from?' he asked.

His home, Bhaderwah, was a suggestion, but he was doubtful. He wanted to contest from Srinagar but only if the Hurriyat supported him, which it did not.

Whether or not it was just an excuse, all these fellows had a reservation at the back of their minds, that the elections would be fixed, that the NC would return no matter what they did, that they just would not win. It was in order to allay that fear and extract greater participation through a transparently free and fair election that the Vajpayee government made a suggestion to Farooq.

It came up during the time that Farooq was promised the vice-presidency. In those days Brajesh Mishra and Farooq talked openly and freely because Farooq was going to be the vice-president.

'Doctor Saheb,' Brajesh said. 'Aisa hai, this time we want the election to be free and fair. Omar toh chief minister banega hi, but we want the election to be free and fair, so we would like to have it under governor's rule.'

Farooq was in a good mood at that time and said: 'Theek hai, laga dena uss time. If we are on the same page and know where we are headed, then okay.'

When developments went in a different direction and Farooq saw what Delhi was up to—that he was overlooked for vice-presidentship—he said: 'What governor's rule? Why do we need it? No. No governor's rule.'

He was feeling more and more insecure, and more and more cheated; what if governor's rule was used against him? He backed out of the agreement.

Brajesh asked me, 'Bhai, woh governor's rule ka kya ho raha hai?'

I spoke to Farooq and he said, 'No need for governor's rule, we're doing all right.'

I told Brajesh that Doctor Saheb was not agreeable.

He became angry and said: 'Omar ko bulao.'

Omar was a minister so I called him up and said the principal secretary wanted to see him. He dropped in and I said, 'I think the boss wanted to have a word with you.'

Unfortunately I had to accompany the young man. Brajesh was curt with him, unnecessarily so.

'Why is your father resisting governor's rule?' Brajesh said.

'I think you should talk to him,' Omar said.

'Please convey to him that if he's not willing to cooperate then we have our own ways of doing it,' Brajesh said, nastily.

It was all over in under two minutes. He came out quite shaken and though we took the lift down together, we did so in silence. The whole atmosphere had changed, and it contributed to the recriminations following the election. Our relationship was never the same again.

The election to the 87-member assembly took place over four phases in September and October of 2002. It was widely seen as credible and because of that there was a lot of violence before the election. The mainstream was targeted and nearly 600 deaths occurred. Pakistan contacted everyone, except, of course, Farooq Abdullah, who it was always wary of contacting since he was unpredictable.

The verdict was a fractured one, and though the NC won the largest number of seats, the number came down drastically from the 57 seats it won in 1996, and it lost power. The NC won 28 seats, the Congress won 20 seats and the PDP won 16 seats. Independents (which included a member of the People's Conference) won 15 seats and the rest were bagged by smaller parties like Bhim Singh's Panthers Party, etc.

It surprised me. I didn't think the PDP would get more than eight seats and never took the party seriously. Ghulam Hassan Mir used to tell me, you're underestimating us, we are in this seriously. But we were all sold on the NC and Omar, to the extent that when I heard that even Omar could lose his family's traditional seat in Ganderbal, just out of Srinagar, I became a bit panicky. I was in constant touch with K.M. Singh, who kept assuring me till the day before the counting of votes that the NC would capture 35 seats. K.M.'s belief was that the NC lost because it had projected Omar as the next chief minister, and if it had projected Farooq, then it would not have lost power.

Omar has many qualities. He's straighter, much more open than anyone else in Kashmir, he's honest, he's smart, he's articulate and he speaks well. Those years he worked at the Oberoi he would have made a good CEO, and yet he was now keen to become chief minister. Before the elections he had had his doubts: about his father's intentions, whether or not he would actually become chief minister, and about Delhi's intentions. He made a great political miscalculation in not being able to win his own seat in Ganderbal. No one would have imagined that he could lose. But he did and that was because he was not in touch with the ground reality, and that has been his problem throughout his political career. Also, he was not easily accessible, unlike his father. Farooq's strength was that he was everywhere, all the time.

Farooq was infuriated when his party lost the elections. On the day of the counting he had flown in from London and he sent me a message to come over and have breakfast with him. I reached his place about 10:00 a.m., by which time the results had started coming in. He was taking a shower, and after he got ready he stormed into the room where I was waiting and stormed out. He was angry. 'Now I know what you guys have been up to,' he said.

He had lost out on the vice-presidency and now he had lost his state. It was not a good year for Farooq.

Though the National Conference had the maximum number of seats in the assembly there was nowhere for the party to turn to, because at that time the Congress was not going to support the NC. The Congress plus PDP together tallied 36 seats and it was enough because they were sure to get the support of some of the smaller parties and independents to cross the halfway mark of 44 seats (in fact, the Congress–PDP combine mustered a total strength of 57 seats when it went to the governor to stake claim to forming the next government). The tie-up was natural in many ways for, after all, Mufti was originally a Congressman.

Interestingly, Delhi preferred that the senior partner in the tie-up, the Congress with its 20 seats, form the government. The BJP was distrustful of Mufti, one of the reasons being the kind of help he got during the elections, and ironically preferred a Congress government over a PDP government. Brajesh Mishra had an effective back-channel with the Congress party's

K. Natwar Singh, and this back-channel was used extensively during the run-up to the presidential election. Word went through the back channel that why don't you people in the Congress form the government?

Natwar came back, however, and said that Madam (that is, Sonia Gandhi) was not agreeable. She thought that Mufti should rule, and overruled the idea. And so Mufti Mohammad Sayeed's life ambition came true. He became chief minister of J&K.

The story went around in Kashmir that I was the one responsible for the defeat of the National Conference. The NC itself cursed Delhi and said there was a conspiracy to dethrone it, and that I was the main villain. This myth persisted and even during the 2014 assembly election, while I was working on this book, Omar publicly stated that it was because of the autonomy resolution that the Centre created the PDP, which was funded by the PMO. Which is hogwash. This keeps coming out of the NC's frustration, most of all Omar's, but it is not true.

I met Irshad Malik—the Pakistan-based militant who fled to London in 2004—in London during the summer of 2014. 'If the NC had not participated in the 1996 election then militancy would have carried on another eight to ten years,' he said. 'Once an elected government was in place, once the democratic process was put on track, then militancy took the back seat. So the NC did you a great favour in 1996. And what did you do of the NC? You demolished it. You put up Mufti Sayeed, funded him, and defeated the NC.'

This was not true at all.

'Who created the PDP?' Irshad asked. 'The ISI, the Hizbul Mujahideen and you guys. The Hizb supported the PDP and they did so because the ISI asked them to.'

The NC chorus against me grew. 'Isne karaya hain,' the leaders said.

I went to Farooq and said point-blank: 'Sir, everybody's saying that you're blaming me.'

'Who told you?' Farooq asked.

'It's not who told me,' I said. 'A lot of people are telling me. I only came to ask, do you believe this?'

'Not at all,' Farooq said. 'You're like my brother.'

And that was good enough for me.

Once he became chief minister, Mufti reached out to Sajad. He wanted the younger Lone in government but Sajad turned it down. Perhaps he felt he would have been selling himself cheap. 'You never know with Mufti Saheb,' Sajad told me. In the case, one of the People's Conference winners who stood as an independent became minister.

Another consequence of the 2002 election was that the British and the Americans, who had till then shown much interest in Kashmir's happenings and its personalities, gradually decreased their overt interest. Till then they would go to Kashmir and inevitably meet separatists like Yasin Malik, Mirwaiz Umar Farooq and Geelani. After 2002, meeting these guys in Srinagar was no longer obligatory, and they avoided Geelani like the plague. Geelani was now too extremist, and so persona non grata.

Even Musharraf told Geelani to step aside: 'We've heard you enough, old man,' he reportedly told Geelani. 'Now get out of the way, we have to move on.' Of course, Geelani was unhappy with Musharraf after that. It was no doubt the impact of the Americans' war on terror following 9/11. But after 2002, Pakistan also made a conscious decision to woo the mainstream in Kashmir, as we shall see.

For now, however, it was Mufti's moment.

14

VAJPAYEE'S LAST CHOICE—MUFTI

Mufti Mohammad Sayeed achieved his life's dream in 2002 and became the chief minister under an arrangement with the Congress party, which had won more seats but which disregarded Vajpayee's advice and allowed the junior partner to assume office. Mufti was to run things for three years and then hand over the chief ministership to the alliance partner. Thus, during the remaining year and a half of the NDA's tenure, we in Vajpayee's team got a good look at Mufti's way of functioning.

He was not a bad chief minister. From our point of view he was a focused administrator, on the ball and wanting to know even small details. Whenever there was a conversation with him and if there was a disagreement, or if you gave him information which he did not have, he immediately picked up the phone and checked with his director-general, intelligence. 'Dulat Saheb hamare paas baithe hain aur yeh bol rahe hain,' he would say. 'Isko check kariye.' And he would add, 'Please get back to me, I want to know.'

That was one of many ways he was poles apart from his bête noire Farooq Abdullah. Mufti was always keen to know what was happening where. Farooq's attitude was, on the other hand, that you don't need to tell me this because he already knew what was happening.

From the Kashmiris' point of view, his tenure was successful at a different level. The 'healing touch' that he spoke of when he formed the PDP was made official policy and Mufti took a few measures. The routine harassment of the common Kashmiri was either stopped or reduced considerably, by keeping the security forces a little more in check; and this was done by curbing the constant frisking or pulling people off buses, etc.

It worked. It had nothing to do with governance or development or matters like that. The crux of the matter is that Mufti was someone who understood and cannily played on the Kashmiri psyche. He turned populism into politics. In due course Delhi understood what he was doing, and the usual hardliners in the NDA were not very happy, but it was getting nearer election time so there was precious little they could do. For the common Kashmiri, it was the defining trait by which they judged Mufti's three years, saying these were the best they had had since 1996.

Mufti has always been a highly ambitious politician, but having always been under the shadow of that great banyan tree—the Abdullah family—his is a complex personality. He has always been highly insecure and he has a fairly narrow way of looking at things. One reason for this is that Farooq, for instance, has always been a Kashmiri with a nationalist outlook, whereas Mufti started his career with the Congress and spent most of his years there. In Kashmiri eyes—even among those who grow disillusioned with the NC—Mufti is ultimately a 'Congressiya'.

This has been so from the beginning when Mufti was a lawyer in Anantnag in the late 1950s and was picked up as a protégé by G.M. Sadiq. If you recall, Abdul Ghani Lone, who was four years senior to Mufti, was another protégé of the last prime minister of Kashmir. Sadiq became the first chief minister in 1965, heading a Congress government that Mufti joined. Lone soon became disenchanted with Sadiq, and Sadiq's successor Mir Qasim, blaming them for eroding Kashmir's autonomy. Mufti, however, made a career at the Congress—at odds with Sheikh Abdullah and company who, first with the Plebiscite Front and then with the National Conference—always spoke of Kashmiri nationalism. And when Sheikh Saheb entered into an accord with Mrs Indira Gandhi in 1975 and became chief minister, Mufti was made the chief of the Congress party's state unit.

Mufti and his bosom chum Makhan Lal Fotedar were always looking to pick a fight with Sheikh Saheb but Mrs Gandhi was not keen to do so (though she obviously changed her mind once Farooq hosted an opposition conclave in 1983). She realised, particularly after the accord, that they had an understanding that the NC would rule in Kashmir and the Congress in Delhi. She wanted it thus so that the Congress need not contest the assembly election and the NC need not contest Parliament.

Sheikh Saheb once referred to these Congress politicians by saying: 'Yeh gandi naali ke keere hain'—they are cockroaches from the gutter.

During the Parliament election in May 2014, I met Mufti and he reminded me of that. He would go on to win all three Kashmir Lok Sabha seats, and though he was perennially on the defensive, on this occasion he was feeling confident. 'Hum toh gandi naali ke keere thhe, na?' he said. 'We have proved today that we are a regional party now.'

In my early Kashmir days, I did not know Mufti. In fact, I had not met him even by the time he became home minister under Prime Minister V.P. Singh and his daughter Rubaiya was kidnapped. During the kidnapping, however, we would have long, long conversations on the phone. In one call he asked me what I thought of Farooq as chief minister. But the calls otherwise were always about the kidnapping and what the latest was. It was a father's natural anxiety.

It has been mentioned earlier how Mufti sent all sorts of interlocutors like the judge Moti Lal Bhat to tell the chief minister how concerned he was about Rubaiya. Bhat and others told Farooq to hurry up. I had just had my most important meeting during the kidnapping, when I met Ashfaq Majid Wani's father, and I told Farooq that we could get her released without giving too many concessions. Farooq had told Mufti's interlocutors that he was not in favour of releasing terrorists, and I told him that since the home minister is so concerned, why not give him a call? Farooq's first reaction was, forget him. 'No, give him a call,' I said. He did, and courteously so.

The day after Rubaiya was released, one of my neighbours on Gupkar Road, Vijay Dhar, warned me that Arun Nehru and Mufti and Jagmohan were gunning for me. I realised that Mufti did not like me at all. Like the others, he thought of me as Farooq's man.

I came face to face with Mufti on the final day of 1989. My son Arjun had gone to Calcutta to look for a job and I went along to take a break. The home minister, however, summoned a meeting for the 31st and I had to be there. Interestingly it was a Kashmir meeting and I sat there without being asked one single question. Also noteworthy was the fact that the Kashmir chief minister was not at that meeting; by then it had likely been decided to dump Farooq.

At the end of the meeting, Mufti asked the IB special director Padmanabhan (the punster from chapter one), 'By the way, where is Dulat?'

'Here he is,' Padmanabhan said, pointing at me.

That was my first meeting with Mufti.

The following month Jagmohan became governor and Farooq resigned, and two months after that I was replaced in Srinagar. Later in the year the V.P. Singh government collapsed and I was installed in the Kashmir group. Mufti was no longer home minister. Soon enough, Narasimha Rao took him back into the Congress.

And then Mufti began coming to Delhi and publicly saying that there was no other way in Kashmir, no other solution, but Farooq. It became his mantra for the next four years, till about 1995: Farooq, Farooq, Farooq.

During this time I was formally and properly introduced to Mufti. A Kashmiri Pandit named V.K. Vaishnavi, who was close to Mufti, came over one day. He was originally a journalist but not a serious one, but he was so close to Mufti that when things were bad, he even went grocery shopping for Mufti. 'Dulat Saheb, aapko Mufti Saheb se milwana hai,' he said.

'Vaishnavi Saheb, you know I meet everyone,' I said. 'But I don't think Mufti Saheb likes me, so kya faayda.'

'Nahin-nahin, Mufti Saheb aapko bahut acchi tarah se receive karenge,' he said. 'Aap chaliye mere saath.'

Mufti was living on Akbar Road. We met and it went well. We got to know each other.

After this Vaishnavi called up and said, 'Mufti Saheb chahate thhe ki aap Farooq Saheb se milwa dijiye.' This was interesting, that Mufti was keen to meet Farooq, who happened to be in Delhi at the moment. It was some time in 1995.

'What is the problem in that?' I asked.

'No, he wants to do it a bit quietly,' Vaishnavi said. 'Aap karwa de toh theek hain.'

I spoke to Farooq, we set it up for dinner at my residence in Kidwai Nagar, Delhi.

Mufti was punctual and arrived at 8:30. 'Sir, have a drink,' I said.

'Nahin-nahin, Doctor Saheb ko aa jaane dijiye,' he said.

Farooq took his time in coming. He did it purely for effect, and he did it deliberately because it was Mufti. They were meeting after a long time, and of course, don't forget that Farooq had been forced out of his job at the start of 1990. He got a kick out of keeping Mufti waiting. At 9:00 p.m. Mufti said, 'Are you sure Dr Farooq is coming?'

'Sir, aap drink le lijiye,' I said.

'Nahin, drink toh koi baat nahin, but are you sure Farooq is coming?'

'Jab woh kehte hain toh zaroor aatein hain,' I said.

Farooq came at about quarter past nine and Mufti was relieved to see him. We all had a drink. 'When Kashmiris talk, it's best that the third man goes out of the room,' I said, and left the two of them in high spirits. Their meeting went off well.

But then after the 1996 assembly election and his swearing-in Farooq came to Delhi and I met him in J&K House. 'I've come to say my thank yous to all the leaders that I know in Delhi,' he said, because a lot of them had come for the swearing-in.

'Who all have you met?' I asked. 'Who all are you meeting?'

He named some people.

'What about Mufti Saheb?' I said.

'Do I have to meet Mufti?' he asked.

'You should meet him,' I said.

Just then Saifuddin Soz, still a member of the NC, intervened. 'My leader will not go to him,' Soz said. 'It's Mufti who should come to him.'

'Soz Saheb, yeh chhoriye,' I said. 'Doctor Saheb ko jaane dijiye.'

But he wouldn't relent. 'Bilkul nahin jaane denge,' Soz said, and that was that.

Similarly, some time later it was Ramzan and there was an iftaar party in Delhi. There was a big crowd, and I also showed up. And again I found Mufti missing. 'Sir, I don't see Mufti here,' I said to Farooq.

'I invited Mufti,' Farooq said. 'Why don't you ask Soz? He said he had sent an invitation.'

So I asked Soz: 'Soz Saheb, Mufti Saheb ko nahin bulaya?'

But Soz insisted he had personally delivered the card.

Later I asked Mufti: 'Mufti Saheb, aap aaye nahin?'

But he said he got the card only in the morning, for an evening invite. 'Is that any way to invite someone?'

So Soz was the spoiler in all this.

After this there was no great love lost between them. I spoke separately to them and asked why they didn't get together, the NC and the PDP. My logic was that they were always cribbing about Delhi but basically cancelling out each other, and that if they joined forces they could get a lot more done for Kashmir. 'Nahin koi opposition toh chahiye na,' Mufti said. Fair enough, perhaps it was a bad suggestion.

In any case, Mufti came to power in 2002 and his three years were acknowledged as good. When we met in 2014, he pointed out that his tenure looked even better after Omar Abdullah's tenure from 2008 to 2014. 'Omar has wasted the last six years,' Mufti said. 'Farooq would never have allowed things to come to such a pass. He has a feel for Kashmir. He had a good cabinet and a competent bureaucracy with him. Omar is over-dependent on security and is far too insular for Kashmir. Here he's called tweet CM.' (This is in reference to Omar's preference for the micro-blogging site Twitter.)

Mufti attained power with the help of his friend Syed Ali Shah Geelani. Both of them are Pirs, who are groups of families from whom Kashmir gets its religious preachers, and that explains their proximity. The feeling among some Kashmiris, however, is that most Pirs are frauds.

Once during Mufti's tenure Geelani was shooting off his mouth and angering the NDA government in Delhi. Geelani was an irritation also because whatever he said was used by the hardliners in Delhi to put pressure on the government. One day Brajesh said Geelani had crossed the limit. 'Why don't we put away this fellow and lock him up?' he said. 'He's becoming a nuisance.'

I spoke to the chief minister but he said no. 'I will not make a martyr out of him,' Mufti said. 'Just let him be. It's better if he lets off steam. He's more harmless outside than he would be inside. We can deal with him politically.' And he was right.

When he was chief minister I made it a point to go and meet

him. He was more relaxed during this time though he never got over his belief that Farooq was the worst thing for him, and that I was Farooq's man. Even nowadays, whenever he comes to Delhi he makes it a point to call me and enquires about Farooq, even if I haven't met Farooq in six months or whatever.

But as chief minister he was more friendly, hospitable. On one occasion he even took us to Dachigam for lunch, which was unthinkable with Mufti Saheb. Even his wife came out. Our relationship was at its best during that period, when he was chief minister and I was in the PMO.

Mufti was a man who loved his Black Label whisky. If after one drink you said you had enough, he'd say no, have one small. Mufti also loved his bridge and played whenever he got a chance at the Delhi Golf Club. Though he fancied his skills at bridge, those he played with were not so impressed. He had a few bridge partners in Srinagar, but I think in recent years he's had less time for it.

Though he made time for me while I was at the PMO, the same was not for those who had stuck by him over the years. For instance, Vaishnavi, his sidekick who used to buy his vegetables and occasionally pay for them as well, got nothing when Mufti became chief minister.

One day I said: 'Mufti Saheb, Vaishnavi feels a bit left out.'

Mufti didn't like it. 'Mufti Mohammad Sayeed apne doston ko nahin bhoolta,' he said.

'Sir, I'm only flagging a point,' I said. 'He's a little disappointed.'

'Nahin, main jaanta hoon,' Mufti said.

Two years later, just before Mufti's term was ending, Vaishnavi was given the chairmanship of some state corporation. He went on a trip to Agra and died, being a highly diabetic and hypertensive man. It was a sad ending.

Then there was a gentleman in Jammu who was actually an astrologer. He hung around Mufti and was like the furniture in his house. Mufti used to call him Kakaji. Once Mufti said, 'Why don't you help him?' We got his son a job in R&AW but when Mufti became CM he disowned Kakaji.

On one occasion Kakaji was sitting here at my place in Delhi and Mehbooba, Mufti's other daughter, who played the main supporting role in the PDP's 2002 win, arrived. 'Main mara gaya,' he said. 'Now it's confirmed that I'm an intelligence agent.'

Poor Vaishnavi and Kakaji and Firdous, all of them got it for the same reason, that they were intelligence agents, even if they were introduced to me by the person accusing them. In fact I called Kakaji in Jammu. 'Aapki sarkar ban gayi hai,' I said. 'Mufti Saheb ka phone aaya?'

'Nahin, saheb,' he said. 'Ab kya phone karenge.'

This is the difference between Farooq and Mufti. If in a crowd Mufti sees Farooq, Mufti won't know whether or not to approach him, or how, because he is so insecure. Whereas if Farooq is sitting in a room and sees Mufti in a crowd he will call out, 'Mufti aao, yahan baitho.' Farooq is confidence personified.

Though Mehbooba, as mentioned, had a role to play in the 2002 election she has been restrained in her ambitions, unlike the youngsters of other political families. Mufti Saheb has made it clear that her time will come but for now, she is to remain subdued.

It may also have to do with perceptions of Mehbooba. When Vajpayee went to Srinagar in April 2003 and famously extended his hand towards Pakistan, a stage was erected high up for the public meeting. Sitting up on the stage were Vajpayee and Mufti, the chief minister. Mehbooba wanted to join them, but she was politely told that there was no place for her on that stage.

Vajpayee did not want her up there. He did not want her projected. There were grave doubts about Mehbooba in Delhi, about her links with the Hizbul Mujahideen and the help it provided to her and her party during the 2002 election.

After a few years, strangely, Kashmiris again began yearning for Farooq's return. There is a particular word in the Kashmiri language, fetir, which means lovable fool. 'Uss fetir ko wapas lao,' became the refrain. In any case, after three years, as per their agreement, Mufti stepped down and handed over the reins to the Congress party, which made Ghulam Nabi Azad its chief minister. It was once again a mistake that Delhi made, not because Azad was not a good chief minister but because of the signal it sent Kashmir that Delhi would not do without its own man in Srinagar. This was unnecessary because Mufti was at the core a Congressman and provided a convenient buffer.

In 2008, the NC won more seats and this time it tied up with the Congress, though Omar ruled for all six years of the assembly's term (the J&K assembly's life is a year longer than that of other state assemblies). Omar's tenure was marked by several lows, including a summer of stone-throwing by youngsters in 2010 in which over 100 boys died. The situation became so tense that it looked as if Omar's government would not survive; Mufti and Mehbooba were summoned to Delhi by Congress president Sonia Gandhi.

A special aircraft brought the father and daughter to Delhi and they met Sonia and Prime Minister Manmohan Singh. Even I got a chance to meet them, and Mufti was upbeat. They hung around for three weeks. But nothing happened. Mufti went back disgusted.

By April 2014 Omar was so discredited that Mufti's party won all three parliamentary seats, and even Farooq lost the Srinagar seat—that too to a former junior member of his party. It was during that time that I had a chat with Mufti, and he made several remarks.

Mufti said that Pakistan had got to everybody in Kashmir. 'They're financing everybody,' he said.

I looked at him.

'Hamein bhi contact kiya hai,' he said.

This was something; the ISI approaching Mufti, former Union home minister. He obviously spurned them.

'The situation is dangerous, there have been aggressive protests, even in the countryside,' Mufti said. 'Pakistan is spreading its tentacles.' For us, Pakistan's influence used to be confined to three assembly constituencies in downtown Srinagar, around the mosque, and in other towns like Baramulla. Mufti was saying that it had now spread into the countryside.

Also, Mufti was concerned for Mirwaiz Umar Farooq. 'He is an asset for both sides but he's more important to us so we need to look after him,' Mufti said. 'His security must be ensured, and we need to engage with him also, as well as with Pakistan in due course.' At that time, Mirwaiz was having a spat with Geelani over who was meeting Modi's emissaries, and Mirwaiz had publicly made various allegations against Geelani.

Possibly he said this because the Mirwaiz had indirectly helped the PDP considering that Farooq had lost in Srinagar. Also, however, he felt that the Mirwaiz had grown in stature at the Pakistanis' behest. Importantly, the separatist Hurriyat 'represented a thought that cannot be wished away, and must be engaged'. The Mirwaiz was the key to that, because Geelani would never come around.

Mufti described Geelani in two ways: a Pakistani and a disruptive force. It appeared they had a falling out, even though the PDP was said to be a brainchild of the two of them. Perhaps Geelani found Mufti, when he was chief minister, to be as dictatorial as the Abdullahs. It could also be that when Omar Abdullah was the chief minister, he helped get Geelani's son, a doctor in Pakistan, back to India. Whatever the case, by 2014 there was a lot of disenchantment within the Jamaat-e-Islami against the PDP. But Mufti and Geelani still have a common bond.

Mufti mentioned that Farooq might lose the parliamentary seat he was contesting, but added that even if he lost, Farooq Abdullah would remain Farooq Abdullah.

The feeling in Kashmir was that Mufti had some

understanding with the BJP for the Lok Sabha election and may have even had some financial help to contest the election. Prior to the Parliament election, Mufti had sent Dilawar Mir, a former minister, as his emissary to meet Modi in Ahmedabad. The PDP suits the BJP as a soft separatist; in the BJP's way of thinking, if it can deal with Mufti then why does it need to deal with the Mirwaiz? Mufti is a nationalist.

Of course the floods of September 2014 changed a lot of the dynamics, and then the BJP began to speak of Mission 44—of capturing power by themselves. It was just rhetoric, but it made Mufti a nervous man.

But not as nervous as the All Parties Hurriyat Conference, who in 2014 were afraid of getting politically squeezed out by Modi. This was a far cry from 2004, during Mufti's chief ministership, when another hardliner, Deputy Prime Minister L.K. Advani, engaged the separatists in talks.

15

THE HARDLINER AND THE HURRIYAT

After the 2002 J&K assembly election was over and as the year was drawing to an end, I went to Brajesh Mishra and said: 'Now what?'

'Now nothing,' he said. 'For the time being.'

'How can you say that?' I asked.

'You tell me.'

'Sir, this is not the end, this is the beginning. We must start talking,' I said. 'Everyone who comes here enquires why we are not talking.'

'Okay,' he said. 'Let me talk it over with the PM.'

That announcement took too long a time in coming: almost a year. In the meantime, though, Prime Minister Vajpayee made a speech at a public rally in Srinagar on 18 April 2003 which changed many, many things. Possibly this speech needed to be made before the talks began; in any case, a lot of valuable time was lost because in May 2004 the ruling alliance did not get re-elected.

Vajpayee had visited Srinagar three times before 2003: in 1999, 2001, and then in May 2002 for a meeting of the unified command. At the time the tension from the military build-up on the border was at its peak so his visit was welcome from the troops' point of view. After his visit was over and as he was leaving Srinagar, a journalist questioned him at the airport. 'Aapne kaha ki sab se baat karenge,' the journalist said. 'Toh kya yeh hogi within the Constitution baat?'

Vajpayee was one step ahead. 'Uski baat kyon karte hein, hum insaniyat ke dairey mein baat karenge,' he said, side-stepping the question of talking within the Constitution by talking of discussions within the framework of humanity.

Kashmiris went jubilant beyond bounds over his 'insaniyat ke dairey'.

And then came his public rally in 2003, the first by a prime minister since Rajiv Gandhi, and which made his prime ministership, especially with his policy of 'insaniyat ke dairey', a benchmark for future administrations in the eyes of Kashmiris.

I was not asked to accompany the prime minister on the earlier visits, but for the April visit I was specifically asked to go with him. What happened on the earlier visits was the PM's speechwriter, Sudheendra Kulkarni, would come to my room and ask me: 'PM is going, what should be said?'

I would say 'let's think', and then we would discuss it.

This time I went to Kulkarni's room and asked him just one question: 'Political?'

'Don't worry,' Kulkarni said. 'This time it's only political.'

I went to Brajesh Mishra and told him I'd like to go a couple of days earlier, just to see the mood. I did and I think by then the prime minister had thought it through.

When he arrived at Srinagar we drove from the airport to Sonawar stadium. As everyone was settling down, I took a moment to ask Kulkarni, 'Let me have a copy of the speech at least now.'

'There is no speech today,' he said. 'Boss ne bola hai, koi speech nahin chahiye, main khud bolunga.'

And then he extended his hand of friendship to Pakistan, which kickstarted the process in which India and Pakistan came closest to an agreement on Kashmir. Once bitten, twice shy, Vajpayee said, but though he'd been bitten twice he did not hesitate to extend his hand in friendship again. The Kashmiris went crazy with happiness. As mentioned before, there is nothing that makes the Kashmiri feel better than good relations between India and Pakistan.

Frankly, I had no idea what the prime minister was going to say. It was something he and Brajesh would have discussed, as with everything else. Whatever happened between Brajesh Mishra and A.B. Vajpayee, only those two knew; there was no third person. Sometimes you would get a feel of it, as I mentioned their disappointment after the Agra summit. Otherwise it was very tight between these two. So who decided all important matters? As I have said Vajpayee spoke very little at formal meetings and Brajesh even less.

We returned from Srinagar and a few weeks later, in May 2003, I had dinner with Mirwaiz Umar Farooq. He had sought the meeting ostensibly to get his passport renewed, but that would have got renewed anyway. So we got down to some talking.

Mirwaiz Umar Farooq became the chief priest of Kashmir at the age of seventeen when his father, Mirwaiz Moulvi Mohammed Farooq, was assassinated in May 1990. The Mirwaizs had their base at the Jamia Masjid in downtown Srinagar, whose surrounding areas have traditionally been a hotbed of pro-Pakistani sentiment (in 1947, Umar Farooq's granduncle migrated to Muzaffarabad). They and other prominent families of downtown Srinagar were known as the Bakras and they were in political opposition to Sheikh Abdullah and his family, which is why Sher-e-Kashmir had the Hazratbal mosque built as a platform to rival the Jamia Masjid (hence their rivalry was known as the Sher vs the Bakras). The Mirwaiz also headed his own separatist organisation, the Awami Action Committee.

You may recall that I used to occasionally meet Mirwaiz

Moulvi Farooq when I was posted in Srinagar, and he lent his help during the Rubaiya kidnapping by publicly denouncing it as un-Islamic. He was assassinated by Hizbul Mujahideen gunman Mohammed Abdullah Bangroo because he was in touch with the National Front railway minister George Fernandes; the militants bumped off several people they suspected to be parleying with Delhi in those days.

Mirwaiz Umar Farooq was a student of Srinagar's Burn Hall school and was planning on becoming a software engineer and all of a sudden he became the chief priest. Though he did complete his studies—he has a doctorate in Islamic Studies—he had no choice but to get involved in separatist politics and in 1993 was one of the founding executive members of the All Parties Hurriyat Conference. Because he was so young, the other Hurriyat founders—Syed Ali Shah Geelani, Abdul Ghani Lone, Abbas Ansari and Prof. Abdul Ghani Bhat—found him to be most acceptable as the chairman (rather than each other, that's how high the intra-Hurriyat trust level was). The other thing with Umar Farooq was that having seen his father assassinated, at home, he was always reluctant to speak too forthrightly against the militants.

Over the years, the young Mirwaiz has impressed a lot of people with his good looks, his youth, his articulation in English, his dress sense. He has been rated very high by everybody, the Pakistanis, the Americans, the British, other foreigners, and by us. It has helped that he remained chairman of the Hurriyat for so long which, as Prof. Ghani once put it, is because Umar Farooq is the only one of the Hurriyat leaders with some standing. The Mirwaiz by virtue of being the Mirwaiz is somebody in his own right. He has the advantage of his position and platform, ideology and constituency. He's been Pakistan's blue-eyed boy. We've also pampered him. He is, among the Hurriyat, a big player.

But the Mirwaiz lacks political courage. Sometimes he gives the impression he's quite happy just being in a mosque or being

at home, leading the Friday prayers; but at some point he needs
to decide whether he wants to be pope for life, or he also wants
to be chief minister. The fact is that he has told people that he
would not mind being chief minister. His tragedy, though, is
that he doesn't realise how highly he is rated, and that too, by
everybody. But staying confined to your mosque has got him
nowhere and will get him nowhere. It is just a matter of
marking time, which eventually doesn't escape the notice of
others. Or, as Prof. Ghani put it: 'Like all rich people the
Mirwaiz wears silk pajamas, and the strings open easily.'

The Mirwaiz on one visit to Delhi in 2001 attended a rally of
the Jamiat-e-Ulema-e-Hind, India's leading Islamic organisation.
He spoke very well.

'You can become a national Kashmiri leader, and you should
aspire to that,' I told the Mirwaiz. 'There's a huge shortage of
Muslim leaders. There's Farooq, and there's you. You should
come out more often.'

The problem, though, is that Muslims in India never speak
up for Kashmiris. I once met Maulana Mahmood Madani at
the India International Centre. 'You never think about Kashmir,'
I said.

'Sochte hain,' he countered.

'Kya sochte hain?'

He thought for a few seconds, but then admitted it was true.
'Yeh hamari kamjori hai.'

'Kamjori ko theek kijiye,' I said. 'Na Kashmiri yahan ke
baare mein bolta hain, na aap waha ke baare mein bolte hain.'

One of the telling episodes about the Mirwaiz took place in
early 2007. He and the other Hurriyat members met Pakistan
president Pervez Musharraf, who told them a few fundamental
truths: that no one could remove India; that India would not
compromise on its sovereignty and that boundaries can't be
changed; and that he had found a formula for Kashmiris. Then,
it is said, Musharraf told the Hurriyat leaders to go back to
Kashmir and prepare for elections. This diktat to the Hurriyat

by Pakistan to get out of its comfort zone was a shock to the Hurriyat.

But our dinner in May 2003 was one of those few occasions when the Mirwaiz provided hope. 'Is Delhi sincere about doing anything?' he asked.

'Of course we are,' I said. 'Why shouldn't we be?'

'Can Kashmir get autonomy?' he asked.

'Why not?'

'Can borders be opened, and can coming and going be easier?'

'Of course.'

'Can we have a bus from Srinagar to Muzaffarabad?'

'Of course,' I said. 'If we can have a bus from Delhi to Lahore, then we can have that too.' (Incidentally, it was aboard this bus that the Hurriyat went to Pakistan in 2007 and were told by Musharraf to prepare for elections.)

I had a counter-question for the Mirwaiz. 'If all this is okay then the Line of Control should be good enough?'

'Yes, it is,' he said.

'Are you willing to say all this publicly?' I asked.

'No,' he said. 'Not publicly.'

The next day I went to Brajesh Mishra and told him about the dinner, and the first question he asked was whether the Mirwaiz was willing to say all this publicly. 'No,' I said. 'In due course we might reach a situation where we may be able to persuade him to say something publicly. But he can't say anything right now.'

It was during this conversation that Brajesh laid out the next stage of the plan. 'Now that you're doing this, carry on,' he said, putting it quite simply. 'We can carry on with Pakistan, and we can merge these two parallel channels at some stage.'

Brajesh had either begun or was in the process of beginning a dialogue with his Pakistani interlocutor, Tariq Aziz, a friend of Musharraf's. Our way of dealing with Pakistan was very straight, in that we'd both put everything on the table and the other side would say what was not acceptable to them and we would say what was not acceptable to us. What was left acceptable to both sides was what we would get into and try to move forward on that. The plan was thus that on one track we would talk to Kashmiri separatists, and on a parallel track we would talk to Pakistan. Once these tracks converged, we would have an understanding on Kashmir.

This was the work I relished undertaking, though there were Kashmiris who told me that it was futile. 'You can try your damnedest but these guys are never going to be in a position to do anything with Delhi,' this Kashmiri, whom I'll keep anonymous, said. 'For anyone who's come into proper contact with the ISI, it's like once you get into a whorehouse you cannot get out.'

Pakistan has always had a lobby in Kashmir, and today that lobby was the Hurriyat. But Pakistan, or the ISI to be precise, is forever nervous of losing control of the separatists, because once it loses control of them there is nothing left in Kashmir in terms of political leadership. And as we saw in the case of Lone, anyone even thinking of stepping out of line gets bumped off. As one separatist said to me, 'What's the worst that you guys can do? Lock us up? Those guys shoot.'

That is why the Mirwaiz sits tight; it's not that he's insincere. Hurriyat leaders in private have said that all they need is a go-ahead from Pakistan and they would be willing to do whatever India wants. 'But please get us an okay from Pakistan,' they plead.

My point is always, why do you need an okay from Pakistan?

To maintain this tight control the ISI's main effort, while I was writing this book, was to reunite the three factions of the Hurriyat—the moderates led by the Mirwaiz, the hardliner Geelani's, and one led by Shabir Shah. The Hurriyat initially split after the 2002 assembly election into a faction led by the Mirwaiz and one led by Geelani, because Geelani pointed out that members of Lone's People's Conference had contested the assembly election as independents which contravened the Hurriyat constitution. At that time, the Pakistanis publicly alleged that India had split the Hurriyat, whereas it was their ISI which had made the split happen.

The ISI wanted to build Geelani at the time, and these are the games that the ISI keeps playing in Kashmir. Pakistan had loosened control during Musharraf's time—he had even told them to get ready to contest elections—but Musharraf's departure from power and the 26/11 attacks on Mumbai meant that insecurity crept into the India–Pakistan relationship, and Pakistan sought to tighten its control again. By 2014 the ISI realised that its effort would be strengthened if the Hurriyat were reunited, which is why there was a constant chorus to the separatists to get back together.

Much water had already flowed down the Jhelum, though. The main players would never join up with Geelani, be it the Mirwaiz or Prof. Ghani or even Moulvi Abbas, or Bilal Lone.

Moulvi Abbas Ansari is one of the seniormost persons in the Hurriyat; he's one of the Valley's prominent Shia clerics who has never advocated accession to Pakistan (he is pro-independence). He's been educated in Kashmir and in Iran, and incidentally he is also the cousin of Iftikhar Hussain Ansari, the politician I mentioned earlier. He's a nice, friendly person. His real rise in politics happened when the Muslim United Front (MUF) was formed in 1986 by government servants dismissed by Jagmohan because he suspected their loyalties. Moulvi Abbas was made chairman of the MUF, and it participated in the infamous 1987 elections. In 1993, Moulvi Abbas was among the handful of separatists who set up the Hurriyat Conference. In July 2003, after Brajesh Mishra gave me the parallel-track brief, Moulvi Abbas was elected the Hurriyat's chairman.

There's an incident that was reported in a gossip column of the *Indian Express* that year. I went to Srinagar and on my flight there were only three people in club class: the Mirwaiz, Moulvi Abbas, and myself. Of course I had a chat with each of them. The problem was when the flight landed no separatist wanted to be seen hobnobbing with a PMO official, particularly one who had been the R&AW chief. We came off the aircraft and we did so in one line, so there was a procession of the Mirwaiz, Moulvi Abbas, and myself.

Someone saw us coming in a single file, so they asked the Hurriyat leaders if we had been discussing something. The Mirwaiz said that there was a third person who said hello and spent time talking with Moulvi Abbas, but he himself had no idea of the identity of that third person. When approached, Moulvi Abbas said, yes he had been talking to Dulat, but only because he was introduced by the Mirwaiz! It was comical, though on a sober note, given the ruthlessness with which Pakistan dealt with anyone who was suspected of dealing with Delhi, their feigning ignorance was not surprising.

The third leader who could never be expected to join Geelani was Prof. Ghani. He hated Geelani, who he claimed had a role in the death of Prof. Ghani's brother, Mohammed Sultan Bhat, in 1995. It embittered him and made him say he was prepared to die at any moment. 'I don't know when I will be shot,' he said. This is why he talks of Geelani's 'narcissism', and that's why Geelani is called Amir-e-Jehad, or even, Bub Jehad (Bub is Kashmiri for father, and Sheikh Saheb was often referred to as Bub).

Prof. Ghani is another 1930s-born Hurriyat leader who worked as a professor of Persian in Sopore before he was dismissed by Jagmohan and joined the MUF in 1986. Prof. Ghani gained prominence as the MUF spokesman and, as mentioned earlier, he was a member of the Muslim Conference which broke away from Sheikh Abdullah in the late 1930s (when he formed his secular National Conference) and went over to Pakistan in 1947, to be led by Sardar Abdul Qayoom Khan, a former prime minister of PoK.

Once the Hurriyat was formed Prof. Ghani was one of its more articulate members, though his frank and direct statements showed him to be less of a politician than the others. He was the most pro-Pakistan of the Hurriyat leaders by virtue of belonging to the Muslim Conference, but when 9/11 took place he turned off Pakistan. 'Who can depend on Pakistan, they can't even look after themselves,' he told me when I met him in 2014, in connection with this book.

The only person who remained pro-Pakistan, and therefore cannot reconcile with the moderate separatists, is Geelani. The irony is that his Jamaat-e-Islami (JEI) was reluctant to take up terrorism and was therefore the last major Kashmiri group to get involved in militancy in Kashmir. In fact there is a story that earlier in the mid-1980s, during Zia-ul-Haq's time, the then JEI chief, Maulana Saaduddin Tarabali, went to Pakistan and discussed the plan to bring militancy to Kashmir.

Apparently Maulana Saaduddin backed off, saying, 'No, if the Kashmiri takes to gun, then Kashmiri will be killing Kashmiri.'

As the story goes, Zia said: 'Bhai, yeh Brahmin ke aulaad hain, inko kahwa pilao.' He basically called them cowardly and useless.

The JEI continued to call it *dashatgardi*; even Salahuddin, who had contested the 1987 election under his real name, Mohammed Yusuf Shah, had argued strongly against the gun, saying he had reservations about terrorism. 'Jehad is not the way to go about it,' he said. And of course Geelani was an MLA till the time the assembly was dissolved. Yet during the 1990–91 winter he and a few others were summoned to Kathmandu to meet the ISI and Ayub Thakur and Ghulam Nabi Fai, who finally persuaded him that there was no choice now but to get into militancy. This led to the creation of the Hizbul Mujahideen, but the JEI as such wanted to stay away from militancy.

Geelani, in fact, wrote a letter to Prime Minister P.V. Narasimha Rao in 1992 saying he was willing to talk to the government if it was willing to concede that there was a dispute over Kashmir. If the government conceded that much, he would talk without pre-conditions.

That was then. Now, the Mirwaiz faction saw him as an arrogant spoiler who would never agree to anything. Probably Geelani over the years became too big for these guys to handle; after he parted company with the Hurriyat and started to come out openly in support of anything that happened, be it a militant act or a protest, he became bigger than the rest of the separatists. He is Pakistan's man in Kashmir and its most effective tool for countering India. He grows bigger every time the moderates are ignored.

Kashmiris interpreted the killing of Prof. Ghani's brother as a signal to the Professor—that he had better start behaving and fall in line. That's why Lone was killed. That's why Mirwaiz Moulvi Farooq was killed. That's why Qazi Nissar Ahmed, the chief cleric of south Kashmir, who was one of the original MUF founders as well as a founder of the Hurriyat, was killed. That's why Majid Dar was killed. That's why Dr Guru was killed. That's why Fazl-haq Qureshi was nearly killed. The list goes on. Some of these killings are attributed to Geelani's brand of politics: it left no room for the moderates and the ISI stepped in to eliminate whoever fell out of line.

Yet, some people, when they think of the Hurriyat, they think of Geelani. For us he has been bad news. This is why the deputy prime minister, L.K. Advani, was against talking to Geelani and restricted himself to the moderates.

A year had passed since the J&K assembly election and I was feeling disappointed that the prime minister was taking so long to decide. With age he had become more cautious and took his time with everything. Yet when it happened, it happened suddenly. It was October 2003 and I was returning to Delhi from Chandigarh because of a meeting on Kashmir called by the prime minister. At the meeting, Vajpayee, who wanted to put an end to the uncertainty, said, 'Haan, hum Hurriyat se baat karenge.'

Everyone was startled. 'Who will talk from the government's side?' Jaswant Singh asked.

'Advaniji, of course,' Vajpayee said. With this masterstroke he nipped in the bud any dissent, by putting the person who was most opposed to talks in the forefront.

The Advani–Vajpayee relationship was a strange one. It was special, and it was not all friction or not seeing eye-to-eye; there were differences because they were different people. The relationship remained special because Vajpayee had sufficient respect for Advani, and Advani had huge respect for Vajpayee. There was so much mutual respect that neither would allow any difference to remain unresolved.

Whenever tension began to build up Vajpayee would say, 'Advani se kehna hamare saath lunch khaye.' And the two men would meet and the tension would disappear. If things had gotten really tense then Vajpayee would say, 'Accha, Advaniji se kehna main unke yahan kal aa raha hoon lunch ke liye.' I don't think they spoke very much at lunch; they simply allowed their chemistry to work things through.

That did not mean there was no tension. People around them created tension, and the greatest source of tension was Brajesh Mishra and his supreme position in the government.

Vajpayee was a politician to his fingertips and he could bluff anybody, Advani included. Everything that he did was political. He had a good mind, as he was a philosopher and a poet; he was also an RSS pracharak; but above all he was a damn good politician. He was a Chanakya, and there was nobody half as shrewd as him.

In comparison Advani was a straight arrow. This was so because he went by the book, by files, by advice. He would listen; he was a patient listener and never interrupted you. He was articulate. If you went and met Advani you would get a pleasurable conversation.

I first met Advani when I took over at R&AW. I called on the home minister and we had a chat, and we would interact whenever he wanted something or whenever he required me. It was rare, though. My colleague at the IB, Ajit Doval, with whom I interacted often on Kashmir, would say to me, 'Why don't you meet Advaniji, or meet him more often, it would simplify matters on Kashmir.'

'Ajit,' I said. 'I'm always there and whenever I'm called I'll go.' On my own I couldn't just cross the road from South Block to North Block, however, because my boss, the national security advisor, didn't particularly dig Advani.

In any case, now the Hurriyat had to be rounded up to talk to the deputy prime minister, and having gotten a formal invitation, they were willing. What also helped was that in the first week of January 2004, Vajpayee went to Islamabad for the SAARC summit, and on the sidelines he and Musharraf shook hands. They also agreed to commence a composite dialogue between the two countries that would lead to a settlement of all bilateral issues to the satisfaction of both sides. To journalists, Vajpayee said that they would discuss Kashmir; Musharraf said Pakistan could drop the insistence of a plebiscite in Kashmir.

As Brajesh Mishra, who had gone to Islamabad in advance to do the groundwork for the Vajpayee–Musharraf meeting, said, the two parallel tracks looked like they were on course to converge at some point.

Advani's first meeting with the Hurriyat was set for 22 January 2004, and it was expectedly a hello, how-do-you-do kind of getting to know one another. The Hurriyat leaders were nervous and came to meet me before their meeting with Advani. The Professor said, 'Humara pajama to nahin utarvaoge!' I assured them that all would go well. It went well. I wasn't there, but the Hurriyat guys wanted the release of some Kashmiris as a confidence-building measure. 'Give me a list,' Advani said. And they agreed to meet again in March.

The next day the Hurriyat wanted to meet Vajpayee. 'What's the harm?' I told Brajesh. 'Let them have a cup of tea together, they don't have to make it an actual meeting.'

So they were invited for a cup of tea and samosas and jalebis with the prime minister. I took them in, and the five of them stood there and one by one said their pieces. Chairman Moulvi Abbas, the Mirwaiz, Prof. Ghani, Bilal Lone and Fazl-haq Qureshi were there and they each had their say and Vajpayee did not utter a word. Once the five had finished they all looked at each other. Prof. Ghani decided he was going to start on his spiel again, but anticipating that the others quickly said, 'PM Sir, you've heard us, what do you say?' One of the five insisted, so the prime minister asked the staff to bring in more samosas.

Vajpayee, as usual, was silent for a long time. Finally: 'Advani is talking to you,' he said. 'Let that go on.'

The tea lasted more than an hour, with Vajpayee doing what he did best, keeping quiet. When the Hurriyat left, I escorted them out and I wondered what the poor fellows would tell the media that was waiting outside. I was feeling sorry for the Mirwaiz, but he acquitted himself well by saying it was a good meeting and that the talks continued.

The Hurriyat went back to Srinagar and in due course passed on a list of nearly thirty guys that they wanted released. I tried to persuade the home ministry to release some of them, but they released only eight, which I felt would satisfy neither the Hurriyat nor the government. 'Why don't you release some more?' I asked the home secretary, N. Gopalaswami. In fact, we had a disagreement and I lost my cool, telling Gopalaswami to get someone else to talk to the Hurriyat instead. I was being unfair to the home secretary. Gopalaswami was a decent fellow and agreed to release twelve prisoners. He then suggested to Advani that I be invited to the second meeting, saying that the meeting with the Hurriyat would not have happened but for Dulat.

The second meeting was on 27 March 2004, and the government said we should now get down to the nitty-gritty. 'What is it that you want?' Advani asked.

Not one single Hurriyat leader said anything.

Finally, Prof. Ghani said, 'Next time we will come prepared with our ideas.'

That was that, and they agreed to meet that June.

The problem was that the Hurriyat was unwilling to bell the cat. Suppose in that meeting, the Mirwaiz had repeated the three points he had mentioned to me over dinner in May 2003, and asked if they could be done. That would have put Advani and the government in an awkward position, for they would have had to deliver. Instead, they kept asking for vague things, like confidence-building measures by releasing twelve persons.

The problem was that the separatist leadership has let down Kashmir time and again. Suppose Farooq were representing the Hurriyat or the separatists, he would have said what he felt he was required to say. Simply because he is not answerable to Pakistan.

After the second meeting I went to Srinagar in May to prepare for the third meeting, and I spent nearly a week with these gentlemen, talking to them. 'Professor Saheb, kucch toh indication de dijiye,' I said. 'Are you going to bring the map, give me some idea.'

'I am preparing it,' Prof. Ghani said.

The truth is that naksha kabhi taiyyar nahin hoga. If you ask me about autonomy, I have dealt with Kashmir for so long, and I have asked at the highest level, is autonomy doable, and I have been told: yes. It is doable. I have never offered anything beyond the Constitution to anybody. I have told different separatists that there are various types of azaadi, but who am I to talk of anything outside the Constitution? And who would have believed me?

And if Delhi has not been sincere about giving Kashmir anything of consequence or substance, then the Kashmiri leadership also does not have the gumption to extract anything. Maybe Delhi was insincere, but then it was up to the Kashmiris to check them out, instead of time and again backing out, whether it was Shabir Shah or Mirwaiz Umar Farooq. The government's game plan would have been to get the Hurriyat engaged, then get Shabir into it, then get Yasin Malik into it.

The only person who would have stayed aloof would have been Geelani and that wouldn't have mattered. All that was now required was sincerity and a bit of aggressiveness of purpose, and in another four meetings or so with the Hurriyat, things would well and truly have been on their way.

I returned on 13 May from Srinagar and the next day the results of the Lok Sabha election were to be counted and announced. I had told the Mirwaiz, 'You've got to come to Delhi.'

'Yeah, yeah, we'll come,' he said. 'But what happens if these guys lose?'

I laughed. 'How does it matter?'

'No,' the Mirwaiz said. 'What if Mulayam Singh is the prime minister?'

'Mulayam Singh will be more keen than Advani,' I said.

And to the great misfortune of the Kashmiris, Vajpayee's team lost the elections.

16

MANMOHAN SINGH'S LOST DECADE

By about 1:30 in the afternoon of 14 May 2004, it became clear that the NDA government headed by Vajpayee was not going to return to power, and that the Congress-led United Progressive Alliance (UPA) would be replacing it. I went to Brajesh Mishra's room, and found him standing by his cupboard, fiddling with things. He looked at me and said, 'Haan, bolo.'

'Sir, ab kya hoga?' I asked.

'Hum sab jayenge,' he said. 'Bistra bandhenge, chalenge.'

And he left the next day. As did everybody else: nicely, neatly, graciously.

I figured it would be appropriate to resign since this government appointed me. I drew up a letter in which I said I would like to be relieved and gave it to Brajesh Mishra. 'You don't have to do this,' he said. 'You're not a political appointee.'

Nonetheless he wrote an instruction on the letter: 'Brief the new prime minister and take further orders.' It thus required me to hang around till the new prime minister came in.

I went back to my room and called my old DIB, M.K. Narayanan, who was in London. Just for that brief moment I may have had second thoughts on quitting. Narayanan gave me the impression that he was not part of the government-formation process, but promised to look me up when he returned to Delhi. Ultimately he joined on 31 May as the advisor (internal security), but in between he did come to Delhi and meet Sonia Gandhi. But he did not meet me.

In the meantime I hung around at the PMO, the last man left, visualising my meeting with the person I thought was going to be the new prime minister: Sonia Gandhi. And I was quite excited about it.

On 17 May, it was announced that J.N. 'Mani' Dixit would be the new NSA. He came down to the PMO and I went and met him. 'Are you serious about leaving?' he asked.

When I said yes, he said he respected my choice, and then said, 'Keep in touch.' He sent for me once in July and enquired about Kashmir and how best to move forward. But that was it. Soon after he passed away.

I bumped into Narayanan at the PMO a day before the swearing-in. Sonia Gandhi was not going to be the prime minister. It would be Dr Manmohan Singh, whom I had first met in the mid-'90s when he was finance minister and I had taken Shabir Shah for a meeting with him at the behest of the prime minister, P.V. Narasimha Rao.

'I'm joining your set-up,' Narayanan said.

'I'm leaving,' I said.

The new PMO came to their offices on 23 May, which was a Sunday. I figured I didn't need to go in on a Sunday, so I did not. When I went in on Monday, I was told, 'You didn't come to welcome the prime minister.'

'It was Sunday,' I said. 'In any case, I'm leaving, I'll meet the prime minister separately.'

When I went to meet the new prime minister, I took along a note I had prepared on Kashmir because Brajesh Mishra had said, brief him, and I did not know how much time I would have. 'Put it down over there,' he said. 'Now tell me.'

We spent 45 minutes in discussion and finally he said, 'We have to continue this conversation.'

'Sir, I will come whenever you want,' I said. 'But I won't be in the PMO, I've put in my papers.'

Dr Singh dismissively waved his hand at my statement. 'Don't worry about that,' he said.

However, I had already sent my letter to the new principal secretary, T.K.A. 'Kutty' Nair. The new gang must have said, Dulat has put it down in writing, why give him so much importance. It was processed and that was that.

Now that I was officially leaving the PMO it was time to make a call on Vajpayee. On one of my last days I went to see him at Race Course Road. One thing about the man was that he was good with his time and you never had to wait more than five to ten minutes, because he did not meet too many people and he never kept anyone waiting. That day I was summoned in immediately.

The old man looked extremely relaxed. What the hell do I say now, I thought. How do I start this conversation. Finally: 'Sir, yeh kya ho gaya?' I asked.

Typical Vajpayee, he laughed heartily. 'Yeh unko bhi nahin maloom ki kya ho gaya,' he said, referring to the Congress party, equally stunned by its win.

We spent a half-hour in relaxed conversation. 'Koi aisi baat nahin,' he said. He was in his light-hearted best element, and there was not an iota of regret.

Then Vajpayee mentioned Gujarat. 'Woh hamare se galti hui,' he said. Perhaps he felt that was the reason he lost power; because he did not stop the 2002 riots.

My last day was 31 May, the day Narayanan joined. We met, and he asked why I was going. 'Sir,' I said. 'This gang brought me here with them so I thought I should go with them. In any case, I never knew you were coming here.'

'Who's going to do this?' he asked, about Kashmir.

'You have two options,' I said. 'Either Ajit Doval or K.M. Singh, these guys are the most contemporary.' In fact, K.M. had just returned from an innings in Srinagar.

'Doval can't be spared,' Narayanan said. 'He's going to be DIB.' That was the first I heard that Doval would become the IB chief.

Eventually no one was put in my job and I don't think they wanted anyone there.

Before I left I also went and met the new minister of state in the PMO, Prithviraj Chavan, who had taken over from Vijay Goel and who would later become the chief minister of Maharashtra. We had two discussions on Kashmir before I left the PMO and he asked me what ought to be the next step. 'There has been a beginning and an opening has been provided,' I said. 'You must take it forward.' I told him he was ideally suited to do so. 'You're the minister here and Kashmiris like to believe that the prime minister or the PMO is dealing with Kashmir.'

'What about the home minister?' he asked.

'Of course you can talk it over with him,' I said. But what mattered to the Kashmiri was that the PMO was involved, which is why Narasimha Rao created a department of J&K affairs directly reporting to him. 'You need to talk this over with the PM on how you want to do it.'

The other thing that I mentioned was that in the 2004 election, the Congress had nearly a dozen absolutely young, bright members of Parliament from different political families, all of whom appeared to have a future. 'Make use of them in Kashmir,' I said to Chavan. 'Two of three should be allotted Kashmir.'

In particular I mentioned Sachin Pilot and Rahul Gandhi. Sachin was a natural because he was Farooq's son-in-law and so related to Kashmir, while Rahul was descended from Kashmiri Pandits. 'These guys should get involved and visit Kashmir regularly,' I said. 'Whenever Rahul wants to go on vacation he should go to Srinagar.'

Even if Rahul didn't want to be connected he ought to go on holiday and like his great-grandfather say this is my land and I have an emotional bond with it. Pandit Nehru even used to go riding in Kashmir. But neither did these youngsters show any interest, nor were they used productively. It was a great opportunity for the Congress party but it was frittered away.

It was my own fault that I did not continue in Dr Singh's administration. Nobody asked me to leave and most were surprised; later I was told that some felt I was being arrogant, which is the last thing I was ever accused of in all my years of government service. Maybe I was being impulsive, but I simply thought it was the appropriate thing to do. Brajesh Mishra had brought me in; he was going and I thought I should also go. A good thing has only that much shelf life.

And in the years to pass, I had no regret on that score. One thing is for sure: Vajpayee's PMO was a very happy PMO. What I saw subsequently was a very tense, stressed-out PMO. I visited a number of times, even on the occasions that Narayanan's successor as NSA, Shiv Shankar Menon, called me over. In the beginning there was a lot of tension between the two guys whose jobs almost overlapped—Mani Dixit and Narayanan. And though Mani departed, unfortunately, there always seemed to be a lot of wrestling going on within. Whereas in Vajpayee's PMO there was no doubt in anybody's mind that the boss was the principal secretary, Brajesh Mishra. I guess it was a matter of Vajpayee and Brajesh Mishra having an exceptional relationship during an exceptional period.

One occasion I went to meet Manmohan Singh was in July. He called me to discuss initiatives on Kashmir, and he asked how the BJP would react. 'The BJP started the process so they shouldn't object,' I said. 'Why don't you just ask them?'

'Whom do I talk to?' he said.

'You can talk to the ex-PM, Vajpayee.'

'He doesn't talk,' Dr Singh said.

'Okay, you can talk to L.K. Advani about it,' I suggested.

'He's very difficult.'

'Okay, you can talk to Brajesh Mishra.'

Brajesh then found a line to the UPA. After we left the government I would go meet the man every five or six weeks and have a drink with him. He was a smart fellow. He supported Dr Singh on the nuclear deal in 2008, much to the unhappiness of his party. When the media asked Brajesh about this he simply said, 'I'm not a party man.' The UPA gave him a Padma Vibhushan.

During the first year of the UPA's government, the prime minister was calling me more often than even Narayanan and so some time in August–September 2004, Narayanan called me up and asked me to dinner at the India International Centre. 'Have you lost all interest in Kashmir?' he asked.

'Sir, why should I lose interest in Kashmir?'

'Can you take up what you were doing earlier?'

'I could,' I said. 'But in what capacity?'

'In your personal capacity.'

I said okay, even though it did not amount to a formal role in the government. It was no big deal, and I didn't even ask for an air ticket. 'I'll go and tell Ajit Doval,' I said. 'I'd like to keep the DIB informed rather than he hear it from his people, so if you don't mind I'll tell Ajit I'm going.'

I think he did mind, but he said, 'Theek hai.'

The prime minister must have said that no one was able to reach out to the separatists, so why not send Dulat, and that's why I was sent. I met the Hurriyat—the guys who had started the dialogue with the NDA were known in Srinagar as the 'Advani Hurriyat'—and had a chat, one by one. I returned and reported my discussions to Narayanan. He took me to the prime minister.

I was surprised to find Kutty Nair in Dr Singh's room. But I suppose everything has some purpose. 'Sir, they're all keen to talk,' I told Manmohan Singh.

The reaction came from Kutty Nair. 'The PM is going to Srinagar next week,' he said. 'Can you arrange a meeting for him with the Hurriyat?' It sounded like he needed P.C. Sorcar rather than me.

'No,' I said, point-blank. 'There has to be a method in this. It will take some time. But I promise you, if Delhi wants to talk I will get them here in three months to talk to you.'

In hindsight I wondered why the prime minister was going and what the rush was. There should be an agenda when you visit, something you want to do or say. But if he felt that as PM he should visit Kashmir as early as possible then he need not have bothered about the Hurriyat. The prime minister can't do everything himself; there are other people to get that process going.

In any case, that was the last time I was officially consulted over Kashmir.

The problem is that they wanted instant results. They wanted me to send a message to the Mirwaiz to meet the prime minister on his visit the following week. The Mirwaiz said: 'Hum itne gire hue bhi nahin hain ki aap thanedar bhej denge aur hum aa jayenge.' (We are not so lacking in self-respect that we will respond to every summons from Delhi.) Ironically, the same Mirwaiz had been happy with his meetings with Sonia Gandhi while she was in the opposition. She's reasonable, he would say. But once the UPA came to power, she stopped meeting the Hurriyat.

The UPA instead got bogged down in what was right and what was wrong. Such initiatives have to come from within; that is what is political will. And the UPA had it on a platter. All it had to do was follow up on the process that Vajpayee started. Since Advani had started talking to the Hurriyat, that should have been the starting point. It just needed following up, patience, time and understanding. It would have been impossible for the Hurriyat to wriggle out, or for the BJP to backtrack on.

But these things never happened. If something had to happen it should have happened in the first six months or eight months or maximum one year. Instead there was a brainwave to broadbase the Kashmir meetings and get more people in. The PMO called a roundtable meeting which was a waste of time. It went on for six hours—and Manmohan Singh sat through the whole thing. Imagine, Vajpayee wouldn't spend five minutes on such a meeting and it required a lot of persuasion just to have tea and samosas with the Hurriyat; and the UPA organised three roundtable meetings to which the Hurriyat did not even show up.

There was no meaningful dialogue and after that everything fell into the usual routine of chalta hai. Then people began saying that the separatists were useless and that there was no point in talking to them. But you have to talk to somebody, isn't it?

They wouldn't even talk to Farooq Abdullah, and I had told them that Farooq was deeply annoyed with the NDA for denying him the vice-presidency and then for his loss of power in the state. It was a good time to win him over. But perhaps Sonia was not interested.

During his decade as prime minister, Manmohan Singh went to Kashmir on at least five occasions and most of those visits were a waste. Kashmir is a political matter, but more than that it is emotive and psychological. That is why 'insaniyat ke dairey' has retained its resonance even after so many years.

That nothing happened on Kashmir or Pakistan is Manmohan Singh's great tragedy, because no other prime minister wanted it more, or was more sincere. But he was a lonely man with no support either from the party or the bureaucracy, and as the government weakened, the BJP took more and more advantage of it, called Dr Singh 'a weak man'. If the BJP had criticised him for being weak towards Pakistan then all he had to do was say that he was merely carrying on what Vajpayee started. After all, despite Kargil, Vajpayee invited Musharraf. Advani did say in 2004 that only the BJP could do something with Pakistan because the majority would never think that the BJP had sold out. Then Vajpayee, surprisingly, in 2005 said the Congress was going soft on Kashmir. It was strange, but basically no matter who is in power the other side doesn't want to concede anything on Kashmir.

Linked to the Kashmir paralysis was the missed window of opportunity with Pakistan, when Musharraf was at the height of his power from 2004 to 2007. This is something Dr Singh himself admitted at his last press conference on 3 January 2014: that there was a golden opportunity for a deal with Pakistan, particularly during the 2006–07 winter, that was missed.

It all centred on what Musharraf himself in 2006 called his 'four-point formula' for Kashmir. It was something that began taking shape when he met Vajpayee during the SAARC summit in Islamabad and gradually evolved during the first few years of the Manmohan Singh era. The formula was: making borders irrelevant by allowing free movement of Kashmiris across the LoC; self-governance which meant autonomy but not independence; demilitarisation; and a mechanism for joint management.

It had big implications for Pakistan's stand on Kashmir: it meant that the LoC was being accepted; that the long-held demand for plebiscite would be set aside; that self-governance would replace the demand for self-determination; that Kashmiris would talk to New Delhi; and that Kashmir was no longer the unfinished business of Partition.

Why did Musharraf do it? From the moment that Musharraf became president he had been speaking about out-of-the-box solutions, about leaving the past behind, and about moving forward. He wanted a deal.

And to that end, he started paying more attention to the political mainstream in Kashmir. Perhaps after the 2002 J&K assembly election he realised the mainstream would have an important role in the future—remember, Abdul Ghani Lone used to say separatism was just a phase—and he reached out to everybody. Mehbooba Mufti was his preferred mainstream politician during the time her father was the chief minister; when Mufti stepped down Musharraf's preference switched over to Omar Abdullah.

In March 2006, Omar visited Islamabad at the invitation of Musharraf, the first mainstream Kashmiri politician to do so, and when he returned I met him for lunch. He was full of Pakistan and full of Musharraf. His thesis was that Musharraf was being much more reasonable than we were. 'Have you met the prime minister and told him?' I asked, which he said that he had.

Musharraf was also very impressed with Omar. From his point of view Omar was a smart, upfront Kashmiri who spoke well and appeared honest, quite the opposite of the wishy-washy Hurriyat guys who said one thing, did another and meant something totally different. Musharraf may have wondered why so much weightage be given to the Hurriyat, if the mainstream guys can do the job for Pakistan.

It was as a fallout of this that he took the Hurriyat to task, telling them to start taking part in elections (advice that, as mentioned earlier, made the Mirwaiz's throat run dry). He reportedly told Geelani that he was an old man who should get out of the way of peace; Geelani was sidelined for the years that Musharraf was in power, not doing much else but criticise Musharraf. Because of Musharraf, Geelani's son Nayeem, a doctor in Pakistan, had to return to Kashmir (which Omar, when he became chief minister in 2008, facilitated). Geelani only regained influence as a separatist once Musharraf lost power.

To illustrate how Musharraf's thinking changed everybody there are two visits to India by Sardar Abdul Qayyum Khan, the former prime minister of PoK and the head of the Muslim Conference, the party to which Hurriyat leader Prof. Abdul Ghani Bhat belonged. In September 2005, Sardar Qayyum attended a seminar at the Observer Research Foundation (ORF) where I also participated in the discussion. When his turn came to speak, he did the usual waffling: that Kashmir was a complex matter, that we need not look at solutions immediately, that confidence building was more important.

When my turn to speak came, I said: 'Sardar Saheb, I've heard so much about you and what you're saying would be extremely disappointing to the Kashmiris sitting here because what you're implying is that there is no solution to Kashmir.'

Sardar Qayyum returned in May 2007, by which time the four-point formula was very much in the air and Musharraf was saying repeatedly that whatever was acceptable to Kashmiris was acceptable to Pakistan. He had built bridges with Musharraf, and his son, Sardar Attique Ahmed Khan, had become prime minister of PoK. Sardar Qayyum said exactly what Musharraf was saying: that whatever can save Kashmir and Kashmiris should be acceptable to both sides. I had a long chat with him and found that all that he said was in parallel to whatever Musharraf was saying. It wasn't Prof. Ghani alone whose tune had changed.

In fact, the greatest proponent of Musharraf's four-point formula was the Mirwaiz. It suited all the separatists.

As far back as I can remember, if we look at the history of Kashmir and if we look at the Pakistani leadership, no other Pakistani has been as reasonable on Kashmir as Musharraf was. Yet Manmohan Singh could not grasp the opportunity. Musharraf is supposed to have sent a message to Dr Singh in early 2007: you're a Pakistani Sikh and I'm an Indian Muslim. Let us get together and unite our people and end this madness of confrontation forever.

The opportunity slipped away, and it was admitted publicly for the first time in 2011 by Musharraf's former foreign minister, Khurshid Mahmud Kasuri. When Manmohan Singh gave his last press conference he too admitted that they had come so close. Yet he could not even visit Pakistan—unlike Vajpayee, who visited twice. Not once during the decade he was prime minister could he visit the place where he was born.

The BJP aside, he was not helped by the bureaucracy around him. If you leave it to the bureaucrats, nothing will ever happen. It made no difference whether Manmohan Singh's NSA was

Narayanan, an intelligence man, or Shiv Shankar Menon, a foreign service man. When Vajpayee took the bus to Lahore, it was not a bureaucratic decision. It was not a whim either, a lot of homework went into that bus ride, but Vajpayee 'drove' that bus to Lahore.

As time went on then the opposition or resistance to forward movement on Pakistan came from within the Congress party itself. Less than two months after Dr Singh won the UPA a second term, he went to the Egyptian resort of Sharm-el-Sheikh where he and his Pakistani counterpart, Syed Yousaf Raza Gilani, issued a joint statement. In that, a mention was made of Baluchistan, where the Pakistanis have suspected an Indian hand in their insurgency. All Dr Singh did was say we have no information, we're not involved, but we'll have a look at it.

This mention brought the prime minister under great criticism from the BJP, as expected, but also from his own party. I can tell you that if Vajpayee had said the same thing, no one would have had the gumption to question him.

Manmohan Singh's inability to seize a deal in winter 2006–07 frustrated Musharraf more than anyone else. By March he was embroiled in a power struggle when he suspended the chief justice of Pakistan, Iftikhar Mohammed Chaudhry. It led to a series of events in which he had to give up being the army chief in November 2007; former Prime Minister Benazir Bhutto returned to Pakistan in December and was assassinated (for which Musharraf was arrested in 2013); and his stepping down as president in the face of impeachment happened in August 2008.

Some people believe that Musharraf was so annoyed at missing out on his place in history that he may have had a hand in the 26 November 2008 attack on Mumbai which killed 164 people. It was a big operation and could only have been an ISI operation, planned in advance. This talk of rogue element is all nonsense. Gen. Ashfaq Kayani, who succeeded Musharraf as the army chief, was the ISI chief under Musharraf and both of them would have been in the know.

Why go from out-of-the-box peace to such a deadly attack that might have led to war? There's a belief that when the generals in Pakistan get irritated they feel that the only thing that Delhi understands is force. Such a thing, like a terror attack, is regarded by the army as a kick in the backside.

Since then the Pakistanis have felt regretful that the attack took place, and in our track two meetings (the unofficial bilateral meetings where retired officials try out suggestions that otherwise would not be brought up in formal meetings) the Pakistanis have wished India would put 26/11 aside and get back to talking peace. I had gone to one such meeting in December 2008 in Bangkok, but despite their genuine wish that the attack had not taken place, I had to inform them that it would take time for India to get over it. For many of us the attack had been like an invasion by sea.

Down the years, whenever Pakistanis have asked me what would happen in the event of another 26/11, I have plainly stated that nobody can predict the consequences.

After 26/11, Shivraj Patil was replaced as the home minister by P. Chidambaram, till then the finance minister and generally seen to be one of the more efficient ministers in the government. He called me in after a little bit of a fiasco with the Hurriyat.

It was obvious that Chidambaram wanted a quiet, meaningful and sustained dialogue, and that he wanted it badly. But like others in the UPA, he was impatient about it. He wanted things to materialise quickly.

The Hurriyat was brought to Delhi to meet the home minister on 14 November 2009. It was arranged by the IB, as per Chidambaram's wishes, but somehow the story leaked and appeared in the *Hindu*. The newspaper stated that the Hurriyat were summoned to Delhi and told to assemble at Khan Market, where they were picked up and taken to meet Chidambaram. So the quiet bit went out of the window with this exposé of the operation, and the Hurriyat was not amused for it claims that whatever it does, it does openly. This was not very open.

'What is so quiet about this?' the Mirwaiz complained to me. 'Aap quiet ki baat karte hain, akhbaar mein aa jati hain.'

The IB figured that the state government had deliberately sabotaged it, meaning the J&K CID. However, if it was intended to be a hush-hush operation then why did the state CID get a whiff of it? How did the state government come to know the Hurriyat men were assembling in Khan Market? They were probably being tailed by the state CID.

The DIB called me up after this and said the home minister would like to see you. I said great.

Chidambaram was very nice. 'I'm told that you know these Hurriyat guys,' he said.

'Sir, we helped getting them to meet Advani,' I said.

'I had contact with them,' he said. 'Can you renew the contact, and give me feedback?'

I went to the Mirwaiz and had a long chat, after which I went back to the home minister and said: 'They're very much on board.'

That was my second meeting with Chidambaram which went well, and later he sent word that we would meet again.

In our third meeting, Chidambaram's frustration came to the fore. He was extremely irritated and said the Hurriyat leaders were not very reliable. I made the mistake of suggesting Shabir Shah.

'You mean Shabir will come?'

'Yes, sir,' I said. 'Of course he'll come. If he's approached he'll talk.'

But Chidambaram was cynical about it because he had negative reports about Shabir. 'Why don't you go and get Shabir?' he said, in a foul temper.

Now Shabir was in jail and I was out of the government. How in the world was I supposed to yank him out of jail? So the home minister got angry with me. And after that, I was not needed.

Chidambaram went to Kashmir in June 2011 and in April

2012, but he did not meet the Hurriyat there. In July 2012, Sushil Kumar Shinde took over as home minister after Chidambaram was shifted to the finance ministry following the election of Pranab Mukherjee as President of India. Shinde made an impression because he was different from his predecessor and more in the mould of a traditional politician. Before he was a politician he was an assistant sub-inspector of police.

Shinde visited in October 2012 and did a couple of smart things: he visited Chrar-e-Sharief and he visited Hazratbal, and he shocked everyone by wandering off into the bazaar at Lal Chowk and asking locals about the price of vegetables. 'Yeh toh theek lagta hai,' Kashmiris said.

Though Shinde's instincts were right there was no follow-up, because a few months later, in February 2013, Afzal Guru was hanged for his alleged involvement in the December 2001 attack on Parliament. Immediately he became a martyr in Kashmir not because he was a fugitive freedom fighter like Maqbool Butt, but because he came to represent the victimisation that Kashmiris felt. In a way, Afzal Guru replaced Maqbool Butt as the main martyr for the Kashmir movement.

Omar, who was the chief minister, was extremely annoyed and protested, asking what was the haste; there were twelve other convicts who had been waiting longer on death row. Yet what choice did he have; Delhi believed it could ram anything that it liked down the young chief minister's throat. It certainly did the UPA government no good, and Prof. Ghani called me up to ask: 'Whose agenda is the government carrying out?'

I immediately asked for a meeting with Dr Singh, because I was receiving a lot of anguished calls from Kashmir. I finally met the prime minister a month later, but by then there was really nothing much to say. Immediately after the hanging I was challenged during a TV debate by Subramanian Swamy and I told him: 'If Vajpayee had been prime minister, this would not have happened.' I added: 'Even if Advani had been prime minister it would not have happened.'

Needless to say, it set things back even further for the rest of India in Kashmir. If India's intention has been to mainstream Kashmir, then not only was progress at a standstill during the ten years of the UPA, they were set back by irritants like the Afzal Guru hanging.

How could there be progress? After Musharraf no Pakistani picked up his four-point formula in fear that they would lose out in Kashmir. Indeed, having come this close to settling it, Pakistan is not interested in Kashmir. Pakistan will gain nothing at this point of time, so it does not even want to discuss Kashmir. Whenever I have asked Pakistanis at track two meetings as to what happened to the four-point formula, they either laugh or look the other way.

And with the hostility shown by Narendra Modi during his first six months as prime minister, the Pakistanis have gone back to talking about UN resolutions—something that Musharraf's four-point formula had promised to render obsolete. On the other hand, Kashmiris, who for the longest time were not all that thrilled with Musharraf's formula, were now desperately seeking it as the political solution to their grievances with Delhi.

The solution to the India–Pakistan–Kashmir Gordian knot was given to Dr Manmohan Singh on a platter in 2004. When he left office in 2014, he had not accomplished what was within his grasp. No wonder Kashmiris call his tenure their 'lost decade'.

17

THE LEAGUE OF EXTRAORDINARY GENTLEMEN

Following the attacks on Mumbai on 26 November 2008, there was a brief period in which anxiety spread that India's anger could spill over into retaliation on Pakistani soil, and there would be a counter-retaliation, and so on, that the thing might spin out of control, to the extent that nuclear weapons would come into play.

Western countries worried the most about it, and when tempers subsided, they were keen that they get a feel of what the thinking was on both sides of the Indo-Pak border. The best way to do that was through track two diplomacy, a term coined by an American diplomat in 1981 to refer to 'non-governmental, informal and unofficial contacts and activities between private citizens or groups of individuals'. Though it contrasts with track one diplomacy, which is governmental, it is not a substitute for it. India and Pakistan have been hosting a track two diplomatic meeting called the Neemrana Dialogue, named after the first venue, a restored fort in Neemrana, Rajasthan, since 1992. The countries have hosted it alternately, and gather together retired defence services officers, retired diplomats, mediapersons, representatives of NGOs, etc.

What had started off as an India–Pakistan initiative was gradually expanded to include Afghanistan and when the process accelerated and stabilised, then someone hit on the idea of having an exclusive dialogue for the two militaries, and thus began an India–Pakistan military dialogue. Retired Lt. Gen. Mohammed Asad Durrani, who was the director-general of the ISI directorate in the years 1990–92, suggested that if the militaries could talk to one another, then so could the intelligence services.

· Peter Jones, a scholar at Ottawa University who was setting up this track two initiative, thought it was a great idea floated by General Durrani and asked for India's response. The R&AW chief who had had successful meetings in 2002 with his ISI counterpart, and who now was retired like me, C.D. Sahay, bounced the idea off me. 'I think it's great,' I said. Hence was born the idea of a meeting of retired intelligence officers from India and Pakistan, sponsored by the University of Ottawa which had been in the business for some time.

One looked forward to these meetings not because we would produce something, but because to the inquisitive mind of an intelligence officer, going to such a meeting would bring you into touch with the other side, you could make a few friends and hear the other viewpoint. It gave you an insight. I must say I learnt a lot.

The other thing is that the question that comes up in Delhi while debating bilateral relations with Pakistan is of who's in control. The Pakistanis acknowledge that ultimately when it comes to foreign policy or national security, the army's approval is required. Within their army, the ISI is an all-powerful institution—perhaps the most powerful spy agency in the world, as far as influence on their government is concerned. So if such a track two dialogue helps us make contacts in the establishment within the establishment, that can only help India–Pakistan relations.

The Pakistanis have been very keen to meet. In these track two meetings we always put down a resolution recommending meetings between the two countries' intelligence chiefs. It makes sense. From the Pakistani point of view, if the intelligence chiefs meet then the army chiefs could meet; and if the army chiefs meet then you could have a summit meeting. One thing follows another. General Durrani and I even wrote a joint paper on it in July 2011. In our thinking, intelligence chiefs can do so much for their governments and their leaders which can remain non-attributable. It can only help the political process.

We've had four rounds of meetings of retired intelligence chiefs. The first two were attended by the future National security advisor, Ajit Doval. The Pakistani side has been better represented than our side, sadly; we find it difficult to muster five people, though we had originally decided that it would be Sahay, Doval, Shyamal Datta, Vikram Sood and myself. Shyamal had second thoughts and backed out, he never attended. Vikram has had better options. So we brought in R.N. Ravi, who used to be with me in the IB's Kashmir Group and who later became the chairman of the Joint Intelligence Committee (JIC). After the second meeting, though, both Doval and Ravi backed out as it had gotten closer to the 2014 parliamentary election. Sahay did not go to the third meeting due to knee surgery so we had to rope in two other R&AW officers, Anand Arni and Rajeev Kumar, as well as an old IB hand, V. Rajagopal.

The significant thing here is that if five people from each country who have handled important positions can sit together and talk frankly, then why can't the intelligence chiefs meet? An American ambassador who attended the fourth meeting called us a 'League of Extraordinary Gentlemen', which is also the name of a film.

My own track two experiences started when Amitabh Mattoo, an expert on international relations who was then with the Institute of Peace and Conflict Studies (IPCS), invited me to participate in the Chaophraya Dialogue in Bangkok in

March 2009. The initiative is named after the main river in Thailand and was organised jointly by the IPCS and the Jinnah Institute in Pakistan, but funded by the British. I had also gotten involved, thanks to former foreign secretary Salman Haider, with the Balusa Group meeting, chaired by high-powered Pakistani-American academic Shirin Tahir-Kheli and named after two villages in Pakistani Punjab.

The track two circuit was also a place where I made what for me was a startling discovery—and one that I passed on to my old organisation, since I was now long retired—and that was a top Taliban functionary telling me that his organisation was not averse to making contact with the government of India.

Mullah Abdul Salam Zaeef was one of the original Talib (students) who was a veteran of the anti-Soviet resistance and who with other Talibs came together under Mullah Mohammed Omar to form the Taliban, which sought to bring an end to decades of strife in Afghanistan by assuming power in 1994. The Taliban government was dislodged by the US invasion of its country in October 2001 in search of al-Qaeda leader Osama bin Laden, mastermind of the 9/11 attacks, but the Taliban undertook an insurgency against the US military, which lasted till America began to pull out in 2014.

Mullah Zaeef was in Berlin in July 2011, at the 59th conference of Pugwash. It was a big jamboree filled with interesting people, one of whom was an Irishman named Michael Semple. He pointed Mullah Zaeef to me and I said I was thinking of talking to Mullah Saheb.

'Yes, yes,' he said. 'You must talk.'

'How much is he in on the Taliban?'

'He's not in the inner core,' Semple said. 'But they've parked him in Kabul and he does have access to Mullah Omar. So he meets people, he listens, and then he reports back.'

I asked Mullah Zaeef if we could talk, not knowing whether he preferred to speak in his native Pashto, but he was quite okay with English. We spoke for about 45 minutes, and he made a number of points.

First, that peace was possible but only after the Americans had left, since they were the core of the problem. 'Once they go, the Afghans know how to sort it out,' Mullah Zaeef said. 'And we will sort it out. Whether it requires a coalition we'll see, but accommodation will be the key.'

The Taliban has matured a great deal, he added. The leaders are getting old.

'Is anything happening so far?' I asked.

A bit of movement has been made, he said, with the help of Arab friends (the opening of an office in Qatar, to explore talks with the Americans, was in the works but not yet public). 'We are open to everybody but not Pakistan and not Saudi Arabia,' he said. 'They have vested interests.' He sounded quite confident.

'So you live in Kabul?' I asked. 'You don't meet Indians?'

'I'd be very happy to meet Indians, but Indians don't meet us,' he said.

I don't know why we in India have such a closed mindset, and why we have never tried to reach out to the Taliban. The government can have a policy, but that should not stop my former organisation from reaching out. While I was heading R&AW we didn't try to reach out because we were so hooked onto the Northern Alliance, but then everything changed once the top Alliance military person, Ahmed Shah Masood, was killed.

Masood's death narrowed down our options. And once 9/11 and the subsequent Afghan invasion happened, we should have tried to reach out. The thing is that this game was similar to what we were doing in Kashmir in 1988 and '89, when we were hooked to Farooq Abdullah but had neglected Mufti Saheb and Lone Saheb, which wasn't very smart. You may think you have the best person, but that is not the end of the matter. In fact, even during the Kandahar hijacking, the messages we got from the Taliban's people was that 'we don't know you guys, you don't want to know us', and this is one reason Jaswant Singh, who flew out there to exchange terrorists for the hostages of IC-814, was totally on his own when he landed in Kandahar.

That's one of the lessons of Kashmir: talk to everyone. And when you broadbase your talks, it keeps all participants from getting too comfortable.

'Do you mind if I take your number and pass it on?' I said.

'You're most welcome,' he said, handing me his card. 'They're welcome to call me.'

And then he said: 'Let me also clarify that Pakistan has been a friend and we are beholden to them for a lot. But we don't trust them. We have no problem with you, we can do business with you. And we'll be happy to.'

Mullah Zaeef was quite bitter about what the Pakistanis had done to him. Though he was ambassador, when the invasion took place in 2001 the Pakistanis locked him up and then handed him over to the Americans, who put him in Guantanamo Bay. He was there till 2005. I don't know whether or not the Americans turned him around, but he was locked up for four years. Even the UN had taken him off its terrorists' list just the previous year, in 2010.

I was quite excited after interacting with him, and when I returned home, I passed it all on to the people concerned at my old organisation. I don't know if anything happened, but Mullah Zaeef did turn up in India two and a half years later, at a conference in Goa in late 2013, where he was in a discussion on the impending American pull-out from Afghanistan with a former CIA officer, Robert Grenier.

In 2013, when I went to a track two meeting in Istanbul I met another Talib, and he was just as keen to interact with India as Mullah Zaeef. He was also based in Kabul, and he gave me his phone number, and again I passed it on to the guys at R&AW. Six months later he called up and said, 'Uncle, I'm in Dubai, this is a good place to meet in case your people want to meet.' Again, I passed the message on, but I don't know if anything happened.

Michael Semple was also a fascinating fellow. He had spent twenty-five years in Afghanistan and Pakistan, could speak Dari and Hindustani fluently, was married to a Pakistani woman, and had a golden beard. He was like Lawrence of Arabia. He was one of the best-informed and knowledgeable people in the West about Afghanistan. He was deputy to the European Union special representative on Afghanistan, though he was later thrown out of the country for what they call 'unauthorised activities'. Basically what I had heard was that he was an MI6 agent, and the Afghans had asked him to go.

I asked him about Mullah Zaeef. 'Look, he's not one of the top guys but he's a useful guy,' Semple said. 'The fact they've parked him in Kabul is significant. It provides a way for other people. He should not be written off.'

In fact, the following summer Semple wrote a piece in the *Guardian* about the Taliban being ready to talk, and lo and behold: it was almost verbatim everything that Mullah Zaeef had said to me in Berlin.

Perhaps our guys are too sceptical of the Taliban. For them, the Taliban is a 'no go', because the Americans are not going to talk to the Taliban. But what happens if the Americans start talking to the Taliban—we'll be left out of that loop as well. That cannot but happen because there is no solution in Afghanistan without the Taliban—even if the Pakistanis are happy to keep their former protégés out. This is what I have been hearing from Pakistanis lately, that there can be no deal with the Taliban. The Taliban have just become too hot for the Pakistanis to handle.

And there will be people in Pakistan who say nothing can be done without the Taliban; like the former ambassador, Rustam Shah Mohmand, who was even on a committee set up by Nawaz Sharif to deal with the tribals in their border areas. In track two meetings, Mohmand openly criticises the Pakistan government. It would thus be wise for us to be talking to the Taliban.

On a personal note, the track two dialogues enabled me to visit Pakistan four times, and I have had the good fortune of making many friends, prominent among them being General Asad Durrani and former Pakistan foreign secretary Mian Shaharyar Khan, who along with his wife has been very kind to Paran and I. Mian and I have a common interest in cricket.

The first time I met Asad Durrani was at the Chaophraya Dialogue in Bangkok and there was a session on terrorism that he and I were co-chairing. It was pre-Mumbai because the mood was different. Everybody spoke their piece and then the two of us were to give our views. I was new at this and I said, 'Sir, after you.'

'No, Dulat Saheb,' he said. 'Pehle aap boliye.'

So I waffled around a bit, saying the usual meaningless stuff: we've borne the brunt of it, etc.

Then it was Durrani's turn. 'People here have been talking of proxies but I would be very disappointed if my friend here didn't use proxies,' he said. 'This is part of your intelligence. I have no hesitation in saying yes, we use proxies, we are using proxies and I presume you're doing that in Baluchistan.'

He was candid about the whole thing, so at the coffee break I went up to him and said, 'General Saheb, what were you saying?'

'Kyon, maine kucch jhoot bola?' he said.

'Nahin, sir, aap yeh keh rahe hain, proxies.'

Don't you use proxies, was his counter. 'Woh Mukti Bahini kya tha, Bangladesh mein kya hua tha? Proxy nahin thi?'

'General Saheb, main samajh gaya aapki baat,' I said.

After that we got along well. He is an incredible guy.

Once at a dialogue held in Istanbul, Turkey, Durrani and I were sitting side by side—which did not normally happen—and this got Malini Parthasarathy of the *Hindu* very excited. She was sitting just beyond Durrani and she took photos of us. 'I've got the two spooks together,' she said.

During a coffee break at the same meeting, a young woman from the Jinnah Institute came up to me and said, 'Dulat Saheb, I marvel at two things. One, you don't look or behave like a spook at all.'

'How do spooks behave?' I said.

She looked at Asad Durrani. 'You're too decent,' she said.

'You mean to say your guys are indecent?' I said, gesturing at Durrani.

'The other is, how do you two get along so well?' she said.

'General Saheb is the boss,' I said. 'I look up to him, he's senior to me.'

Besides the paper we jointly wrote on intelligence cooperation, we prepared a paper called 'Kashmir: Confrontation to Cooperation' for the October 2013 Ottawa Dialogue. I told Durrani, 'General Saheb, you write it whatever way you like, I'll go along with it.'

When I saw the paper, though, it looked like it was written more by a diplomat than by an intelligence chief. 'This is a diplomatic story that you're writing,' I told him. 'I want you to include Kashmir in it. The last four paragraphs I will give you.'

He said okay, but when I sent it to him, he hemmed and hawed on Musharraf and we got stuck. 'Musharraf is finished here,' he told me.

'He may be finished there, but he's not finished in Kashmir,' I said.

'Do we have to use his name?'

'Yes,' I said. 'We have to mention his name.'

Finally he agreed.

Another of our meetings must be mentioned, which was sort of a track two of track two meetings. We were in Islamabad in 2011 for a two-day dialogue. On the second day, I was expecting the session to end a bit early so that we could take a round of the bazaar. It was June and it was hot, and Durrani had said, 'When this is over we must sit down together and have a chat.'

But it broke only at 5 p.m., and he said, 'I guess you'll go shopping now.'

'Yeah I was hoping to go shopping but it's become too late because at 6:30 p.m. I have to attend a cocktail at our high commissioner's place,' I said.

'You're sure you're not going shopping?'

'I'm sure.'

'So,' he said. 'Would you care to have a drink?'

'General Saheb, it's five in the afternoon and so bloody hot,' I said. 'In any case, where is the drink here?'

'I've got a bottle in my car,' he said. 'If you're interested I'll bring it up to your room.'

He brought a bottle of Black Label, and at five in the afternoon we had a drink. We enjoyed taking digs at each other. 'Sir, I can never disagree with you,' I would say.

'Amarjit Singh, you're very smart,' he would respond. 'You always start by saying you'll never disagree with me, and after that you disagree with whatever I say.'

After our drinking session he dropped me to High Commissioner Sharad Sabharwal's place. 'Why don't you join us?' I said.

'No, no, I know this will be an exclusively Indian thing but do give the high commissioner my regards,' he said. The former ISI chief seemed to get along with all our high commissioners.

Most of the time Durrani and I discussed how bilateral relations could improve, and what were the chances on the Pakistani side. He was frank. He would ask about the chances on our side, and sometimes he would say, things are looking very good; and sometimes he would say, things are not looking so good, I don't think anything will move. That was his view when we last met in November 2014.

When I first went to Pakistan, I was invited by Salman Haider and I was sceptical I would get a visa. 'We will get it done,' he said. I got my visa, and I never had a problem getting one. India, on the other hand, is very stingy with the visas; General Durrani did not get a visa to visit India until November 2014. I think this phenomenon of India being tight with the visas is a post-26/11 phenomenon: because David Headley, the Pakistani-American who got a visa, came to Mumbai and did a recce for the 26/11 attack, nobody wants to take a call on giving someone with a Pakistani background or connection a visa.

As for me, I got my visa and I went with Salman and Paran to Lahore in January 2010. We stayed at a guest house of the Lahore University of Management Sciences (LUMS), which has a beautiful campus and can match any American university. We had taken a Pakistan International Airlines flight on Saturday and on Sunday they took us sightseeing to the old fort and the mosque (there's also a gurudwara there). My maternal grandfather had a house in Lahore so on that visit I asked the conference's coordinator, General Durrani (he was briefly the NSA in Pakistan in 2008), where 4 Zafar Ali Road was and whether we could swing by there. 'I remember it used to be near the canal,' I said.

'There's no water in the canal, only a ditch,' General Mahmud said. 'But yes, there is a Zafar Ali Road, we'll go via that side. Number four has probably changed.'

We had a look but I couldn't recognise the place. I was also keen to see the Government College, Lahore, where my father studied, and also the great Aitchison College, but hardly had time to spend. We managed a bookshop and then it was back to the conference for two days.

Mani Shankar Aiyar was also there, and after one of our sessions in which I did a lot of blabbing he came up to me and said, 'What a useful life you've led, and what a useless life I've led.'

Former Pakistan foreign secretary Shaharyar Khan, whom Nawaz Sharif appointed the track two interlocutor with Satinder Lambah, was also at the Balusa conference. Our wives hit it off pretty well. In fact I asked her once, 'Come to Delhi, come and stay with us.'

'Baba, you'll get me into trouble if I stay with a former R&AW chief,' he said.

There was also a fellow running a TV channel, Ejaz Haider. He called me up while I was in Lahore and asked me to come on the show. I said, 'Sure, what's the big deal, who else will be there?'

'I'm trying to get Gen. Mahmud Durrani,' he said.

But Durrani wouldn't come on TV. He already had Mani Shankar Aiyar and Manvendra Singh, former BJP MP and son of Jaswant Singh, so I said, why do you need me, you've got the bigwigs.

'No, no, I need you, please come,' he said.

After the discussion on TV was over, he said to me: 'This is a big thing for me. This is the first time a R&AW chief has been on a Pakistani TV channel.'

On one conference I even visited Karachi, and one night Paran and I were invited, along with a few other colleagues, by Sherry Rehman, former ambassador to the US and PPP MP, for dinner. It was at the poolside at her lovely home in Clifton, where she lived with her third husband, a most charming person, in great luxury and style. There were a handful of us and she had even invited her second husband to the dinner; she obviously knew how to deal with men. There was another TV journalist, Nasim Zehra, and they began calling me Casper, which I understand is the name of a friendly ghost on an American TV show.

Which goes to show you that for the Pakistanis, once a spook, always a spook.

This brings me to Yasin Malik, who went all the way to Pakistan to depose that he had never met A.S. Dulat, R&AW chief.

That was technically true: we had never met while I was at R&AW. However, we did meet when I headed the IB's Kashmir Group. Basharat Peer the writer has referred to Yasin as the Che Guevara of Kashmir, and in many senses he was a romantic in that he had taken to the gun and headed the JKLF, the first real militant group that dominated when the movement was full-blown in the 1989–90 period. If Shabir was the headmaster of the movement, then Yasin was its headboy. No one raised higher expectations, or disappointed more. He was a member of the leadership of the JKLF known as the HAJY group—the acronym standing for four militants, Hamid Sheikh, Ashfaq Majid Wani, Javed Mir, and Yasin Malik. The boss was Ashfaq—whose Dad came and held the important meeting with me during the Rubaiya kidnapping—and he was considered a gutsy, courageous guy. Unfortunately, he was killed. In fact, JKLF boys now say that Ashfaq was angry with the Pakistanis and took them on, saying this was the Kashmiris' movement and so on.

In January 1990 Yasin participated in the shooting of thirteen Indian Air Force officers who were waiting for a ride to their base in Awantipora. Four died, including a squadron leader. A few months later, he was arrested during a raid downtown; he jumped off a roof and hurt his ankle. He was arrested and eventually brought to Delhi, where he was kept in the Mehrauli sub-jail. People began meeting him here and he then came into the limelight.

The first occasion I met Yasin was in a house in Delhi. He was already there when I walked into the room, and the first thing he did was put his feet up on the coffee table and light a cigarette. I was not impressed and it did not bother me because by then I was familiar with Kashmiri gimmickry. Then he uttered the standard line that all the Kashmiri boys used, even Shabir, to the effect that they had nothing to say to me, all they wanted was freedom: 'Hum aap se kya baat kar sakte hain? Hum toh azaadi chahate hain.'

It is something my son wants too, I told him. 'Azaadi toh mera beta bhi chahata hain,' I said. 'Aur agar joh azaadi aap dhoond rahe hain, aapko mil sake toh main bhi naara lagaoonga ke hamein kya chahiye, azaadi. Woh azaadi aapko nahin milne wali hain. Ek azaadi hain joh hamare Constitution ke dairey mein hain, uske baare mein sochiye.'

He was very sceptical about the whole thing but during the 1991–94 period he mellowed down and became a Gandhian. There were two reasons, each involving a doctor.

While he was incarcerated at the Mehrauli sub-jail, he was visited by Dr Farooq Abdullah. Farooq took him out on to the lawn, and said: 'Come on, let's do some plain talking.'

I don't know exactly what he said, but I was told Farooq gave Yasin a piece of his mind. And for two days after that, Yasin lost his appetite and hardly ate. He was that demoralised.

The other reason was Dr Upendra Kaul, a Kashmiri Pandit. Yasin developed serious medical problems and required a valve placement in his heart. Dr Kaul performed the heart surgery on Yasin. Dr Kaul would become extra-protective about his fellow Kashmiri: anyone critical of Yasin would not be allowed near him in the hospital. Because of that surgery the two had a special relationship: when, some years back, Dr Kaul's mother died, Yasin especially came down to Delhi for the cremation.

From 1991 to May 1994, when he was released, Yasin softened. Che Guevara became a Gandhi and began talking about giving up the gun and adopting peaceful forms of agitation. Upon his release he went back to Srinagar and he announced that he was giving up the gun and sitting on dharna. One day, while he sat on dharna outside his house, some boys from the Hizbul Mujahideen came in a three-wheeler autorickshaw, picked him up, took him somewhere and soundly thrashed him.

After that he never spoke of Gandhi, and he ended his dharna. Later dharnas were all held in Delhi, at Jantar Mantar, where Rajinder Sachar, the former chief justice of the Delhi High Court and human rights activist, and Kuldip Nayar, eminent journalist, would offer him juice for him to break his fast.

Many people, however, considered him a cold-blooded killer for his role in the killing of IAF officers. Years after Yasin was released, Sachar took him to the India International Centre for the weekly meeting of IIC intellectuals called the Saturday

Club. When Yasin entered there was an uproar. A lot of members, most of whom were elderly, objected and told Sachar: 'How dare you bring a killer to the IIC?' The two of them had to beat a retreat.

The second time I met him I realised he had a great chip on his shoulder: he thought that we were responsible for the break-up of the JKLF. What happened is that while Yasin was in jail another JKLF fellow named Shabir Siddiqui had formed a breakaway faction of the front. Siddiqui in fact was later killed in a shoot-out at the Hazratbal complex in 1996, when he laid siege to the mosque. Unlike the siege in 1993, the militants were not given safe passage in 1996.

Yasin thought that we had set up Siddiqui as the leader of the breakaway faction. 'Yeh sab aapki game hai,' he said.

'Yasin Saheb,' I said. 'Aisa hai ki yeh hamari game nahin hai. Aap unse puchh lijiye. Aur main toh Delhi mein baitha hoon, aap Srinagar walon se puchhiye.'

We met once more after that but we never hit it off. His discomfort with me stemmed from the fact that he knew I talked to many Kashmiris, and he wanted an exclusive relationship. That was okay because Yasin was great friends with two other people: IAS officer Wajahat Habibullah, and my IB colleague Ajit Doval. I'd heard Wajahat speaking to Yasin over phone: 'Haan, phir sunao beta kaise ho.'

But for many years, Yasin was going nowhere. He was pretty unstable, not knowing which way he was to go. But because he was gradually the only one left talking about azaadi, he got a lot of support from expatriate Kashmiris. Either the expatriates would send him a lot of money, or in the case of Majid Tramboo and company, who came here and met us in 1994, urged us to give Yasin financial support. In fact, some of his colleagues began whispering allegations of misappropriation of money. His long-time sidekick, Javed Mir, fell out with him; Javed went over to the Hurriyat under the Mirwaiz.

This was one problem Yasin had with the Hurriyat: he could

never come to terms with supremacy in the separatist movement. He was uncomfortable with the fact that the Mirwaiz was the Hurriyat chairman for many years; Yasin and Mirwaiz don't see eye-to-eye. Yasin was so opposed to Umar that from 2002 to 2003 he drew close to Sajad Lone. Both were anti-Hurriyat and anti-Mirwaiz. I was in the PMO at the time and Sajad suggested that he and Yasin could link up. 'That's a great idea,' I said.

'How do we go about it?'

'Get Yasin here,' I said. 'The three of us will get into a room and we'll stay there no matter if it takes 24 hours or 48 hours or whatever. We can find a formula which is acceptable to you guys.'

Sadly that did not materialise.

Bizarrely, the reason Yasin had to deny that he had ever met the R&AW chief had to do with a controversy in Pakistan and the United States that broke open in October 2011, called memogate. This involved a memorandum that had allegedly been written at the behest of Pakistan's then president, Asif Ali Zardari, and addressed to Admiral Mike Mullen, the chairman of the joint chiefs of staff. It spoke of the need to avert a military takeover of the civilian government following the deep unhappiness in Pakistan over the secret raid in May 2011 which led to the execution of al-Qaeda chief Osama bin Laden. The memo was with the Pakistani ambassador in Washington, Husain Haqqani, and a Pakistani-American businessman named Mansoor Ijaz claimed that he was asked to deliver the memo to Mullen.

Ijaz fashioned himself after Farooq Kathwari, the Kashmiri-American who met me soon after I joined R&AW. He has claimed that he was the one who arranged the ceasefire announced by Vajpayee in 2000, shortly after Majid Dar defected to India, but this is a lot of nonsense. The fact is that Mansoor landed up here claiming to have contacts with Yasin and with Pakistan and that he could get a peace process moving.

Yasin, however, had a different take. He narrated a story that both he and Mansoor attended a seminar on Kashmir held in Gurgaon, near Delhi. Yasin says that Mansoor said something derisive about Kashmir, whereupon Yasin picked up a table lamp and hurled it at Mansoor.

That would have been the end of Mansoor but in 2011 he surfaced again with memogate; Mansoor wrote a piece in the *Financial Times*, which brought the whole affair to light and as a result of which Haqqani had to resign as ambassador. Somewhere in the fallout of this whole memogate thing Mansoor mentioned Yasin, and took credit for introducing Yasin to R&AW during the time that I was chief. Yasin in his defence said he was pressured by R.K. Mishra, a well-known journalist involved in peace initiatives, to meet the R&AW chief, but refused to do so.

Then, inexplicably, Yasin went to Pakistan and deposed before the investigation that the Supreme Court was conducting. 'I have never spoken with the R&AW chief,' he said, which was true in the narrow sense that when we talked, I was not the R&AW chief.

But when I went over to the PMO, then another character who was a great pal of Yasin's popped up: a half-American, half-Kashmiri fellow by the name of Usman Rahim. He suddenly showed up, saying he was a great supporter and great friend of Yasin's, looking after Yasin's assets and property. Amitabh Mattoo, then an academic at Jawaharlal Nehru University in Delhi, came to me and insisted I meet Usman, so the three of us had lunch together.

After lunch Mattoo asked me for an opinion, and I told him: 'I'm not impressed. He doesn't understand Kashmir, he doesn't know Kashmir.'

Mattoo was very disappointed.

That was the only time I met Usman Rahim though I kept hearing about him until he was deported from India for being up to no good. I bring up Usman Rahim because of Yasin's marriage.

Yasin married a Pakistani named Mushaal Hussein Mullick, a very good-looking and smart woman. Her mother Rehana, a former member of the women's wing of the Pakistan Muslim League, is even smarter. They have a lot of influence on Yasin. Mushaal's brother, Haider Ali Hussein Mullick, is a professor at the Naval War College and a fellow at the Joint Special Operations University in the US. But more importantly, his mentor throughout his career has been David Petraeus, the former military commander who also served as CIA chief under Barack Obama.

Hence the talk here is that Yasin's mother-in-law is a big influence in his life. She's been to Kashmir, and she apparently holds all the levers and controls everything.

Though strange, one theory doing the rounds is that Yasin's marriage is a CIA operation to get him to marry a Pakistani girl. The reasoning is that this is to get Yasin dependent on someone they know and trust. That is the story, no matter how weird it may sound. And now, like the American Usman Rahim who is also married to a Pakistani, Yasin draws most of his strength from Pakistan.

No matter what is the truth in this, the undeniable fact is that Yasin Malik is no Che Guevara. Burnt out as a separatist, having lost his street power, he has been unable to master the art of politics; Yasin Malik may pretend to be a Kashmiri leader, but he can't suddenly become Farooq Abdullah. He is now a rebel without a cause gradually gravitating to his original moorings in the National Conference. I'll always think of Yasin as the James Dean of Maisuma.

Everyone gets taken up with James Dean at one point or another, and in this the venerable Agha Ashraf Ali was no different. When Yasin had begun his Gandhi phase, he one night landed up at Agha Saheb's house and narrated to the elder his change of heart. Agha Saheb was an educationist from an illustrious family of Kashmir; he was a liberal and a Shia, and three of his brothers had joined the civil services—Agha

Showkat Ali left the Indian Civil Service and joined the Muslim League in Pakistan following Partition; Agha Nasir Ali joined the IAS and became a secretary to the government of India, passing away at the age of 96 in November 2014; Agha Muzaffar became chief secretary of Kashmir before shifting to Pakistan in the 1970s.

Agha Ashraf Ali himself was close to the future president, Dr Zakir Hussain, who was Jamia Millia Islamia University's first vice-chancellor for two decades from 1928; Agha Saheb taught courses at the university. He also served his state both as commissioner of education and as head of the education department of the University of Kashmir.

Agha Saheb was impressed with Yasin for several years, until he became disillusioned with his lack of direction and inability to grow as a leader, even though the two maintained relations to the extent that Yasin's wife and mother-in-law were occasional visitors to Agha Saheb's house in Rajbagh. I visited Agha Saheb when he turned ninety in November 2012. He is a fascinating man, a sharp intellect, and a reservoir of history, as well as being a committed Leftist and humanist. During the floods of September 2014, he was rescued from his rapidly inundated house in the nick of time: 'I escaped death by two minutes,' he told me when he reached Delhi, on his way to the US with his son Agha Iqbal Ali, a management professor at the University of Massachusetts, but Agha Saheb because of his age and delicate health, never could make the long journey and spent the winter in Delhi itself.

In fact, during the 2014 parliamentary election I asked Agha Saheb who he would have voted for (it was increasingly difficult for him to walk around in his old age, so he did not). 'Farooq, of course,' he exclaimed, as if it was a no-brainer. 'He's the only one who can stop Modi.'

For many people, however, it is Agha Saheb's late son, Agha Shahid Ali, who is famous for his poetry, who comes to mind when you mention Agha Saheb. Some in the literary world believe that Shahid opened the gates for many young writers in the subcontinent; Kashmiris like Basharat Peer, who drew the title of his book *Curfewed Night* from a poem by Shahid, are steeped in debt to this deep and original thinker. Shahid died at the young age of fifty-two in the US, where he lived and taught.

When I read his collection of poems *The Country without a Post Office*, I was struck that one of the early ones, 'Farewell', is actually a love poem to the Kashmiri Pandits. Or perhaps it is to India–Pakistan. He says: 'In your absence you polished me into the Enemy./Your history gets in the way of my memory./I am everything you lost, you can't forgive me.'

Call it a love poem or an apology, he asks: why did you have to go?

Yet not all Kashmiris are like Shahid or even Dr Farooq Abdullah who told me Kashmiris had failed Kashmir and Kashmiriyat when they did not prevent the 1989-90 exodus of Pandits. Kashmiris are hypocritical. Like Yasin Malik or the Hurriyat Conference they mouth platitudes about how they feel incomplete without their neighbours who have gone away, and that they would love to have them back. But there are two things here: the damage to the Pandit psyche, and the Muslim fear of being swamped by non-Muslims.

The Kashmiri psyche has been shaken up. The Pandit used to think that because he was more educated than the Musalman, he was the real Kashmiri. That is one clock that truly cannot be turned back. The Pandit has to pay a huge price for the clout he once wielded in Delhi. They are no doubt smart but after deep introspection one has to admit that the Kashmiri Musalman outwits him. The converts are after all the same breed.

The fact is that Vajpayee never seriously talked about the Pandits. No Kashmiri has seriously talked about the Pandits except Farooq when he returned to power in 1996 and said his government would provide security, etc. Not much happened though, whatever his intention was. The Mirwaiz keeps talking about the Pandits, saying he'd like them to come back, and even

Geelani has said, 'The Pandits are a part of us.' But since so many who were a part of you got bumped off, it's not easy.

I would like to put on record the fact that though I'm no fan of Jagmohan, when he was governor in 1990 and I was heading the IB in Srinagar from 21 January to 7 March, I saw no evidence of him pushing out the Pandits, as has been alleged by many Kashmiris. Pandits had started escaping before he was appointed. They were dead scared, because there had been targeted killings of Pandits (some of them IB officials, as mentioned earlier in the book).

My friend, lawyer Ashok Bhan, a Congressman, came to me one day suddenly in those dark days. 'Can you get me out of here,' he said. 'I'm under threat.'

'Okay, I'll get you out of here,' I said.

'No, today,' he said. 'I want to go today.'

'But what about your belongings, your furniture, your house?'

'I'm making arrangements for that, but can you get me, my wife, my family out of here?' he asked.

I gave him a car and sent him down to Jammu the same day.

Despite this threat, the IB was revived during those difficult days in 1990 by a couple of Pandits. We had three Kashmiri boys at the sub-inspector level: D.J. Handoo, A.K. Braroo, and R. Qazi. I called them the three musketeers. They were truly extraordinary gentlemen. They sneaked in and out of all sorts of places, and got the humint (human intelligence) flowing again. They rendered yeoman service to the nation.

All those who could afford to leave, left. A lot of others got stuck in camps in Jammu. And a few refused to leave. When you have terrorism of that kind, where people are targeted— and the Pandit was being targeted—what has happened ever since is that neither are the Pandits very keen to go back, nor have the Muslims been keen to bring them back. Yes, once in a while someone will make the nostalgic trip back to his former home, and his former neighbours will shed tears. But that is just in the moment.

The final Kashmiri insecurity, which they never talk about, is that there is a plan in Delhi to reduce Muslims to a minority in their homeland. The day that happens, they are finished. It took a Kashmiri a long time to tell me this. That's why they get worried whenever talk of abrogating Article 370 of the Constitution (which grants special status to J&K, and allows for certain restrictive laws on residency). That's why the Kashmiri is very sensitive about the Amarnath Yatra, whose pilgrims and duration increase every year. They feel it may be a Trojan horse for repopulating the Valley.

It is not a coincidence that the Hurriyat, which sheds tears about being incomplete, does not have a Pandit member in its executive. It is not a coincidence that since 1996, there has not been a Kashmiri Pandit in the state cabinet. Till then, there had been Farooq's sidekick, P.L. Handoo, from Anantnag. Why didn't the Congress, under Chief Minister Ghulam Nabi Azad, not have a Pandit in its government? Mufti had Raman Matoo but he was a non-entity.

There was one Kashmiri Pandit whom Prime Minister Vajpayee wanted me to regularly brief when I joined the PMO. This was P.N. Dhar. I first met Prof. Dhar at a Pandit wedding in Jammu in January 1989 when militancy was just beginning in the state. As Indira Gandhi's principal secretary, Prof. Dhar was a key advisor on Kashmir and played a pivotal role in the mainstreaming which resulted in the 1975 Sheikh–Indira accord. A sensitive man of great culture and wisdom, Prof. Dhar loved his homeland and despite all the tumult in the state never lost interest in Kashmir. His home in Old Delhi was a regular meeting place for Kashmiris including separatists. My friend Ashok Bhan told me that on the night of 24 December 1999, the night of the Kandahar hijacking, Prof. Dhar was dining with A.G. Lone in Delhi. Between 2001 and 2004 we interacted a great deal, and we got along well. He was never overly critical of the Musalman, was always balanced, and didn't have any grudges. He asked me about personalities, saying what do you think of Yasin Malik, or what's your view on Sajad Lone.

One day he landed up at the PMO and he could hardly climb up, being an octogenarian. 'What are you doing here?' I said, startled that he had bothered to come all the way.

'I'm going to meet the prime minister and I'm going to propose your name for governor of J&K,' he said.

I had a hearty laugh. 'It's never going to happen,' I said.

After Manmohan Singh became prime minister, Prof. Dhar visited Kashmir and gave him a report. Before he submitted it, he called me home and showed me the three-and-a-half page report. I was going through it and again I saw a paragraph which said it was necessary to send me as governor to J&K. 'Sir, this will not happen,' I said, embarrassed.

'This is not Vajpayee, this is Manmohan Singh,' he said. 'Manmohan Singh has been a student of mine.'

That was P.N. Dhar.

When the Kashmiri Pandits are sent back, both sides should show extra sensitivity. Farooq Abdullah had said in 1996 that Pandits should be welcomed back and if necessary we'll build a separate colony for them. Again in 2014, the new BJP government was talking about setting the Kashmiri Pandits up in a high-security zone.

I don't think building a Chanakyapuri for Kashmiri Pandits is really the way to get them back. Those who want to go back must go to their own surroundings. A lot of Pandits used to live in Habba Kadal, so why not let them go back to Habbakadal, and live in the thick of security. Don't try to get 3,000 or 10,000 all at once. Let it be gradual. It's not necessary to build a Pandit township; that would be an artificial and insecure way of doing it and would also create community tensions. Those who go back should be willing to go back, and the Muslims should be willing to take them back. It has to be organic. There are some Kashmiri Pandits who are very well off. Vijay Dhar has rendered yeoman service in the field of education, setting up the first Delhi Public School in Srinagar. There are other wealthy Pandits as well who could help in setting up badly needed hospitals which could earn them huge goodwill, facilitating their return.

I don't think Kashmiriyat is dead, nor is Sufism. If we don't support the idea of Kashmiriyat or the Sufi tradition, it will fade out eventually, because radicalism is increasing.

Sheikh Saheb was said to be a pure Musalman but he kept the Jamaat-e-Islami at bay, telling them they were not going to meddle in political life. After him, Farooq was the same way and in fact more aggressive about it, saying that they should close down all the Jamaat schools and that if Delhi funded the state, it would set up its own schools. But he did not get that much support.

This is getting compromised. If you don't do anything about Kashmir, then more and more Wahhabism will come in, as petro-dollars, etc., with their mosques growing and the lectures from their mosques increasing. A couple of years ago I was leaving Srinagar on a Friday and I was startled. Every road I passed had a loudspeaker blaring for the jumme ka namaaz. This never happened earlier.

To my surprise, one of the breeding grounds of the fast-spreading radicalism is the Srinagar jail. A Kashmiri who was detained twice under the Public Security Act told me that the atmosphere of radicalism was so suffocating that you felt that you were in a jail inside a jail. So long as the likes of Masarat Alam and Qasim Fakhtoo are given free rein radicalism will grow.

While Pakistan remains a factor in Kashmir, the real danger is that radicalism will end up as the lasting political legacy of Kashmir.

18

MAINSTREAMING THE FUTURE

Agha Ashraf Ali, the nonagenarian who is one of the most extraordinary Kashmiris I have met, once told me: 'Sheikh (Abdullah) had a heart of gold, but no brains.'

Agha Saheb felt that Sheikh Abdullah was unable to fathom the fallout of the Partition in north India; or what India's first prime minister, Pandit Jawaharlal Nehru, was trying to do in Kashmir in order to save Muslims in the rest of India. The fallout of Partition was an onslaught of political conservatives in the Congress party, against whom Nehru had to wage a series of continual battles—which ended when he lost the 1962 war to China—and make a series of concessions. One of these concessions was the August 1953 dismissal of Sheikh Abdullah as prime minister of J&K and his immediate arrest in the Kashmir conspiracy case, for which he spent eleven years incarcerated.

Agha Saheb believed that the Sher-e-Kashmir also did not seem to understand that for Nehru, Kashmir was of prime importance because of the Muslims who did not leave for Pakistan; Kashmir was a demonstration that the Indian State could and would fairly treat its Muslim citizens. If Sheikh

Saheb had grasped this, he could have helped Nehru; if not fight some of the battles being waged in Delhi then at least not add to the skirmishes in Kashmir.

After Sheikh Abdullah was arrested, IB Director B.N. Mullik happened to meet (then) Madras chief minister C.R. Rajagopalachari. Rajaji, as he was known, had taken over as India's home minister after Sardar Vallabhbhai Patel's death in December 1950 and served for less than a year, as differences with Nehru forced him to quit on health grounds. (Like many others, Rajaji believed India's greatest threat came from the Communists, whereas Nehru believed the Hindu Mahasabha to be the main threat.) According to Mullik's memoir, *My Years with Nehru: Kashmir*, Rajaji asked the DIB: 'Why has it become necessary to arrest Sheikh Abdullah?'

Rajaji told Mullik that the Sher-e-Kashmir ought to have been given other options of autonomy in order to maintain a good relationship, and the door should never be shut on Sheikh Abdullah. The Madras CM prophetically apprehended that continued uncertainty and unrest would prevail in the Valley. In fact, Mullik in his memoir felt that if Rajaji had continued as home minister, then events like Sheikh Saheb's arrest would have been avoided.

The home minister at the time was Kailash Nath Katju (whose grandson, Markandey Katju, was a Supreme Court judge who in 2014 completed his term as the chairman of the Press Council of India); and Sheikh Abdullah pinned most of the blame for his arrest on Nehru. Unfortunately, the fact is that these two men were Kashmiri Pandits (even if their families had left the Valley and settled elsewhere in India), and contributed to the perception in Kashmir that the Pandits with their disproportionate clout adversely impacted Kashmir policy in New Delhi.

There is a school of thought that believed that Sheikh Abdullah was secretly pursuing independence, but the fact is that he was walking a fine line and could have been handled with more subtlety. For instance, in October 1948, the National Conference held a special convention in which it unanimously passed a resolution affirming J&K's accession to India. While moving the resolution, Sheikh Abdullah said: 'So far as I'm concerned, the political, economic, social and cultural interests of Kashmir demand an immediate and final accession to India, and to India alone.' And speaking at an Eid gathering after the convention, he said, 'the pledge I gave to Pandit Nehru that Kashmir will be a part of India has now become an eternal bond . . . Our decision to accede to India is based on the fact that our programme and policy are more akin to those followed by India.'

Politics followed a different trajectory, and Sheikh was arrested. For Kashmiris, it was a big deal. As Hurriyat leader Prof. Ghani pointed out to me once, even Hindus came out to protest. This was an important turning point, the first of four 'what ifs' that mark out Kashmir's history since 1947.

1. 'What if' Sheikh Abdullah had not been arrested in 1953? One consequence of Sheikh Abdullah's arrest was that two years later his right-hand man Mirza Afzal Beg set up the Plebiscite Front (the National Conference cadres joined in droves); in effect, that was the 'mainstreaming' of separatism in Kashmir, something that has remained a fixture in Kashmir ever since.

The Plebiscite Front was in existence for twenty years, and was wound up only after the 1975 Indira–Sheikh accord— which the Sheikh agreed to once he saw, after Pakistan's defeat in the 1971 war and the creation of Bangladesh, that Pakistan was no match for India. For Kashmiris the 1971 war had a huge impact: according to Prof. Ghani, the break-up of Pakistan made Kashmiris more sullen towards India. 'Kashmiris even abused God and said there is no God, no hope, no justice,' Prof. Ghani told me. The Kashmiris felt further let down by the accord; when Sheikh Saheb returned to J&K after the accord and reached Jammu, the Valley observed a hartal in protest against him and his 'compromise'. Ironically, when Sheikh Saheb reached the Valley the next day, massive crowds turned out to see him. That is the way of the Kashmiri.

If Sheikh Saheb had not been arrested, there would have been no mainstreaming of separatism in Kashmir. That does not necessarily mean there would not have existed a Kashmir problem—after all, a lot of other disputes in our neighbourhood still linger. But had there been no mainstreaming of separatism, then when the Plebiscite Front was withdrawn in 1975 there would have been no first wave of separatists that included Shabir Shah.

While Sheikh was in jail for his first stretch, China defeated India in the 1962 war and this left Nehru a broken man (besides bringing China and Pakistan close). He also began to regret what had happened with Sheikh Saheb—they had a correspondence which would prove a goldmine of history, but whose letters have not been made public by either man's descendants. Sheikh was released by 1964 and sent by Nehru to Pakistan to work out a solution, but while he was there Nehru passed away.

After Nehru, there was no stopping Delhi in its desire to erode Kashmir's autonomy in stages. And in 2014, when Narendra Modi and the BJP came to power, ministers openly spoke about abrogating the Constitution's Article 370, which gives Kashmir its special status. It forced Farooq, who was in London waiting for doctors to decide whether he ought to get a kidney transplant from his wife Mollie or whether he ought to go on dialysis like his brother Sheikh Nazir, to state that the BJP's stand on 370 was worrying. 'For Kashmiris it is a matter of life and death,' he said, warning that its revocation would weaken the integrity of the country and pose a threat to peace.

India and Kashmir have travelled a long distance since 1947, with important milestones in 1952, 1953, 1975, 1980, 1987, 2001 and now in 2014. By now, there is nothing great about Article 370; what is great about the special status that Kashmiris enjoy now? Article 370 is by now merely symbolic. It is a fig leaf for Kashmiris—so why would anyone want to take that away from them? Perhaps if Sheikh Abdullah had not been arrested in 1953, we would not have be having this debate in 2014.

2. 'What if' Farooq Abdullah had not been dismissed in 1984 at the behest of Prime Minister Indira Gandhi? It was a terrible mistake, and the only reason Jagmohan came to J&K as governor was to dismiss Farooq. The way I see it, there would have been no need for Farooq to enter a political accord with Prime Minister Rajiv Gandhi—which President Giani Zail Singh immediately said was a bad idea—and there would have been no formation of the Muslim United Front (MUF). Remember that in 1984, Farooq and Abdul Ghani Lone and Mirwaiz Moulvi Farooq were all on one side. Suddenly Jagmohan was there, dismissing government employees he thought were separatists (like Prof. Ghani, who was among those who formed the bulk of the MUF).

Farooq's dismissal suddenly woke up Kashmiri regional sentiment. A Kashmiri think tank came together with an idea from the *Aftab* editor-in-chief, Khwaja Sanaullah Bhat, that Kashmiris had to get together to resist the Delhi onslaught. That they had to build a counter to it. And when the MUF faced a rigged assembly election in 1987, then their boys went across the LoC and took part in Zia's war of 'a thousand cuts', the one that the ISI used to successfully drive the Soviet Union out of Afghanistan. Possibly you would have had one-off incidents of terrorism, like the hijacking by Hashim Qureshi, but it would not have been on such a large scale.

In fact, when militancy erupted, then even the Pakistanis were surprised by its magnitude, a former militant once told me. They were as surprised as India as to how big it had grown. Yet for the Kashmiris, as former militant Firdous Syed once pointed out, the boys who went across thought of themselves as freedom fighters and took affront at being treated as agents of the ISI; this was probably why a lot of JKLF boys picked fights with the ISI at the time.

We in India wasted so many years in containing the Kashmir militancy. And once it was contained, we sat back and were happy with the status quo, instead of taking advantage of the situation to forge a political solution. The status quo has gone on a long time, with a lot of vested interests having been developed: the army, the police, the paramilitary, the bureaucracy, and politicians of every hue. Even separatists like Shabir Shah, whose career is over, are still well off; ones like Yasin obstinately cling on to the rebel identity, because they are unable to grow.

Today, Kashmiris want peace, and they are very clear that 1990 cannot be repeated. War is not an option and neither is another arms struggle. As Firdous says, it would be disastrous. Also, there aren't many Kashmiri boys available; recruits are only available in Jamaat pockets, and those that get trained do so locally, without a need to go to Pakistan. Now that boys do stone-pelting—this caused a major crisis for Chief Minister Omar Abdullah in the summer of 2010, when nearly 120 youngsters were shot during stone-pelting—you don't need to use the gun. Stone-pelters can even enforce election boycotts in Srinagar.

3. 'What if' Shabir had contested the 1996 J&K assembly election? If he had then it would have provided an excuse for the other separatists to join in. As it were, had he known how to run the thing there were already a bunch of fellows ready to join up, like Nayeem Khan, our friend Firdous, and others on the periphery. A substantial separatist participation would have changed the atmosphere.

But by Shabir not participating, Pakistan only tightened its control on the separatist movement, particularly the Hurriyat. It has not loosened its grip after that; it has always been a carrot-and-stick, stick-and-carrot thing with the separatists. On the Hurriyat side, they are forever waiting for someone to 'bell the cat' as far as going mainstream is concerned. They are happy with the status quo; for instance, after the September 2014 floods, in the name of relief, several of them have received a lot of money, some from Saudi Arabia but most from Pakistan.

During my summer of 2014 visit to Kashmir, a local journalist called separatist politics a business, and he put it like this: there were three Hurriyats and three-four groups of the JKLF; the manufacturers are in Pakistan or in Delhi; the distributors are in Srinagar, particularly Hyderpora (where Syed Ali Shah Geelani resides); and the retailers and dealers are in the districts. It is a business without any conviction, the journalist said. It only depends on whatever sells during a particular season.

In Delhi, however, there is still this hang-up that the separatists are Pakistanis, but my point is that if Pakistan has influence on them or controls them, it is because Delhi won't talk to them.

And suppose they are the worst form of Pakistanis, then ask yourself: what is India's problem in Kashmir? It is Pakistan. So either you bomb and finish off Pakistan—a strategy that even the Americans could not successfully pull off in Afghanistan or Iraq, and which we certainly can't do—or you talk to Pakistan. And while you're deciding on whether or not to talk to Pakistan, it's easy to use that time to talk to the Kashmiri separatists. Again, when you mention separatism, there are people in Delhi who argue that Mufti Sayeed is soft on separatism, and that's 'theek hai', which is a whole lot of rubbish. Even if the Hurriyat's credibility hits rock-bottom in Delhi, a message has to be sent: that (a) we're always willing to talk, and to talk to anybody and everybody; and (b) we're always willing to listen, that we have the time to hear whatever your grievances are, which we will look into and rectify.

In fact, I have always felt that Delhi should engage Geelani. Even if nothing comes out of it, you lose nothing by engaging with him.

Further, it is strange that no Kashmiri separatist has ever

been called for a national day function in Delhi, be it 15 August or 26 January. Not even the J&K governor invites them for a cup of tea. (At his own investiture he invites his relatives, etc., but never the Mirwaiz.) They may turn it down, but they have never been invited. I'm willing to vouch for it: if you work on it, they will come.

There is a fundamental point to this that Delhi overlooks. Kashmiris feel let down by Pakistan and the ISI because there is no consistency in the Pakistani or ISI position on Kashmir. India, on the other hand, whether it is the dovish Kuldip Nayar or the hawkish Ajit Doval, is consistent that we will never let go of Kashmir. Many Kashmiris I've spoken to believe that while the containment of militancy could be attributed to the good work by the armed forces and the intelligence agencies, they feel it is more because of the arrogance of the ISI. Whether it was creating more than a hundred tanzeems, or criminalising the movement, or creating-splitting-reunifying the Hurriyat, Kashmiris say that Pakistan has never understood or tried to understand Kashmir.

4. The last 'what if', and as big as the first, is what if Vajpayee had not lost power in 2004? He had visited Pakistan for the second time in January 2004, and President Musharraf began talking about out-of-the-box solutions and eventually came up with his four-point formula. The opportunity that Manmohan Singh squandered would have been seized without delay by Vajpayee, because by his second term he had already spent a lot of time checking Musharraf out. Just imagine—a settlement acceptable to India, to the Pakistan army, and to the Hurriyat. That would have settled the Kashmir dispute for the foreseeable future.

(Additionally, if Vajpayee had returned as prime minister, he would not have had his stroke in early 2009. After we left office, I used to visit him twice a year: on Diwali and on New Year's. The last time I went to see him was 2008's Diwali; after the stroke he could not hold conversations, and his household discouraged visitors. So much for the 'what ifs'. But, so long as 'what is' dominates, we will remain where we are in Kashmir. Almost everyone connected with Kashmir has over a period of time developed a vested interest. So the 'shops' and 'businesses' that we are sensitive to also continue to flourish.

Whether you think Pakistan is moth-eaten or weakened and vulnerable, it remains a factor in Kashmir because of the anger and alienation against India, and it provides Kashmiris with a convenient fallback position. Pakistan has been in a mood to move forward, but as mentioned in the last chapter, the question Delhi bogs itself down with is of the reliability of those in control in Pakistan. The army is not against moving forward, and it is not weak; it is what counts in Pakistan. Pakistan's fall-back is its special relationship with China, so it can't be underestimated. Hence the track two dialogues ought to be encouraged and given proper direction; they ought to be institutionalised and recognised.

As Prof. Ghani told me privately, it is impossible to conceive of another Vajpayee, but Kashmiris expect his policies to be followed by whoever is in power in Delhi. And the time, in 2014, was ripe for moving forward on Musharraf's four-point formula, but Vajpayee cannot be replicated. The BJP was blessed to have Vajpayee and Advani as prime minister and deputy prime minister together.

Finally, a solution to Kashmir has to be found between India and Pakistan, and because it will involve a compromise on the part of Pakistan, Pakistan will have no choice but to fall back on Kashmir and that's where the Hurriyat will come into play. This is why Delhi needs to talk to the Hurriyat. And it should let the Hurriyat talk to Pakistan. And then the real talking can be done between India and Pakistan.

As Prof. Ghani put it: 'Modi's rule can be epoch-making if he can carry everybody with him.'

Vajpayee is over. Brajesh Mishra is gone. Advani is sidelined. Jaswant Singh is lying in a coma. Farooq has been in poor health since 2012. Mufti will now have his final innings, or a benefit match, if you like. Shabir has wasted his chances. Geelani has credibility but he's an old man who has swung from one side to the other; during an escalating spat in April 2014, the Mirwaiz bravely asked a press conference: 'Who the hell is Geelani?'

The Pakistani high commissioner once asked me, 'What do we do with Geelani?'

'Take him to Pakistan and give him a farm in Raiwind or something,' I said. 'That's his ultimate desire, so bury him with a green flag or something.'

The four likely players for the future in Kashmir are Omar Abdullah, Mirwaiz Umar Farooq, Mehbooba Mufti, and Sajad Lone. With the exception of the former chief minister, the rest are untested.

Omar started off with great hope. He made a huge impact in Kashmir and in Delhi with a statement he made in Parliament during the July 2008 debate on the Indo-US nuclear deal, when he declared that it had been a mistake not to resign from the NDA after the 2002 Gujarat riots, and when he declared that Kashmiris would never let any harm come to the Amarnath Yatra pilgrims (in May 2008, the state government transferred 100 acres of forest land to the Amarnath Yatra board but had to reverse its decision following widespread protests in the Valley). During the 2008 assembly election, even the Pakistanis let their supporters know that they wanted to see him as chief minister (remember, he greatly impressed Musharraf during his visit to Pakistan in 2006). And when he became chief minister, he began by writing letters to people interested in Kashmir, asking them to come to Kashmir as his guests. It enthused many.

But Omar had this hang-up about his father. He felt Farooq was gullible, that Farooq was misled by bad advisors, and that he was going to do things his own way. From what he said it sounded as if Farooq was bad news, and Dadaji (Sheikh Saheb) was everything. Which was fine, except that he forgot that if it hadn't been for his father, he would not have become chief minister. Ultimately, his repeated reference to Sheikh Saheb, while ignoring his own father, did not go down well in Kashmir.

Rubbishing Farooq ultimately became counterproductive because Omar's biggest problem became that he was not like his father in the matter of reaching out to his fellow Kashmiris. You cannot reach out to Kashmiris via the smartphone, iPad or Twitter. This made Omar look more like an Englishman than a Kashmiri. On top of which, Omar dealt with everything through the security paradigm. You don't need to be a genius to know that unemployment and development are not dealt with through the security paradigm.

Then came the two big disasters of Omar's tenure: the stone-pelting of 2010, and the failure of his government to provide visible relief during the 2014 floods. Those people who were enthused by Omar's youth and freshness and energy were deeply disappointed.

Yet I would not write off Omar, because of the great legacy he has. He has plus points, and as he has said during the 2014 assembly election campaign, time is on his side. There's a huge legacy on his side, so long as he doesn't squander it. The way Kashmir is, the way Kashmir functions and the way Kashmir politics is, even in the long run Omar is the most likely to succeed. This is simply because politics in Kashmir is so bogged down. Mehbooba will have a head start at the moment because after the 2014 election she will be a key player in the ruling combination. As I was concluding this book the election results in J&K which satisfied no party in particular were announced. The obvious coalition staring one in the face was a PDP–BJP alliance. But when I asked a Kashmiri who understands politics what he thought, he felt they would get together but it would always be a rocky relationship—'Shaadi to hogi lekin nikaah nahin.'

Omar is honest, he's straight, he's transparent: he's different.

But he needs to learn politics a little more, and he needs to become a little more Kashmiri. He's willing to wait it out and he's reconciled to sitting in the opposition; in a way he's looking forward to that because it'll be a different experience. Omar definitely needs another chance.

The Mirwaiz has to make up his mind, as mentioned earlier, whether he wants to be pope for life or whether he wants to be chief minister. I've told the Pakistanis that they're doing him a great disservice by holding him back, because as a politician he remains untested. As a human being he has all the qualities. But you have to be tested in the field; you have to be tested in power and you have to be tested out of power.

Sajad is a wild card. He has many qualities, but he's a little unpredictable. As mentioned he had been offered a senior ministership by Mufti Sayeed in 2002, so he had by the 2014 assembly election wasted a dozen years, when he could have used the time to mature into a seasoned politician. During the 2014 election I spoke to him and advised him that when the results came in, despite his having gone and met Modi, he should not jump into anything. 'Maybe you've made some commitments, fine, but see what happens,' I said. 'If you want to be a player, then you have to come on to the board. There's no point in being in the fringe or on the outside.'

Though Sajad was a borderline separatist—remember, he learned from his father that this separatism wasn't going to last very long—he was Delhi's favoured separatist. But he has looked for extraordinary favours from Delhi, and because of his temperament, Delhi has not been able to handle him properly. Thus the desperation in November 2014, when he went and met Modi; Sajad was thinking that he had to get on Delhi's right side. Like every other Kashmiri, Sajad believes that what Delhi wants is what will happen. Now that he's arrived on centre court it is up to him to prove that he has the mettle to get to the top.

The Mirwaiz could be a big player if Pakistan gave him freer rein. Mehbooba is a bit quirky. But I have felt that a government with these, Omar, Umar and Sajad—and they could accommodate Mehbooba as well, why not—would be the best combination for Kashmir. It would take care of every shade of opinion: the pro-Pakistan, the pro-Indian, the pro-regional, etc. It would automatically take care of the problems of engagement. As Omar used to say whenever there were talks about the Hurriyat, 'Why are you asking me about talking to Delhi, I'm talking to Delhi all the time. Delhi should be talking to these guys.'

Modi is in a position to do what neither Vajpayee nor Manmohan Singh could do, because he can't blame anyone. The welcome Modi got from Kashmiris when he became prime minister was unprecedented: a BJP-RSS guy was being welcomed by the Mirwaiz. If Modi wants to waste the opportunity, then fine. He has no excuses after this 2014 assembly election.

Some would say that to find a solution to Kashmir one must understand the Kashmiris' collective psychological personality. Kashmiris are said to have descended from the Nagas but are basically Saraswat Brahmins who were converted. And after suffering at the hands of the Mughals, the Pathans, the Afghans, the Sikhs, the Dogras, and currently, India, they fight with their brains. Their brains make up for whatever they might not have.

Neither Pakistan nor India understands the Kashmiri's remarkable adjustability. An old Kashmiri woman will tell you whom she voted for, but she will not give up on azaadi. The Kashmiri will not accept defeat in a hurry.

Even in the worst of times the Kashmiri has never lost his sense of humour. When Rubaiya Sayeed was released from captivity on 13 December 1989, a popular saying was: 'Mufti Saeben gab, panch duh lab,' meaning Mufti's lamb found in five days. And when they began to tire of Mufti's rule in 2004, they said about Farooq: 'Uss fetir (lovable fool) ko wapas lao'. Mirza Afzal Beg was said to be the wittiest of his contemporaries and his jokes are a legion.

But times have changed: as Modi said during the 2014 parliamentary election, India has changed, and the corollary to that is that Kashmir has also changed. Many of today's youth don't know Sheikh Abdullah, and some don't even know Farooq.

Another illustration of the change before my eyes is in two flights that I took to Srinagar from Delhi: one in 1990, the other in 2012.

In 1990, all hell had broken loose: central government employees deserted Srinagar, the Pandits made an exodus, our officers were getting bumped off, anti-India crowds were on the streets every day, and you never know whether you would make it home that evening. I was transferred out in March and I left in a hurry, leaving my baggage behind.

I went back for my luggage in May and it was an unforgettable experience because there was so much tension in the aircraft. At that time there were only two flights to Srinagar, both operated by Indian Airlines. Nobody spoke on the aircraft, not even a whisper. Kashmiris sat grimly throughout the flight. There were only two non-Kashmiris: myself and a Border Security Force (BSF) officer in uniform, who coincidentally sat next to me.

I was in no mood to talk to anybody; the atmosphere was so stifling. But the BSF officer said: 'Are you going to Srinagar on work?'

'No,' I said. 'Not really.'

He paused and then asked: 'Are you going on holiday?'

'Not really.' And the conversation ended there because I didn't want to carry it forward and explain why I was going there and tell the entire story.

When the plane landed, the BSF officer was first off and I followed him on to the tarmac. The IB has a presence at the airport so a couple of guys were there who received me. The BSF fellow was obviously posted in Srinagar and so recognised the two, and figured out who I was or where I was from. He looked back at me and smiled.

The other flight was at the end of April 2012. Now there were 26 to 30 flights to Srinagar, and when I boarded the aircraft I could have sworn it was a charter from Bangalore, because it was filled with south Indians going on holiday. I talked to a couple of fellow passengers and they said they were from Bangalore. I sat in the back and there was only one Kashmiri man, with two women.

The Kashmiri was a little inquisitive; he thought I was a Kashmiri. 'Aap kahan se hain, kahan rehte hain?' he asked me. He wanted my Srinagar address.

'Main Delhi rehta hoon,' I said.

But he wouldn't believe I lived in Delhi. He asked me for my Delhi address.

'Nahin sir, aap toh Kashmiri lagte hain,' he said. 'Toh aap Delhi address bataye kyonki main nahin manta hoon ki aap Delhi rehte hain.'

I told him that I lived in Friends Colony and he was finally convinced.

The atmosphere was completely different: lively, a lot of tourists, relaxed. Everything had changed.

If you go to Kashmir now during season, which extends from April to October, Srinagar is full. You can't get a ticket, you can't get a hotel room. Hotels keep mushrooming. There are seven-star hotels now; in Gulmarg, which sees another tourist season in the winter, there's a new place that is said to be better than anything in Srinagar. If you walk down the Boulevard, it's packed with strollers. At the end of the high-security Gupkar Road, where the IB office is as well as Farooq's house, there are dhabas that have opened, some of them Punjabi dhabas. The most frequent visitor is the Gujarati, and during Puja it is the Bengali. But there is a continuous flow of tourists.

Irshad Malik, the Kashmiri militant now in London (who Firdous had wanted me to bring back to India when I was at R&AW), once said to me about PoK: 'Uss taraf kya hai? Pakistan mein kya hai? Aap kyon fiqar karte hain? Inko jaane dijiye, paar dekhne dijiye, udhar kuchh bhi nahin hain.' He said that Srinagar airport—and he obviously hadn't been to Srinagar airport in at least twenty-four years—was better than any Pakistani airport. Hotels in Kashmir are as good as any in the world. 'They have nothing there,' he said. You should publicise these facts, he said to me: 'Aapko toh film banani chahiye.'

Kashmir is as normal as normal can be. The crisis of 1989–90 has long blown over. Separatism has receded, or as one of their own kin put it, their lottery is over.

Kashmir and Kashmiris have moved on. Agha Shahid Ali, the Kashmiri-American poet, has inspired a whole generation of writers from South Asia including Basharat Peer and Mirza Waheed, who have made their mark in the West. S.A.S. Geelani's son-in-law, Iftikhar Geelani, who started as a small-time journalist, is heading the Delhi Bureau of the popular Mumbai-based daily *DNA*. More promising youngsters are making their mark in the national media. Kashmiris are regularly figuring in the All India Civil Services list. A couple of years ago a Kashmiri topped the list. Kashmiri doctors are travelling for jobs not only to the Gulf and the Middle East but the US as well. Cricket has picked up since Parvez Rasool was included in the national one day squad. For the first time J&K defeated Mumbai in the Ranji Trophy this season.

But sadly radicalism has moved apace and signals from the neighbourhood are ominous. Not only is Pakistan in turmoil and Afghanistan yet to unravel but which way the Taliban is headed and how Islamic jihad will finally play out is difficult to say. Al-Qaeda may no longer be the force it was but is still clearly inspiring. The ISIS is attracting more and more Muslim youth the world over. Kashmir can hardly remain immune from what is happening all over the Islamic world, more so because the violence it has witnessed in the last twenty-five years. Significantly, of late Kashmiri boys involved in militancy are more highly educated and from better stock. Not surprisingly, pro-ISIS graffiti has appeared in Srinagar city and its flags flown in the university. The proclamation of a caliphate is likely to be the most significant development in international jihadism since 9/11 which is beginning to impact worldwide. Nearer home, Taliban's terror factory is on auto pilot and all the more dangerous when there is no communication with Pakistan.

Nothing is constant; least of all Kashmir; it could change overnight. The Kashmiri has suffered for the last twenty-five years and though he largely blames himself, he is not internally at peace with the status quo. The peace with honour he bargained for still eludes him; he made a dignified exit. Why can a Kashmiri not be an Indian? We need to look deep into this question which disturbs us when a shopkeeper in Srinagar enquires, 'Aap India se aaye hain?' The Indian State is big enough to breach this psychological barrier. What Kashmir needs is not magnanimity but hard-nosed commonsense which Vajpayee displayed. Had he been around for a few more years or had Dr Manmohan Singh not missed the window of opportunity in 2006 or 2007, a solution around the Musharraf formula would have disposed of the problem for the foreseeable future. Now we need to engage with Kashmir (not just Mufti Saheb) and with Pakistan as well. The reason that people in Delhi have reservations about talking to separatists and Pakistanis are the very reasons we need to talk to them for. As Mufti says, there is no other way.

In closing, I must say this: if anyone who reads this book has any doubts about the path I took—of talking, talking, talking— and how unbeatable dialogue is as both a tactic and a strategy, then I will tell them of what Agha Saheb said to me during a meeting in May 2014: 'You were sent to disrupt the (Kashmir) movement . . . in the friendliest possible manner.'

INDEX

ABOUT THE AUTHORS

AMARJIT SINGH DULAT served as the head of the Research and Analysis Wing (R&AW), India's spy agency, under Prime Minister A.B. Vajpayee. He later joined Vajpayee's Prime Minister's Office (PMO), where his job was to 'monitor, manage and direct' the government of India's peace initiative in Kashmir.

Dulat was born in Sialkot, Punjab, in December 1940. With India's Partition, his father Justice Shamsher Singh Dulat, ICS, was posted to Delhi. Dulat was educated in Bishop Cotton School, Shimla and Punjab University, Chandigarh, after which he joined the Indian Police Service (IPS) in 1965, and then the Intelligence Bureau (IB) in 1969, where he served for almost thirty years. At IB he headed the Kashmir Group during the turbulent 1990s till he joined and headed R&AW.

Since leaving the government in 2004, Dulat has been active on the track two circuit, and has visited Pakistan. He has co-authored a paper with former Pakistani intelligence chief Lt. Gen. Asad Durrani on the benefits of intelligence cooperation between India and Pakistan.

During service, Dulat accumulated a vast reservoir of goodwill with Kashmiris of all shades. As *Jane's Intelligence Digest* put it in 2001: 'Well known for his social skills, Dulat prefers dialogue to clandestine manoeuvres. He has built up an impressive network of personal contacts in Kashmir including militants.' A decade after retirement, that goodwill remains intact, with Kashmiris dropping in on him and his wife Paran at their Friends Colony house in Delhi, to share gossip, information, and advice.

ADITYA SINHA is a journalist since February 1987. He has been Editor-in-Chief of *The New Indian Express* and of *Daily News and Analysis* (DNA). His published work includes the biographies *Farooq Abdullah: Kashmir's Prodigal Son* (1996) and *Death of Dreams: A Terrorist's Tale* (2000).